WE WERE WARRIORS

Johnny Mercer served in the British Army for twelve years. A captain in 29 Commando, he was deployed on three tours of Afghanistan, and weathered some of the heaviest fighting of the campaign. No longer prepared to tolerate Britain's treatment of her veterans, he retired from the Army in December 2013 to run for Parliament. He was elected in May 2015 for his home seat of Plymouth Moor View, and used his maiden speech to bring the realities of his generation of warriors to the floor of the House of Commons, in a speech hailed around the globe. Johnny and his family settled near Plymouth, where he continues to serve as an MP.

Praise for *We Were Warriors*

'A highly charged, vivid and moving account of frontline combat, and then an even harder fight to honour the sacrifice of so many. Utterly compelling throughout'

Tom Newton Dunn, Political Editor, *Sun*

'One of the great British accounts of close combat, matching Orwell in Catalonia and MacDonald Fraser in Burma. It is the inner conflict, as much as closing with a shadowy enemy, that gives the book its edge . . . His exploration of fear, and the dread of fear, is profound . . . a remarkable book by a man remarkable in his humanity and courage'

Standard

WE WERE WARRIORS

JOHNNY MERCER

PAN BOOKS

First published 2017 by Sidgwick & Jackson

First published in paperback 2017 by Sidgwick & Jackson

This edition first published 2018 by Pan Books
an imprint of Pan Macmillan
20 New Wharf Road, London N1 9RR
Associated companies throughout the world
www.panmacmillan.com

ISBN 978-1-5098-5302-1

3 5 7 9 8 6 4 2

A CIP catalogue record for this book is available from the British Library.

Typeset in Warnock Pro by
Palimpsest Book Production Limited, Falkirk, Stirlingshire
Printed and bound by CPI Group (UK) Ltd, Croydon, CRO 4YY

For Felicity.
It was all worth it.

PROLOGUE

Nad-e Ali, Helmand Province, 2010

I took a brief moment to rest. I knew it would be short-lived. The enemy were close and it wouldn't be long before we would be in action again. Holding my rifle by my side I gulped as much water down my throat as I could, spilling most of it down my front in the process. The temperature was unbearable, forty degrees, and I was sweating so much that my body felt lubricated, as if covered in oil. I constantly shuffled the two radios, spare ammunition, spare batteries and water in my rucksack to allow the air to get up under my shirt, albeit briefly. I glanced at my watch. We'd been on the move for four hours now. I was going to have to change my radio batteries soon.

It was late summer 2010. The previous year alone had seen a hundred and eight British servicemen killed in this sweaty, stinking, blood-soaked acreage. We were on eighty-eight, and it wasn't even the end of August. Joint UK/US operations in the spring had cleared a lot of enemy from key districts around Marjeh but also squeezed many of them up to northern Nad-e Ali, where I was now plying my trade for the third time in four years.

Firefights can be long or short, ferocious or rather quiet. Sometimes they just become a deadly game of cat and mouse.

1

Today was like that. We moved slowly, carefully; avoiding obvious ambushes and channels for IEDs – improvised explosive devices. After a few hours like that the senses dull, but I could still hear my pulse in my ears as the hairs on the back of my neck began to rise again. I knew we were approaching the climax of this patrol.

I leant against the forward edge of a ditch and peered through the grass along the lip; I could see across the field straight to the compound that lay between us and our patrol base. The high mud walls of the compound enclosed a simple square building that peeked over the top. It was quiet. Bullet holes around a small aperture in the wall marked the location as a previous Taliban firing point, also known as a murder hole. It was perfect for the enemy, just big enough to aim a rifle through, looking directly over our patrol base with an easy escape route into a treeline and another crop of compounds to the rear. They used these holes to pour murderous machine-gun fire onto our patrol base. I should have destroyed the compound months ago. Two five-hundred-pound bombs would do it, or a couple of guided rockets. Last time I attempted it we waited for six hours in this ditch, while battalion headquarters worked out the 'environmental impact' of me turning it into dust. What would happen to the watercourses? How would the trees recover afterwards? British soldiers' lives were tumbling down priority lists out here.

I rubbed my eyes. The fucking sweat always blurred your vision after a while.

Looking at my watch, I worked out it would have been 0710 in the UK. Families would be waking up, getting ready for school. The morning commute would be well underway – trains packed out and roads jammed. All listening to the

2

Today programme on Radio 4, Nicky Campbell on Radio 5 or even Chris Moyles on Radio 1. All the suits, picking up their coffees. I could have been one of them, but for some reason I chose this instead.

I glanced left along the patrol group. I was the 'tail-end Charlie' – the last guy. The section commander was looking at me. He was a young lad; bright, engaging and determined. We'd been intercepting the Taliban's radio comms and knew they'd been tracking us for more than two hours now.

'Are you pushing through it?' I asked him.

'Roger, boss. What do you reckon?'

'I'm happy if you're happy,' I lied.

There was no real way of bypassing this compound without getting into further trouble. We knew the enemy was very likely to be inside. In this crazy fucking war, we were about to advance across open ground, no doubt containing IEDs, towards a murder hole in a compound that was almost definitely going to fire on us. We'd been patrolling out twice a day every day for four months now, trying to create space for peace to take hold, and every day the Taliban had told us to go away, in their own inimitable style – with their AK47s.

I heard retching and saw the young soldier at the front of the patrol bent over his Vallon metal detector, throwing up.

I scrambled along the ditch, winked at the section commander on my way past, and scuttled in next to the lad at the front. His puke was just bile – no food. It was fear.

'You all right, bud?' I asked him.

'Yeah,' he replied.

He can't have been more than eighteen or nineteen, but had been patrolling for the last four hours not with his weapon looking for the enemy, but with a metal detector looking for IEDs buried in the ground. We had stopped a few times while he had fingered a suspicious mound of dirt to see what lay beneath. He had risked injury, if not death, every single day of his tour.

We'd had a good patrol, despite being heavily 'dicked' – followed around by young men on motorbikes who were reporting our movements back to the Taliban. By being careful, and taking it slowly and methodically, we'd avoided contact thus far. But patrols always got hit in this area eventually – it was a question of when, not if. The Taliban knew you had to return to your PB and they usually left a present for you on your way back in.

I looked back at the patrol; they were all quiet, sucking on CamelBaks. As they gazed at me I thought some of them looked like pandas – the dust on their faces interrupted only by the sweat around their eyes. Salt had crystallized on their cheeks. Yet their eyes were wired; they knew what was coming as well as I did.

'Give me the Vallon,' I said to the lead man. I don't know why. I didn't even know how to switch it on.

'No, boss, I'm fine,' he said.

In his eyes I saw nerves, but also a steely determination. I wasn't going to get that Vallon off him.

'We'll advance together, side by side, and I'll put shots into that murder hole the moment he opens up,' I said. We both knew that, being at the front, there was a strong chance we'd be dead before I heard or saw anything.

'Sounds like a plan,' he replied, wiping his mouth.

'Let's get this done,' I said quietly to the patrol commander. We all stepped out of the ditch together, advancing on the compound very slowly.

As promised, I kept my weapon up and trained on the murder hole, waiting for it to flash. It was hard to breathe.

I thought I saw the curtain behind the murder hole move and felt bile in the back of my throat. It was just the wind, I decided. Another step, then another.

Whack-whack-whack!

That was incoming 7.62 rifle fire.

I kept scanning. Someone to the right of me returned fire.

I couldn't see the flash but I could see the curtain moving rhythmically. He was in there. I fired six shots, fast and deliberate, into the murder hole, and then took a knee.

The firing stopped. The patrol froze where we were, in the open. We couldn't break left or right, for the IED threat. We couldn't rush the firing point for the same reason. We couldn't really see the firing point properly so had no idea if he was dead. It was fucking frustrating.

In the sudden quiet I could hear my own breathing. I looked at the Vallon man in the prone position on his front. He stared back at me. I should have been lying on the floor too, but I couldn't see anything from down there, and in this lethal game of cat and mouse, I smelled blood. I wanted him to take another shot and expose himself. Turning my head to the right, I caught the patrol commander's eye and gestured to indicate that we should go around the left-hand side of the compound and head straight up to our base. The gesture wasn't in any manual, and I got a puzzled stare in return.

Giving up, I called over to him.

'Don't go in there,' I said. 'I reckon it's riddled.' The Taliban's tactics were nothing if not cunning. Entice the Brits in with a shoot and scoot; lace the place with IEDs.

'You happy to lead us back in?' The section commander said.

'Yep. Follow me,' I replied.

In single file, me and the Vallon man at the front, we moved slowly around the side of the compound. About five minutes later, exhausted and wild-eyed, we entered the patrol base through the rear gate. We gathered around and had a quick wash up. I made sure everyone understood what had just happened.

'Don't flap; always think,' I said. 'Good work.'

I went back to my camp cot and opened another carton of cigarettes. Drawing the smoke deep into my lungs, I wondered if I'd killed the shooter. Probably not, but I didn't really care either way. Another patrol chalked off.

I saw the company commander having a piss into the piss tubes that ran through the wall of our compound. Still in his pants and T-shirt, he was up late – I'd actually got the day wrong. It was a Sunday. There would be no morning commute. Instead, my family would be going to chapel. A few years ago, I had been a nervous, confused little boy sat in those pews on a Sunday, trying to understand and live within a very strict set of rules. It almost destroyed my mind.

This Sunday morning, I might have killed someone – the ultimate sin apparently.

I exhaled. I couldn't give a fuck. One day less. One day more. Not many more months left in this war.

1

I remember little of my childhood. Some say I have chosen to forget which is probably true. I was born on 17 August 1981 in Dartford General Hospital, the sixth of my parents' eight children. I had four older brothers, Neil (14), Keith (13), Stuart (11) and Sam (6), and just the one sister, Heidi (3). My father worked in the local branch of Lloyds Bank and my mother was a retired paediatric nurse. We were not well-off at all, which was a source of anxiety for my parents.

We lived in a small terraced house in Dartford – two up and two down. It was a tight squeeze, and managing our daily lives meant my mother was run off her feet. A military routine was adopted to ensure baths, showers, mealtimes and bedtimes ran as planned.

This disciplined approach to life was nothing new for my parents; my father in particular came from a harsh home which was anchored by religion. In fact, my family history on both sides is marked for at least three generations by a strong religious devotion. My parents' Strict Baptist faith governed every minute of every day for them and had done so for their entire lives. It was an impressive – if at times destructive – devotion that defined my very early years and shaped our family relationships.

But there came a moment in time where this traditional religious life and modern British society collided. As the

1970s became the 1980s, and then the 1990s, it became impossible to insulate one's family from the rest of society, its culture and behaviour. My parents found the encroachment of the outside world very difficult to deal with.

Strict Baptist life was dominated by Sundays, or the Sabbath as my father would call it, greeting it each week like an old friend. And Sunday would be dominated by the chapel. A Strict Baptist chapel is not a church; we did not think much of people who 'went to church'. It is a 'brethren' built around a common, strict and literal interpretation of Biblical texts. Those who worked for the chapel were called 'deacons', but the whole set-up was commanded by the Pastor, who was held in almost mystical adoration by some. According to our Pastor, having a late night on a Saturday was the devil's work because full focus and concentration were required on a Sunday. And he wasn't wrong: three ninety minute services, plus some Sunday School, needed serious effort.

Most churches in the UK have services spread through the course of a Sunday to enable those with varying commitments, and perhaps children, to attend one at their convenience. My father saw it rather differently. In his eyes, these services simply presented multiple opportunities to plug into some Old Testament truths, and we attended as many as possible, to the extent that we sometimes took a packed lunch so we could remain in our pews between the services. As a very young boy full of pent-up energy, with hairless legs that stuck to the varnished mahogany benches, I felt as if I was spending most of my life in chapel.

The ceremonies, or 'services', themselves generally all followed the same format. An opening hymn would be followed by a longish reading of ten or fifteen minutes from the gospels. We would then sing again and that would be followed by a long, single prayer of over twenty minutes in length. This seemingly endless prayer was an opportunity for the Pastor to improvise around a number of topics linked loosely to the reading we had just heard, but could also run to local and world current affairs.

During this eternity, the congregations would be seated, heads bowed and eyes shut. This was of great amusement to us children, who saw it as our opportunity to communicate with each other through glances and perhaps even pictures. But woe betide you if you gave cause for one of the worshippers – in your family or not – to break from their prayer and cast you a killer look.

Strict Baptist chapels can be frightening places; large and cold and usually filled to five or ten per cent capacity. It was rare to meet another family our age; if we did, friendships were either chased desperately in order to seek solace in shared experience, or avoided to miss the awkward conversations about why we were so strange.

Most worshippers wore very sober colours to chapel. As a family we mirrored this; us boys in shorts or trousers (if over the age of eleven) and a plain shirt and tie, while poor Heidi often looked like she'd just stepped off the *Mayflower* with the Pilgrim Fathers. Whether on the Sabbath or not, Heidi was not allowed to wear trousers, and none of us were permitted to wear jeans. Pop music was 'rubbish' that was not to be played in our house and the radio was not to be switched on at all on a Sunday. When I began my short-lived career as a chorister, I did an interview with the local BBC radio station which was broadcast on the Sabbath. I remember very clearly the angst betwixt my very strict father and my ever-so-slightly more relaxed mother, and then the novelty of firing up the wireless on a Sunday, all of us wondering what on earth was played on a Sabbath that prevented us from listening to it. Television was banned, as was a great deal of literature that would sit in the traditional 1980s or 1990s family home. The things children or 'non-believers' our age knew about – TV shows, politics, pop music and so on – were totally foreign to us.

My father was and remains a very complex man. He knows that I think he is driven almost exclusively by guilt, be it guilt over spending money or enjoying the odd earthly pleasure. He wrestles with it daily – I can still see the fight in his face. He possessed and demonstrated an iron will and commitment to a literal interpretation of scripture that inevitably revealed itself in a quick temper. He could be extraordinarily attentive – once building me an entire train set for one of my birthdays as I slept – but he was not happy, and our home life suffered for it.

The truth is, he longed to live in a society swept by the evangelical fervour of Charles Wesley or Martin Luther – so much so that I was given Luther's surname as my middle name. He was entirely ill-equipped to deal with modern society in almost any sense. Children, home, women, immigration, work – almost anything outside of chapel – challenged his matrix of views, and he simply could not cope. He was one of those most confusing of men – those who believe that God's will is unchallengeable, that we are all doomed unless we commit ourselves ever harder to the literal translation of the gospel, but who also draw hard at the ATM of forgiveness for their own contradictory shortcomings.

My mother was slightly (if not enough of) a different person. She was extremely subservient – as she was instructed to be in the scriptures – and always deferred to her husband's wishes, especially on any matter pertaining to disciplining the children. Her love for her offspring was clear, but she too was commanded by a higher calling – seemingly a 'hotline' to God – and that drove her behaviour. But at the same time, she had an uncanny ability to mask any unpleasantness in front of people outside the family – she would have been an extraordinary actress – and cover and excuse my father's moods. At the time, I could not understand her silence; in later life my view did not change even as her behaviour changed towards me.

Apparently, I was a very naughty child who needed strong discipline, but this may have just been an attempt to excuse the inexcusable. The presence of our parents' Christian faith seemed to legitimize this 'discipline' – God was in control, after all – and because this faith would simultaneously speak of ultimate forgiveness and inability to challenge God's will, I was left feeling confused, scared and vulnerable. I developed coping mechanisms that still cast shadows to this day. All this before the age of ten was not healthy.

At a young age, I decided that my parents were more concerned with the world's perception of me than they were about ensuring I was a well-rounded, secure, stable little boy. Understanding their true priorities made things around me easier to understand, but the insight brought its own kind of deep sadness.

Home was not just a physical test to get through; it was also wildly inconsistent. There is no doubt that I can recall some good times, when the clouds would part and the sun would reveal itself. I remember being taken away by my father for a couple of nights in a bed and breakfast; I remember laughing as I jumped on the autumn leaves in the bin, squashing them down so that we could fit more in as we cleared up the garden together. But – and it is a deep regret of mine – these memories were swamped by others less pleasant. My family could embark on a fantastic day out without any cross words, which would end with sudden explosions of temper, for reasons I as a boy simply did not understand, but were usually to do with the impending Sabbath. And yet on the rare occasions I was listening at chapel, I heard tales of qualities which could have changed my life at home: gentleness; peace; forgiveness; children sitting on Jesus's knee.

When things were good they were good. When the moments were bad, they were very hurtful and scarring, and it is these memories that endure.

The first real collision between the 1980s Mercer family and the outside world happened when my two eldest brothers, Neil and Keith, went off to join the Royal Navy. We had a strong family heritage within the Senior Service: Jack 'Boy' Cornwell, who was killed winning a VC at the Battle of Jutland in 1916, was a relative of mine. My grandfather was a radio operator in the Second World War. My father then signed up my two older brothers on their sixteenth birthdays and both attended HMS *Raleigh* in Torpoint, Cornwall, as ratings.

It is hard to comprehend, yet alone describe on paper, the soul-chilling contrasts that my brothers experienced in the weeks that followed their first days of naval service in the early 1980s. It was tough enough joining back then simply on the grounds that if you didn't have an eye-patch from the Falklands War you weren't really worth talking to. Added to that, Royal Navy basic training was famed the world over for being intrusive, destructive and degrading. Tough for your average young man then; indescribable for my brothers, whose upbringing meant they were entirely unequipped for any of it.

In chapel as children, we were encouraged not to mix with the 'unbelievers'. School was manageable, in that its influences were necessarily limited – we all went home afterwards. But for Neil and Keith, thrown together with the unbelievers full-time for military basic training and reluctant to tell them that they were going to hell for – amongst other things – not observing the Sabbath, the experience was deeply challenging.

Venturing beyond the confines of home was a tremendous shock for me and all my siblings, as it became clear to our young minds that not everybody in the world was a Strict Baptist. Shortly after we understood that other people were not the same as us, we realized we were going to have to get on with them anyway – and that these people could actually be our friends. It gradually dawned on us that some of them might be more stable anchors than our own points of reference – our parents or church groups. These 'friends' would end up looking out for us and some – as mad as it seemed – would end up loving us. This journey of emotional discovery was both remarkable for us and very hard to understand.

Neil and Keith were the first to grapple with these issues, and I will never forget the unique and deep challenges they faced, that dull but do not disappear with time.

In the early 1980s we moved from Dartford to Purley in South London, where my sister Naomi was born, before settling when I was five in Crowborough, East Sussex, the home of Sir Arthur Conan Doyle, the creator of Sherlock Holmes.

In Crowborough, my mother had one more daughter – Mary – finally bringing an end to my father's reproductive efforts. We lived in the old parsonage on the main road running up to Crowborough Cross, which is still there to this day. The two older boys had left for the Navy, so there were six children all crammed in as we got on with growing up.

There was a small personal benefit to me from Neil and Keith leaving, and widening their horizons, so early in my life. They were home on shore leave for Christmas 1987 when my father took issue with me again, this time for feeling Christmas presents under the tree. Neil and Keith caught my father disciplining me, and made it clear to him that if he didn't calm down he would come to regret it. They saved me that day, and although the discipline did not disappear altogether, there was certainly less of it.

It was around this time that my father became the area manager for Lloyds Bank. (I wouldn't have fancied going to him for a loan; reckless borrowing and lending was not a problem in south east England in those days – he single-handedly took care of that.) Simultaneously, my parents decided to set up a nursery school in our home. Crucially for me, this process made our home life more public, which was a very good thing.

It was a lot of work running a highly regulated Montessori nursery, and we all had to get stuck in to some extent. I had to get up early every day and clear either leaves or ice from all the paths around the house. I would then put out the toys for the children to play with in the garden, and put them away again when I got home from primary school. In those days I attended St John's primary, a mile and a half's walk down the road. I also cleaned out and fed the animals with which we now shared our lives, including some surprisingly aggressive guinea pigs and rabbits.

Life was definitely changing. Thanks to the nursery, my mother and father had to employ and engage with members of the general public more than they had ever been required to before. My parents were beginning, very slowly, to relinquish control over our lives, as their older children's independence made them realize the limits of their influence. At the same time, the stress this caused them was almost intolerable, and we all felt it in various ways.

I have a number of memories scarred on my mind. The time Keith drove up from Royal Naval Air Station Culdrose in Cornwall to see us at the parsonage, only to be shooed away from the door with a chair by my mother until he paid for his accommodation for the night. I remember another brother coming home for Christmas all the way from Derby on the train and asking for a lift from the station from my father. My father refused, and my brother re-boarded the train and returned to a lonely Christmas on his own. My parents' reaction to their loss of control became desperate; it was heartbreaking to watch and is still upsetting to recall.

These are rather distant memories now, but I cannot forget them. My parents have grown old, changing physically and emotionally as life has taken its toll. But crucially for me, I now have children of my own, on whom I obsessively check in whenever I wake in the night. I had hoped that being a parent would expose me to the sort of stresses and frustrations that I assumed lay behind my father's behaviour, and that I'd gain some insight into and perhaps a bit of peace with what went on. Unfortunately, it pushed me the other way, and I still can't comprehend much of my childhood. I love my parents; they have indeed changed and time heals much. But it can never change what actually took place, or the effects of what happened to me at the most formative and precious stages of a child's life.

2

A combination of my father's career upturn and the lucrative Montessori nursery school in our home meant that when I was seven my parents could afford to send me away to boarding school.

Temple Grove preparatory school was in Heron's Ghyll, just three miles from home in the opposite direction to my primary school. It is now converted luxury accommodation for the wealthy of East Sussex; then, it was a delightful old country house. My younger sister Naomi went to the pre-prep, but Heidi and I boarded. Our parents could have sent us as day pupils or weekly boarders, but chose the option of full boarders who stayed at the weekends too. Although I was pretty devastated at the time to be separated from my mother, it was probably best for all of us.

I'm told I loved some of the boarding experience, but my memories can be somewhat hazy. I remember corporal punishments, such as being made to eat a bar of soap for saying 'shit'. I remember plenty of 'double baths' with my male friends – the sort of thing that would perhaps land a school in trouble these days. I also remember the first time my mother bought me a Kinder egg for getting a 'plus' certificate. I rarely saw her, so when she did things like this it melted me.

It wasn't all such raucous fun. The weekends, when most

of the other kids would go home, were staggeringly lonely, and I'd cling onto my poor sister Heidi like Velcro. I loved the outdoors where I could go and do whatever I liked without recourse. I was never scared outside on my own and I was fascinated by the darkness where no one could see me. I could be as odd as I liked, repeating identical prayers like a mantra or reading my 'Olde Englishe' King James Bible, which I had won at Sunday School for reciting long parts of scripture by heart. I did find almost everyone else at the school intimidating, at least to some extent, and darkness gave me the opportunity to hide from a world about which I was extremely confused. Some of my form masters seemed to enjoy holding a position of authority more than actually stabilizing a child who was clearly deeply affected by his early years. My friends were so much more worldly wise and able to cope with school than me. I struggled to find my feet and, bizarrely, longed to run away home.

I used to work out how I could walk cross-country to the parsonage, how long it would take and what food I would need to sustain me. This was indeed odd, given the unhappiness of family life, but I think I missed the routine and regularity of home. In addition, now that Mother had opened a school and we had 'outsiders' coming in every day, the parsonage seemed a slightly more appealing prospect than boarding school.

I was eight years old when Heidi outlined the folly of making my way home – I would only be driven back to school again. I had to adapt and overcome, and forced myself to do so. She was in the choir, and invited me to join, promising me it wasn't like singing hymns at our Strict Baptist chapel down the road. Singing treble was easy for me, and I seemed good at it. It was a gift; one I did nothing to earn.

I had made friends at school and knew they were good people. But I also found it tough to have friends who did not share my family's beliefs; the Church taught that it was wrong and my guilt was simply too stifling. I felt pulled in two distinct directions; one minute I could be having fun with my friends, the next I'd be hating myself for breaking God's rules by playing football on a Sunday. Looking back, I couldn't have asked for better friends. I think people had an inkling about my home life and instead of bullying or teasing there was simple sympathy meted out by most staff and pupils alike.

Lots of people say that they don't care what others think of them; in my case being seen as so odd already by other children and their parents meant that by the age of nine I genuinely didn't give a shit what people thought of me.

So when it came to singing, I just got up there and did it. And I seemed to make people really happy. Some would cry when I sang, others would clap and get on their feet. I moved to Stoke Brunswick, an idyllic little prep school in West Sussex, that was better for music. There I was taken on by an inspirational and extremely talented music teacher called Mrs Barber. She managed to craft a pretty ordinary group of children into an award-winning choir that starred in BBC documentaries and won through to the finals of the Choir of the Year competition. Individually, I entered an *X Factor*-type competition to find the best chorister in the land – the National Choirboy of the Year Competition. I won the regional finals and came runner-up in the national final in 1993 to a boy whose voice broke shortly afterwards. As a result I fulfilled some of his singing commitments, while being trumpeted as Choirboy of the Year and instructed not to tell of his demise!

I sang at the Royal Festival Hall, for the Queen at the

Albert Hall and at the VE Day fiftieth anniversary celebrations in 1995 in Hyde Park, and abroad at international competitions for my school and on my own. And, of course, I sung in almost every bloody church in Sussex at Christmas.

In the process, I gained admiration and respect in spades; just not from the two people I, for some reason, still wanted to impress. Outwardly things looked great; once the car doors slammed life was still very different.

Heidi was extremely gifted on the piano and went to Wadhurst College to advance her music skills there, but I was joined at Stoke Brunswick by my younger sister, Naomi. Bizarrely, my homesickness remained chronic. I had a wonderful matron called Miss Warriner who consoled me through some excruciating scenes involving my parents as my sister and I were dropped off again, usually on a lonely Sunday afternoon, at the huge, empty prep school. Miss Warriner often let me watch some TV (yes, even on a Sunday) to calm my nerves, despite telling my friends and parents she didn't. She had a special place in my heart.

I enjoyed much of Stoke Brunswick – particularly the sport – and made some friends, but I never really saw them outside of school. I seemed to be popular enough, but remember feeling desperately lonely, particularly when Naomi seemed to settle in so much easier than me. Quite simply, I felt I was very, very different to my peers; most were extremely wealthy and privileged, and had home lives to return to that were entirely dissimilar to my own. Regrettably, I began to wonder what was wrong with my head: Why did I find being away from home so tough when I didn't even really like being at home in the first place?

The main thing I did enjoy as a boy was breaking free from the confines put on me by authority figures other than my parents. My parents' rule was so fearsome that others held no terrors for me, and I treated their rules with a distinct lack of respect. I would lead 'dormitory raids' from the boys' to the girls' dormitories in the small hours. Having achieved our objective, I would sit triumphantly on some poor girl's bed before leading the raiding party back to our room. I was completely disinterested in the girls; I simply enjoyed the excitement of potentially 'being caught', whatever consequences that might have. I also managed to pick the lock on the tuck cupboard and regularly led a night-time patrol to raid some tuck, which I would then sell on to raise cash for all sorts of things I did not have – including a pair of jeans.

Despite my bad behaviour at Stoke Brunswick, in 1995 I sung my way to prestigious music scholarships for myself and Naomi, who was by now my closest and dearest friend, to Eastbourne College, a beautiful Victorian secondary school.

I was the first in my family to go to public school, something that caused consternation amongst my brothers. They were so deeply scarred by their upbringing that they almost resented any opportunity, however self-earned, that was presented to the younger members of the family. Because I was the only boy in the younger half of siblings, their resentment fixated on me. But I still saw the scholarship as an opportunity. Towards the end of my time at Stoke Brunswick I realized the folly of my homesickness; by the time I got to Eastbourne College it was largely cured, although the mental challenges of dealing with an unorthodox upbringing would manifest themselves in another way. Eastbourne College meant I could be truly away from home, and aged fourteen on a top music scholarship I thought musical greatness beckoned.

It didn't work out quite like that.

For one thing, although their children's musical talents had started off as something to be nurtured, they ended up as an obsession for my parents. We were required to perform as a family whenever relatives or friends from chapel would come over to our home. There was a rigidly enforced timetable for music practice, and some quite bizarre rules to go with it. I had taken up the violin by now. My mother was impressed at a recent concert by how high a violinist had held her violin; for many months afterwards I had a round pencil eraser placed (not attached) under the bridge of my violin. It was not to fall to the floor as a result of the violin not being perfectly flat under my chin, no matter how many hours I practised. Bizarre, and bloody torturous. It was even worse when my sense of guilt made me continue the exercise at school, in case God was watching and told my mother. Humiliating doesn't cover it. My interest in music waned somewhat, and I focused on other aspects of school life.

I particularly loved sport, where I didn't have to interact verbally with others but could just run my guts out and collapse at full time. I couldn't play enough football, rugby and cricket. My rugby and football skills were poor compared to everyone else's but I wasn't too bad at cricket, and did a summer school to beef up my skills. I was very good at striking things in general and my father also introduced me to a pastime where you could stare at something and hit it as hard as you can without having to go and get it – the golf driving range.

With no children left at home except Mary, my father's outlet for his frustrations was said driving range, and I would go along too. Eventually he bought me a half set of clubs and I was hooked. I used to break in to the Royal Eastbourne at hole four and play until hole seventeen, where I would duck out and walk the four miles back to the school campus without paying a penny. Everyone at the club must have known what I was up to, but they let me get on with it; I was never challenged.

I represented Eastbourne College at football, cricket, hockey, tennis, rugby and golf. Despite never being the most talented, I was usually made captain. I wasn't loud – quite the opposite – but I found it easy to self-motivate, and others would simply follow my lead. Looking back, perhaps the leadership bug had infected me already, without me knowing it.

While outwardly I was the popular sports captain getting stuck-in and appearing relatively 'normal', behind closed doors I was enduring a sort of mental, religion-based torment. I felt the heavy hand of religion on my shoulder wherever I went. Before bed every night I said the same prayer in my head that my father had taught me, thinking the right things at the same time. If my mind wandered I would have to start again, lest harm come to someone. I believed this would be my fault, and that my father would find out. I was to read the Bible every day, and I did so, petrified of misunderstanding it and thinking thoughts in my head that were wrong, and of God judging me.

Whenever I shut my eyes and tried to sleep my mind became a battleground, as I wrestled with growing up in a world full of 'temptations' such as television on a Sunday, while being haunted by the contradictory and guilt-driven religion I had ingrained into me. My mother and father were very clear – deviating from what was taught at our Strict

Baptist chapel would result in 'eternal flame and gnashing of teeth'. It is difficult to articulate the effects of this on an adolescent boy, and I developed quite a case of obsessive compulsive disorder. Nights when everyone else was in bed, I was staring at taps, flicking light switches on and off, and washing my hands to the extreme, sometimes emptying a 500ml liquid soap container in one go. I was terrified people would find out and realize I wasn't coping with home life as I should be, and I tried to do most of it in private when everyone else was asleep. Weirdly, the days were an entirely different matter, and none of the guilt really bothered me. It was just when I shut my eyes. I was an extremely disturbed young kid who went through boarding school barely getting more than four or five hours' sleep a night.

I made some extremely good friends at Eastbourne. I was still very different to them, and rather ashamedly begrudged their 'normality', but on the whole they didn't judge me for my 'different' home life, and I didn't end up in too many scraps with the posh kids. There were four of us in particular – Olly, Dan, Mike and me – who always seemed to end up in the same sports teams and at each other's houses (except mine) when time allowed. From sixteen onwards we were also trying to get into pubs and drink, pretending to be the adults we most certainly were not.

I completed my GCSEs and then A Levels with lower than average results – ten GCSEs grade A–C and three A Levels C–E. I almost completed my Gold Duke of Edinburgh Award (my mother had already bought her hat for the palace) but got caught taking a taxi when I'd had enough on one of the practice yomps and was thrown off the scheme. I wasn't too upset; by then I was starting to pay a little more attention to females and had mainly used the expeditions as a chance to chat to girls in a captive environment – their tent on a rainy night – and to get away from bloody music practice.

I remember the dreaded day when my A Level results came through. I had been working a series of jobs and saved some money to go abroad after I'd finished the exams, so I was away from home when the results came through. I don't know why I was shocked by how poorly I had done, but I still was. My wonderful sister Naomi kept ringing up UCAS clearing, trying to get me a university place that I didn't really want. In the end, I called off the chase. I was done with full-time education.

It wasn't that I was lazy – I was a bloody hard worker – I just found concentrating on one thing particularly difficult when I had such mammoth internal battles going on. I had no idea what I was going to do with my life. Only when I was physically exhausted did I seem to manage a modicum of internal peace, when my mind would stop ticking over. I needed to try and get to grips with it all. There was very little awareness about 'mental health' in those days. I just felt like I was mad.

3

I got my first job at the age of fourteen, as a paperboy. The early starts, coupled with the criminal pay, were only ameliorated by the chance to flick through the latest *Playboy* with the other lads in the newsagent. We'd have about five minutes before we'd be sent on our way to deliver them through people's letterboxes, together with the *Kent and East Sussex Courier*. It was always awkward when I recognized the name from chapel.

Being a paperboy was followed by working as a waiter and slops man on the washing up machines at the Spa Hotel in Tunbridge Wells. Being a waiter was harder work than I hoped for, but I made up for it with regular sit-ins inside the walk-in refrigerator, tasting the delicious yoghurt or wolfing down a cold croissant because I hadn't got up early enough to eat breakfast.

When I was eighteen, I progressed to Lighting Department Manager at a department store. I say I was the manager, but I didn't manage anyone. What I did manage to do was get together with the head of the menswear department, who was a very attractive girl five years my senior. Unfortunately, she was also the girlfriend of a notorious hard man, who was quite upset when he found out. Overhearing a conversation between her and the regional manager in the store cafe, when he told her that being with me was 'not good for her career', was a low point.

Luckily, I found a more serious job through Olly from Eastbourne College, who had essentially became my surrogate brother as we went through our teens. His father owned a farm in Sussex, and I could stay there during school holidays, for as long as I wanted, in exchange for chores. I spent most of my summers there. Olly Pile overlooked the many oddities that I had developed in my childhood, and was still trying to shake off in my adolescence, even though I reckon they made me pretty hard work to hang around with. We spent long, hot summers driving illegally across the South Downs on his motorbikes or drinking ale for the first time, listening to Oasis and Blur. One thing I had to put up with was his family's determination to drink milk straight from the cow, without any skimming or treatment. We often went shooting, with mixed results. I was no dead-eyed Dick, but Olly really struggled with a gun. I would often drive the truck right up next to a rabbit in the dead of night, only for Olly to shoot the wing mirror off. Awkward conversations at breakfast with his long-suffering father were the norm.

Somehow Olly managed to get us both a job in London through some rich uncle of his. We'd be working for a fund manager in Farringdon, and our role there was to answer the phone, do the admin for some of the fund's products and try to start a career in finance.

We lived with one of Olly's family friends just off the King's Road. I passed the financial exams but found the rest of it mind-numbingly dull, and consequently messed around far too much in an attempt to escape my mental wrestles. By day, I looked at my fellow workers and was filled with sympathy that this was their lot in life – an office in London, the daily commute, a very small world. By night, I was drinking far too much in an effort to sleep, and being a dick in the process.

I spent the majority of my time trying to get with a girl who worked in the office, but had once been a dancer in one of those gentlemen's establishments. I wore her down and eventually she taught me a thing or two. I always pitied my partners in those days; my nocturnal pseudo-religious behaviour meant they must have thought me very odd indeed. *Her* boyfriend was rather unhappy with me as well. Incidentally and rather ironically, he was also some sort of hard man from Essex. Looking back I'm not sure what sort of girls I was going after . . .

Before long, it was clear that spending far too much money, drinking a fair amount and chasing posh girls down the King's Road, while trying to build a career in something that failed to hold my interest at all, was not enough for me.

My father, who had relaxed a great deal by now after many years of strict adherence, wanted me to join the military like my brothers. I agreed that this might be something I'd be interested in, but I certainly wasn't set on it. While I wavered, he succeeded in getting me an interview with a retired General he knew through his work at the bank.

The General got the measure of me within a few minutes (it wasn't hard), and told me he had a plan for me. He paid for me to spend two days in February with a couple of his old soldiers, who had left the Special Air Service to set up a civilian training and leadership company. The course was held in the woods not far from my family home. We dispensed with the teambuilding tasks and high-wire courses pretty early on, and spent much of the day and late into the night chatting.

They outlined how much they had enjoyed the military, and were very honest about why they left. They had achieved what they had wanted to as young men, and they carried the air of confident, self-assured professional and personal satisfaction that I longed for but found entirely missing in London. They had lived a boy's dream – friends, the SAS, operations, war, holidays. And, crucially, they seemed stable and happy. I wanted that.

They made me feel that even I could join the Army, despite knowing so little about it. I should join a specialist unit, and then I could be the outdoors loner of my youth on exercise and operations but a 'normal' person in barracks – a perfect mix, it seemed to me.

I said I wanted to sign up as a soldier and do it 'properly'. I didn't really fancy being an officer. I didn't want the responsibility, or the discomfort I'd already experienced at Eastbourne College of spending my time with much wealthier, and better educated and bred men than me.

But the two men told me not to be such a prick. If I was good enough I should be an officer – the Army needed good officers from all sorts of backgrounds – and who was I to judge where I best fitted in? I could, after all, spend all my time with the blokes if I wanted to. I didn't have to become a moleskin-wearing, corduroy-jacketed wonder overnight.

I asked what was the most pressurized and demanding role in the Army. They suggested that controlling joint fires – meaning coordinating aviation, air, artillery and mortar fire – while people were being shot, was very testing. It came with a lot of pressure and responsibility. I would have to master multiple technical and communications skills and operate at the highest professional standards; mistakes killed people. And I would get to scrap with the enemy too. Apart from the last bit, I was sold.

I did some research and found the only unit of the Army that I thought ticked all of these boxes. In Plymouth, on the south coast, there was a specialist unit called 29 Commando Regiment, Royal Artillery. The mix of soldier and seamanship that my family history demanded was a bonus. You had to pass the notorious All Arms Commando Course to join them, and then work your way up through the guns and reconnaissance jobs before you could become a fires controller – the job I was after. Training would take a few years and I could build a career. What came after that, I would have to wait and see, but I would always be a Commando. I might have a wife and a family by the time I had finished, who knows? One thing was certain – Plymouth was a long way away from Sussex.

That was what I was really after, if I'm honest. A family of my own in my own part of the world, where I could stand on my own two feet and perhaps put the past behind me. Home still defined everything I did. I found Christmases extremely sad; epic fall-outs were inevitable as we all struggled to readjust to a changing family dynamic – parents and siblings alike.

The battleground in my mind had become debilitating, and interfered heavily in my daily life. I felt I had blown it: by attending Eastbourne College, I had been given academic opportunities that were beyond so many; I simply had not made enough of them. My fear of my parents was now replaced with an almost sympathetic view of them. Despite their shortcomings, they had worked hard to earn money to enable me to go to that school. I felt like an incredibly wasteful kid sometimes.

But it was out of my hands. I was unstable and unhappy, and I longed for some inner peace from the religious torment that engulfed me every time I went to bed. Despite slowly becoming an adult, I felt like a boy emotionally. I thought that I struggled inordinately due to some strange lack of robustness. I had moments – days even – when the battles would leave me. But they always returned. My self-esteem was affected enormously.

As I turned nineteen, I knew I had to leave all this stuff behind and re-shape myself before my mind was lost. The Army was for me.

I sat my Regular Commissions Board – the entrance exams for officer training – in 2000; for the first time I really wanted to pass something and perform to my capacity, rather than let my performance be shaped by my internal struggles.

Inevitably, I totally cocked it up. If one could simply leave one's internal struggles behind at the flick of a switch, the world would be a very different place. I was shy around the other candidates – all these 'hooray henrys'. I would have happily sat there and taken the piss out of them all day, but struggled to discuss the finer points of Field Marshal Slim's principles of war. Insecure piss-takers were not really what the Army was looking for.

I felt like a bit of a fraud, and let it show. Having taken on some significant 'timber' during my time in London, I was painfully slow during the physical assessment. I went home convinced that for the first time I had had a lifeline hung out for me and I had thrown it away.

While I was at Westbury, where the RCB was based, I was

told about a course for those who hadn't failed the Board outright, but were generally considered 'below par'. Those who passed it would win a place at Sandhurst. Called Rowallan Company, it was the sort of course around which countless legends brood and was designed to build character through leadership for those a bit rough around the edges. It was made for me.

By now I was living with my brother Keith in Lewes, Sussex which had a good rail link to get to London for my job with the fund manager in the City. Keith had given up his career as a naval aviator to earn some money and have some fun flying for Virgin Atlantic. And having fun he was. He would often take me on trips with him, but what we got up to cannot be committed to paper. Keith also introduced me to curry, and we had a cracking local pub, full of Sussex hippies. There we would while away the evenings, putting our piano skills to good use and singing old songs, updating them with ruder and ruder lyrics about hippies until we were inevitably asked to leave, laughing as we were booed out of the door. We did have an extraordinary fraternal bond, borne out of the shared experiences of our upbringing.

I remember the summer morning at Keith's when I got my results letter from Westbury. The words on the posh paper were shouting out at me. I had scraped through with a 'Rowallan Pass'. They even sent me a video of the course, showing some lads my age running around in rugby shirts carrying what looked like a telegraph pole. It seemed like fun. Life was a little bereft back then.

When I informed my father, to his credit he was adamant I should attend Rowallan. I wasn't so sure, by now only half-committed to a potential career in the Army. Then something happened that changed the world profoundly, and cemented my decision to join up.

I returned early from working in London one day and flicked on the TV. It was 11 September 2001. I watched the first plane, and then the second, crash into the Twin Towers. Then the first tower fell. I saw a couple of jumpers – those faced by the agonizing choice between burning in the building or falling to their death. I was talking to Olly on the phone as the second tower came down.

If I'm being entirely honest, there wasn't much nobility in my initial decision to join the Army. The idea of travelling the world, playing sport and getting away from home life was enough for me. However, in the immediate aftermath of 9/11 those motivations began to be rivalled by another; one that affected many that day, and that had affected generations before me in times of great national change.

I grew up with the IRA creating havoc in the UK and dominating our news agenda. Their victims were often unconnected to the province and wholly innocent of wrongdoing. On 9/11 a lot of those who died hadn't even heard of Al Qaeda; many were Muslims. Dead for going to work.

The world could be a very dark place. Dark men with dark ambitions could only run amok if your average man like me stood by, and allowed this evil to spawn. I didn't know much about being a Muslim, but I knew enough to understand that killing three thousand innocent people in New York on a bright September morning had nothing to do with it. These cowards didn't *believe* in anything. It was all about power and selfish ambition trading on man's inhumanity to man.

As I was maturing and relinquishing the bonds of home life, I started to develop a real need to stand up to those who preyed on the weak and the vulnerable in society, perhaps unsurprising given the way my siblings and I entered the real world after growing up in our family. Even now, when I think of those who took the piss out of us back then . . . I would like to meet them again.

So back then on that infamous day, and in my own way, I still wanted to fight back against what I was seeing, however desperately ill-equipped a messed-up young man like me may have been. I knew I wanted to contribute. Something was growing inside me – a combative spirit. I was beginning to feel like a bit of an animal – at my best when physically exhausted, when my mind would finally rest somewhat. I thought if I could learn to tame it I might become a good soldier.

These motivations propelled me forward in those few months before I did something life-changing like entering the Army, a time when everyone wants to change their mind.

The Royal Military Academy Sandhurst is the premier military academy in the world. My father drove me to the gates. By now I was very well-informed about the course I was about to undertake. It cost half a million pounds to run, produced very few officer candidates, and because of this low pass rate (six of forty-two on my intake) it was being discontinued. I was going to be 'fortunate' enough to be part of the final class. It was, as the training team would never let me forget, a 'privilege'.

Dad and I were slightly early on 28 January 2002. We went and sat in the Camberley Marks and Spencer across the road for a cup of tea. I had never been to the area before in my life. Through the academy's gates we could see an imposing, palatial facade with some immaculately kept lawns running up to it.

The nausea was almost overwhelming. At twenty, I was a good seven years younger than the average age of people attending Sandhurst. I was considerably underqualified too – four out of five had degrees, and those that didn't had a decent business background behind them, or had already entered the Army in the ranks and were now looking to commission.

My father, I think, saw himself as the general who never was. I distinctly remember part of our conversation over that M&S cup of tea.

'What if I don't like it, Dad? Lots of people don't.'

'You *will* like it, son.'

That was that.

4

It was cold that January afternoon when I arrived in A Block, Rowallan Company. The staff were very pleasant to our parents. However our parents were quickly shepherded out of the door at which point we were ordered out of our civilian clothes and into our uniform for the next three months – denim trousers, a rugby shirt, combat high boots and a 1958 pattern webbing belt with a black army-issue water bottle on it. We put our civilian clothing into a holdall, which was then locked away.

After that, we were summoned for parade and split into two platoons. When speaking about myself, I was to refer to myself as 'Cadet Mercer'. We filed into a classroom with the smell of fart hanging heavy in the air; someone was scared already. We were introduced to the platoon commander, a lanky sort from the Parachute Regiment who seemed unable to make facial expressions.

'However tough you fuckers think you are, this course will break you. It will form you as new men – ready to enter the commissioning course to become an officer in the British Army. If you get there.'

He seemed to like the grand announcements – I think we all knew why we were there.

I did feel like telling him that breaking me wasn't going to take particularly long. Perhaps we could get on to the re-forming part of the course sooner? I had no idea how this process was going to work.

A platoon sergeant got up after him. He was small – never a good start. Small people in the Army generally over-compensate. He smoked heavily, which in the following weeks would give me hope that he might suffer a heart attack during some exercise and be replaced by somebody a bit nicer.

'This is the hardest fucking course outside Special Forces in the British Army,' he politely bellowed.

Yeah OK, I thought. Fifteen years later, I can safely say that he was absolutely right, although I would remove the Special Forces bit.

I made friends pretty quickly. Cadet Oscar was a beast of a man, who I would come to respect above all others for his ability to keep going when others – literally all of the rest of us – could not take another step. There was Cadet Matthews also. Our friendship became so deep that I was the best man at his wedding five years later. He drove a blue, still-immaculate 1985 Ford Escort. He came from Essex and in his own words was a 'pikey' like me, so we got on well amongst all the university types.

The conditions were fairly austere. We could have one radio stereo per platoon in our twenty-one man rooms, provided that the dial did not move off BBC Radio Four. We were 'so fucking thick' we couldn't pass the RCB properly, and this way we might be educated. This was according to a platoon sergeant who, I think, left school for borstal at age fourteen.

Mobile phones were handed in on day one and were banned. So was leaving the 200-metre parameter of the Rowallan Company complex. Watches were banned too, so there was no way of telling time or date. Moaning wasn't banned.

The physical exercise was brutal. On the first day, we were given an induction into something called the 'pain machine'. I'm pretty sure this would have been banned had the course not been discontinued. It involved lifting tractor tyres, doing heaves (pull-ups) for five minutes and seemingly interminable crawls through all the shittiest areas of the camp. The crime that warranted this punishment always varied, and was not always understood. Often it was for a collective untidy accommodation, sometimes a 'general malaise' in the platoon, or some equally unaccountable reason.

The course was brutal and much of the early days passed in a blur. The physicality of the course was something beyond what I was expecting. Strapped to a log for miles and miles; endless route marches at just a slightly quicker pace than I could cope with; 'robustness tests' through ice-covered lakes and survival exercises that genuinely felt like a quest for survival rather than the controlled, sanitized examples you see on television these days.

But the strange thing was, I liked the pain; it cleared my head. It required real mental discipline to not give up and I enjoyed the challenge of never letting my mind cave in, despite my body doing so. At night-time I found that I finally slept; granted not for long, but I slept, and things began to change for me.

The instructors had this nasty trick of waking you up at three in the morning. Bedtime wasn't until all our tasks were done, which was usually around 1 a.m., and with reveille every day at 5 a.m., sleep was at a premium.

Sometimes the instructors would come in screaming and take us on exercise for a week, right out of the blue. They never told you where you were going on these exercises, so you always took maps of each of the seven different training areas in the UK with you. When you arrived at a training area, you had to work out where you were using the ground in front of you.

This sometimes followed thirteen-hour trips in the back of a Bedford truck – an open-ended lorry used to transport troops. They have a top speed of 41 mph and are rigidly sprung, so one feels every bump through the spine and has little protection from the elements. I can remember some of those journeys through the night like they were yesterday.

People dropped off the course like flies. The intelligent ones quit. The weaker ones were trampled on, literally, while carrying logs around the training area. I didn't really fall into either of those groups at that stage and seemed quite well-liked by the directing staff; they had probably seen my type before – strange boy from a strange home – and been overcome by sympathy. Or so I hoped.

The first weekend's leave came after four weeks. We were unsure of the date or the time, so it came as a surprise. The course was paraded in civilian clothes, and – mother of all privileges – we were marched to the pay office on camp and given £50 for the weekend's leave. Fifty pounds, I jest not.

Just before we were allowed to 'fall-out' for the weekend, four names were called out. Mine was one, as were Oscar and Matthews. Stood there in our civilian attire ready to go home, we were singled out in front of the course.

'Ha ha! You're not going home at all. Your equipment was not up to the standard in this morning's inspection!' bellowed the platoon sergeant.

I thought it was a joke. My kit was fine.

'Get your fucking denims back on and get outside the platoon commander's office for a chat.'

We stood in silence, stunned, before he started manically shouting again. The four of us ran upstairs.

I snapped, as did Oscar. I went down to see the staff to put in an 'official complaint', whatever that was. I didn't bother knocking, but walked in and asked what the hell was going on. Bad move. I was dragged outside for a personal training session with the company sergeant major.

You only spoke to the company sergeant major if you were really in the shit. On this occasion, he was very much speaking to me.

I remember only parts of the next hour and a half. I have a mental snapshot of hanging on a heave bar for an interminable amount of time, tears not far away due to the sheer pain in my arms, with the sergeant major spitting his angry words in my face:

'You are pathetic; weak and pathetic. Why are you here, Mercer? Just fucking leave.' He managed to drag this theme out for what seemed like the entire session.

I physically collapsed at the end of it, was ordered back to my feet and collapsed again, seemingly drifting in and out of consciousness with my face stuck to the dead leaves and mud. I could just about hear the sergeant major:

'You are a pathetic little fuck, Mercer. Pathetic. Be under no illusion – pull that trick again and I will take you around the other side of the block.'

I didn't know what this meant, but the threat of further, more concentrated violence was pretty clear.

'Yes, Staff,' I mumbled.

He walked off, leaving me on the ground.

That weekend was tough on the mind. The staff were

clearly trying to get us to quit. The four of us were given some work to do to present to the rest of the course the following Monday, fresh from their weekend off. I led the presentation, which was on Ernest Shackleton. I casually dropped into my talk that when Shackleton joined the Navy he was given adequate leave, and that this contributed to his success.

There was an explosion from the back of the room where all the staff were sitting. They took this as a direct jibe at them, and although it wasn't, I could see where they were coming from. I was made to stand and watch both platoons (their numbers diminished significantly by this stage) while they were systematically destroyed on the 'pain machine.'

'Have you seen *A Few Good Men*, Mercer? Heard of 'code red'?' said the horrible little colour sergeant from the other platoon. He was small, too. And angry. 'Good luck tonight!'

'No, Colour Sergeant,' I said. 'I do not have a television at home, Staff.'

'You don't have a fucking television? What are you, some sort of monk?'

'No, Colour Sergeant. My parents are religious, Staff.'

'Your parents are religious? Is this a fucking joke?'

'No, Colour Sergeant, it is not a joke.'

I think this course thrashing was designed to get my mates to rally against me, but it had the opposite effect, and while afterwards I was sorry, they wouldn't hear a bit of it.

'Funniest thing I ever seen,' said Matthews.

'I actually enjoyed it,' said Oscar.

I wasn't entirely sure why the staff had suddenly taken against me, or if they were simply pretending. I think I must have been quite eccentric, or really bloody annoying. Probably a bit of both.

Later that bruising week I was summoned downstairs to the directing staff's offices. All seven instructors were in their little hang-out room when I walked in.

'Relax, Mercer, you're just here for a cup of tea,' one of the platoon sergeants said. This made me very nervous indeed.

These instructors had been vile to me for six weeks now, and now they were being friendly. They didn't even baulk when I said I'd prefer coffee. With sugar.

'How's it going?' they asked, as one of them put a mug in my hand.

I felt like being truthful and telling them what a group I thought they were. I tried to stop wishing I had a grenade on me that could take out the whole room.

'Yeah, fine. Think the worst of it is over now, but as ever I don't know. I don't even know what day it is,' I said, trying to garner some sympathy.

This was a clever answer, making them feel good that they were fucking me up, and at the same time showing I hadn't given in and was just hoping for the end. I was just prolonging the conversation – the coffee was rather nice.

'So, Mercer, who are the troublemakers? We are getting to the point now where we need those who are unsuitable to go. Tell us who is causing the problems. What about Hillmoor?'

There were some problem people on the course, but I only hated one of them, Cadet Hillmoor. He was lazy, posh and weak and we spent interminable hours in the evening helping him with his kit. The staff knew I didn't like this guy. But they must also have thought I was very stupid.

Thinking fast, I mumbled some nonsense to buy me some time and they all fake-laughed. I took a deep breath.

'Unlucky, lads,' I said. 'I'm not going to come in here and grass anyone up I'm afraid, Staff. But thanks for the coffee.'

I put the empty cup down and went to leave. I had a second to wonder why I'd called them 'lads' before the company sergeant major exploded again. It was worse this time – he was in front of his training team. Time for him to show off, I think. He destroyed me verbally – or so I assumed, he had a heavy northern accent and I only caught bits of it – but just about kept his hands off me this time. As soon as he paused to draw breath and looked like he was winding down, I beat a hasty retreat.

One of the two platoon commanders was from 29 Commando. He followed me out.

'Mercer?' he said quietly. When I looked back he added, 'Good for you. Go away.'

He winked, and I knew I just had to get through the next four weeks and I would pass the course.

The remaining weeks were as tough physically as anything I can remember, but the staff behaved completely differently to me. Smiling, taking the mick. My waterproof trousers and jacket were old and shit – doing nothing against some of the epic weather we were working through that winter. I asked for a new set and was handed a brand-new pink ensemble. I was given the option to refuse and get wet. I took the new Gore-Tex and looked ridiculous.

The exercises were hard – they all started with rain-sodden two-day solitary marches across Dartmoor and Otterburn, carrying significant weight made heavier because it was so wet. The North Sea blows in hard and wet across Otterburn, and it had broken many souls in its time. I certainly saw my soul on those nights, and what it took to keep it going.

Just surviving in some of these conditions was tough.

Hallucinations were regular. We had wet and dry drills – keeping one set of dry clothes to wear for a couple of hours in your sleeping bag at night, and putting your wet, ice-clad clothes on again in the darkness before the dawn. These experiences ground away at us, mentally and physically. But for some reason I was resolute, and even became a source of strength for others. I would pass huddles of quitters, who had put up a tent and were waiting for the staff to come and collect them, but giving up never crossed my mind. I used to keep thinking of the 'yardage' I was putting between myself as a disturbed, vulnerable adolescent and who or what I was becoming on this course.

They were teaching us independence, discipline, an unyielding attitude and the ability to simply keep going. Many dropped by the wayside. From a course of forty-two, seven of us lined up against each other in two teams to complete the final race – twenty-six miles across the entire Otterburn training area, with two 20kg ammo boxes per man. Somehow I was one of the six finishers.

Unbeknown to us at the time, the original Rowallan Company course – on which the modern version was entirely modelled – was used to select the first commandos before they entered full commando training during the Second World War. It was the traditional 'naughty boys' course, but it produced brilliant results in those who stuck with it. Some older men had visited us at irregular intervals, often with the course officer, but I didn't take much notice in my various comatose states. I found out later that these were veterans from the original course.

At the end of the final march in Otterburn, we formed in a hollow square and were addressed by one of the veterans. His words were between us and the hills, but they have stayed with me for the rest of my life. He was from a generation that defined itself by the qualities we learnt on that course. In my wet, muddy, sweat and piss-stained clothing, I felt deeply privileged for the first time in my life.

I experienced a strange new emotion too. I felt a deep and warm sense of security – pride even. It was the first time in twenty years I had felt that way.

When we returned to the accommodation block at the Royal Military Academy, we were informed that we were going to close this historic course in style. The symbol of the course is the stag's head that had hung above the office of the Commanding Officer (CO) since the very first Rowallan Company almost sixty years earlier. That deer was shot in the area around Spean Bridge – where the first commandos trained in the 1940s. We were going to turn it into a backpack and carry it, entirely on foot, from Sandhurst back to the Highlands of Scotland.

An interesting ten days followed. Not many of us could run properly any more, but we did trot a half marathon each, every day in a relay, 24/7. My running partner was the platoon commander from 29 Commando, who became a friend of mine. Running at a pace that allowed us to talk, I learnt a lot about him and his motivations, and was even more determined to join that unit. He is an impressive guy, who has had an equally impressive career. Like the CO of the course, he is now a general, and reached that rank in a very short space of time.

We always did the night shifts – I liked being out at night. Night-times were destroying me before the course, yet now I loved them. The staff couldn't see you put your hands in your pockets in the freezing winter and you could wear a soft hat, provided it was gone by the first shards of dawn.

And so, the most formative months of my life came to a close. I made friends for life and found myself brutally but firmly changed from boy to man. I had learnt hard and painful lessons that I would carry with me through the battlefields of southern Afghanistan, the jungles of Belize and Brunei, the Arctic wastes of Norway, the mountains of south Wales and into the Houses of Parliament.

All these years later, the truth is that nothing came close to Rowallan.

The Commissioning Course at Sandhurst was a sausage machine, and a deep disappointment by comparison. I hated it. It was all uniform, marching and soft exercises – I wouldn't put it down as more than some slightly aggressive camping. You had to 'play the game', and I wasn't great at this particular game. I needed to develop a 'career laugh' to get on, it seemed.

However, I did make some truly great friends, and coped with some relatively significant challenges, such as completing fitness tests while still drunk. But, all in all, I was delighted to leave and move on. I graduated in April 2003, as UK forces went over the border into Iraq for the second Gulf War.

Tony Blair attended my passing out parade.

'Yours is a noble calling,' he told us.

When he got to me in the line he asked me why I joined the Army. Good question.

'For the boys,' I said.

The company started laughing. The drill instructors started getting very upset.

'I didn't mean it like that, sir,' I said.

Blair laughed.

In order to join my chosen unit – 29 Commando Regiment Royal Artillery – I had to commission into the wider Royal Artillery Regiment first, and then hope I got selected for service as a commando.

Some of my peers were getting pulled out early to go and fill jobs that were urgently needed in the Operational Order of Battle (ORBAT) for Iraq. I wanted to go to war. My brother Stuart wrote to me at Sandhurst. He was a medical officer onboard RFA *Argus*, and had treated three wounded British soldiers engaged by a United States Air Force A-10 ground-attack jet. He wanted me to stay away from Iraq.

Rather than the frontline, the Army decided to task me instead with completing Young Officer Training for the Royal Artillery at Larkhill in Wiltshire. If Sandhurst was relatively relaxed after Rowallan Company, this was a barely disguised student's union. While the finer points of gunnery were lost on a lot of us, the opportunity to let off some steam after the confines of Sandhurst was not.

I loathed much of the Commissioning Course and Young Officer Training, but I regret this now. I was a machine after Rowallan Company and I wanted to kick on again with another tough course. And, if I'm honest, I did find the 'officer thing' rather uncomfortable. I was terribly self-conscious and I'm embarrassed about it now. I should have just enjoyed myself a bit more, and made the most of the privilege.

I did make good use of my time at Larkhill in some ways; I made friends with my fellow officers, got fitter and earned some money to buy a car, which would allow me to expand my hunting ground for girlfriends beyond the public transport network of southern England.

During this training cycle, I became close friends with

someone who I could tell was also a bit uncomfortable with the whole 'officer thing'. A tall, gangly, badly coordinated but very funny man called James Goddard. Jimmy and I were to become close friends for life, and my friendship with him has had a deep and lasting impact on me.

I was asked to put down three choices of regiment I wanted to be posted to in the Royal Artillery, and filled out all three spaces with '29 Commando'. There were two slots available at 29 Commando that year and Jimmy and I both wanted one. Plenty of others did as well, but we were determined to stick together, and when the forms came round he did the same as me.

'You're a bit silly aren't you?' said the ever-so-condescending chief instructor. 'You can't even complete a form properly.'

'I just want to go to 29, sir. I'm not sure what I'll do if I don't. Sorry to be so firm,' I replied.

'For not filling out the form correctly you can polish the gun outside the office for half an hour every day before parade. But you can go to 29.'

He never got in early; I wasn't going to polish the gun. But I was off to 29, as was Jimmy.

I had spent a lot of time at Sandhurst and Larkhill trying to recover from Rowallan Company, so I had my work cut out if I was to pass the Commando Course. First time passes were a requirement for officers in those days.

5

On a warm, late summer's evening in September 2003, I arrived in Plymouth and walked through the imposing gates of the Royal Citadel on the Hoe – home to 29 Commando Regiment Royal Artillery. I remember very clearly the first time I ascended the ramparts of this famous sixteenth-century fort, which dominates the Plymouth foreshore, and looked out across the iconic natural harbour that is Plymouth Sound. The Royal Citadel is the longest continuously military-occupied fort in Europe. The guns predominantly point out not towards the sea, but the City itself.

29 Commando Regiment remains a unique unit in the ORBAT of the British Army. Formed to provide close all-weather fire support to the Royal Marines, each man was expected to pass the All Arms Commando Course in order to stay in the regiment. With operations from Aden to Northern Ireland and prominent roles in the Falklands, Sierra Leone and Iraq, the tales emanating from this place were the stuff of legend. The evening I arrived I was fully aware of the personal challenge that lay ahead, but I also felt that I had arrived somewhere that I just might belong. I didn't know, then, that this place would one day become my spiritual home, and that these soldiers and officers would become my family.

First, I had to go and earn my Green Beret and become

a qualified commando. I was instructed to turn up to a place called Okehampton Battle Camp on the very northern edge of Dartmoor in Devon. Okehampton is an isolated Army outpost built largely during the Second World War, which looked as if it had received precisely zero development since. The camp itself is perched on a small area of flat ground on the northern side of Yes Tor. Instructors on any course there would happily dispatch you for a quick run for any infraction, deserved or not, with the bonus (for them) of the site being on a steep slope and close to a prominent tor that disappeared into the clouds.

Jimmy and I turned up two weeks into the six week pre-commando course run by the regiment. This wasn't our fault. At our stage in a military career, you simply do what you are told by the individual who is most likely to cause you harm – it could be the commanding officer, but more often than not it was the senior non-commissioned officer (NCO) who was shouting at you.

The CO of 29 Commando had insisted Jimmy and I be allowed to buck the system, as there was an urgent need for two commando-trained officers in the regiment after some successive failures.

'Jimmy, you've got to understand that the course staff aren't going to be at all happy that you don't have to spend as long at Okehampton as the rest of the course do,' he had said to me in my initial interview.

'It's Johnny, sir,' I replied.

'I thought it was Jimmy?'

'No, that's the other one,' I said. Jimmy was waiting outside for his initial chat with the CO too. I wouldn't have minded, but his letter welcoming me to the regiment had also been addressed to 'Jimmy Mercer' and I was beginning to worry that he might be a bit 'off the pace', so to speak.

He definitely wasn't wrong about the Okehampton staff, though. My simply being there was apparently 'a crime'. The sergeant running the course personified the staff's collective anger that a couple of 'fucking officers' could bypass the first two weeks of 'his course' and still expect to pass-out from it.

His name was Pete Simmons. With a body ravaged by twenty years of operations, and no hair whatsoever, Pete was an iconic figure in the regiment and would become one of my closest friends. He was, however, clearly determined that friendship wasn't going to start now.

Pete told us that there was no room in the officer accommodation block (there were six free beds), so Jimmy and I were sent to the ranks block with a wink and a nod, and some sniggering from the other instructors. Given the choice I would have gone into the lads' accommodation block anyway. I enjoyed helping the others with their kit (on the rare occasion that theirs was worse than mine) and I enjoyed the banter. I was young for an officer – I had just turned twenty-two – so was a curiosity for the lads if nothing else. The physical training was hard, but nothing I hadn't seen before.

Officers stayed at the back of the groups on the early morning squadded runs around the granite tors and misty valleys of Dartmoor. Apparently it was tougher at the back, but I quite enjoyed it there because you could pretend to help the slow ones while catching your own breath. I can't have been the first, or the last, to figure this out.

There are four commando tests that a soldier must complete to earn his Green Beret, which have all remained unchanged since the war. The infamous Thirty-Miler is the last and probably most famous one. The Tarzan Assault Course, the Nine-mile Speed March and the Endurance Course are the others. The Tarzan Assault Course is held on 'bottom field', where one is also required to climb a thirty-foot wall on a rope, with weapon and webbing.

To ensure recruits are suitably prepared for the rigours of the Commando Training Centre, Royal Marines Lympstone, this rope-climbing serial is completed at Okehampton, where I struggled very much with it. I could not for the life of me get more than halfway up the rope using the instructors' preferred technique. Eventually, Jimmy and I went down to the ropes one evening and he showed me an entirely different technique that would help me until my arms were strong enough to repeatedly climb to the top. The technique worked, and I used to practise it well into the night on my own on the vertical ropes on the assault course, while everyone else was in bed. I could not afford to fail.

Come the final day of the course, I had to demonstrate that I could pass this test. I climbed using Jimmy's method, not the one taught by the instructors. I would take a couple of shimmies up the rope, lock on with my legs and shake off my weak but strengthening hands; a couple more shimmies and rest again. The instructors were like a sea of angry piranhas below as they hurled the most vitriolic abuse at me, a couple of them completely losing their tempers. I didn't care; it wasn't like they were going to come up the rope and get me. And I also knew there was no time limit. Eventually I passed, much to the mirth of the lads, who liked anyone who stuck up two fingers at the instructors.

Jimmy and I drove to Commando Training Centre, Royal Marines Lympstone that weekend, to be greeted by the new course officer, who bore a striking resemblance to Bruce Willis. He knew it as well, and overplayed his hand.

Lympstone is an intimidating place to turn up to if you are not a natural fit for the military. There is an ever-present tension in the air; a sense of careers starting, or failing with a thump as another 'sprog' marine falls off the rope from thirty-foot up and gets transported away on a stretcher. There were no women on camp (none that I saw anyway); it was a school of 'masculinity' that simply awakened each day and produced commandos. The loud blokes were hammered; the arrogant ones snapped; the weak ones were trained up; the nervous ones were inspired with confidence. I loved it.

As an officer, you were expected to lead. If you couldn't they would tell you and you would soon be leaving the course. There was none of the tolerance of Sandhurst. The Royal Marines prided themselves on being 'better' than the Army (or *pongos* as they called us, because our 'personal admin' – hygiene – was so bad that we persistently stank). We countered these aspersions with an equally determined belief that these marines were land-loving sailors who spent far too long in the gym preening themselves, and could learn a thing or two about soldiering from us.

This delicately balanced rivalry helped keep standards very high, from kit husbandry to marksmanship on the range; from speed over the ground with weight on your back to resilience in foul weather. Professional standards were the currency we traded in, and again I learnt a great deal.

And, of course, there were the foggy mornings on the banks of the River Exe when the tide was out, when we took part in the infamously brutal 'mud runs'; the staple of any commando's diet. If you ever take the train from Exeter to

Cornwall along the western side of the river Exe, squint through the fog and across the estuary towards the newer collection of industrial buildings on the far eastern side. If you are early enough, you will catch recruits still suffering it today.

At Lympstone, Jimmy and I became firm friends with a chap called Goose. As with 'pongos', nicknames are not overly cerebral in the military; he did literally look like a Goose. Goose was part of the detachment of the Royal Electrical and Mechanical Engineers attached to 29 Commando Regiment. They kept our vehicles on the road, and generally fixed anything we broke. Goose was very much like Jimmy, except he was equipped with a significantly higher dose of common sense. But that was why I liked Jimmy in the first place, and why we were such firm friends.

Goose was probably the toughest bloke I've met; annoyingly so. I recall one particular march on the Commando Course when I tried to take all of my team's radio equipment in my Bergan to help ease their load on what was to be a difficult day for my section.

Marching – known as 'yomping' or 'tabbing' – is a strange art. Sometimes done 'in step', the military uses marches to move a body of men from A to B at speed, with full equipment – usually in the region of 120lb in a rucksack, excluding weapons. With marches lasting anything from a few hours to a few days, they require determination and strength of character to push through the discomfort, blisters and fatigue.

For some reason, on this occasion I was nowhere near strong enough to pull off carrying my men's spare batteries. I had written a cheque my body was not going to cash. I tried. I pushed it bloody hard. The embarrassment was keeping me going, long after I would normally have asked for help. But about six miles in and drifting in and out of consciousness, I had to approach Goose.

He teased me relentlessly about this for a long time afterwards, but the truth is he didn't bat an eyelid at the time; he simply loaded some batteries into his already topped-up Bergan, before giving them back to me at the end without a word. I felt dwarfed, literally and metaphorically.

Goose, Jimmy and I made a very odd threesome. They were both six feet four, and I most certainly wasn't. But we became known as a unit, and eventually we all passed the notorious commando tests together, earning our Green Berets by Christmas 2003. We were inducted into 29 Commando in the usual manner – we were dropped off by helicopter – with nothing but what we were wearing – in the very middle of Dartmoor and given a series of embarrassing tasks to complete, before meeting the CO and the rest of the officers in Plymouth's premier gay bar. What followed on Union Street is largely forgotten, which I am assured is a good thing.

Christmas duties that year were neatly split between us. Goose and Jimmy and I were generously given a week each to get to know our way around the Citadel. It was better than searching for a dropped weapon in a freezing pool on Dartmoor, so I didn't mind. My first duty was perhaps the most eventful, but for all the wrong reasons. One of the Junior NCOs had passed his leadership course and celebrated by drinking heavily in Plymouth. He died in his sleep in the lads' accommodation that night. His girlfriend couldn't rouse him, and ran across the square emitting the most howling scream to get the attention of the guardroom. Nothing could be done for him. I was largely shielded from the ensuing inquiries and Coroner's Courts, but they were a horrendous ordeal for his family and the regiment.

January 2004 arrived, and back in those days, 3 Commando Brigade, which was the higher formation of which 29 Commando was a part, went to Norway every winter. NATO expected the UK to help defend the 'northern flank' from Russia. It was a point of principle that this fell to the Royal Marines and 3 Commando Brigade – it was considered 'too tough for non-specialist units', according to my Commanding Officer. Precisely how much of the 'too tough' Norwegian winter he was personally going to see from his office was up for debate.

He wasn't wrong, though. The entire regiment headed off to Asegarden Camp in northern Norway, which was to become our regimental home for the next three months. Soldiering in the Arctic was tough. It's bloody cold for a start. Depending on how far north you were, temperatures ranged from minus eight degrees centigrade to minus thirty. Your eyelids stick together and your piss freezes before you've finished. You have to have your wits about you if you want to survive in the field without long-term after-effects.

Those of us on our first trip to Norway had to complete the infamous NIGS (New In Gunnery) course – a rather brutal three weeks in the Arctic wastes trying to keep all of your fingers and toes. The Arctic Winter Warfare course followed. Both were notorious in commando circles, and often considered the 'proper Commando Course', to the extent that some old-timers in wouldn't consider you a full member of the regiment until you had completed the Norway training as well.

I learnt how to ski for the first time. For those of us who had never skied before, the approach to teaching was robust. The regiment hired a ski slope for the day. Once we had figured out the button lifts, we were taken to the top and told to get on with it. The wimps like me spent most of the day learning to 'snow plough' our way down, before the more adventurous learnt some parallel turns and the show-offs learnt how to Telemark.

Even at this stage, it was clear to me that one of the best things about my regiment was the characters you met. There was an officer in another battery to mine who had taken a bit of a shine to me, and me to him. His name was Jim Philippson.

Jim's approach to learning to ski was different to mine. He took the first lift of the day, got to the top, pointed his skis down the slope and let gravity take over. He careered faster and faster down the slope, entirely out of control. To the amazement of the rest of us, and himself, he remained upright. The mountain leader instructor, a Royal Marine who we despised for his undisguised pleasure in making us suffer, saw the impending accident before we did and started threatening Jim with some un-pleasantries as he hurled past. Jim ignored him.

Just at the point of highest velocity, and without the strength to absorb the flattening of the slope signalling the end of the run, Jim simply disappeared into a huge cloud of snow. We all expected the worst, but he got to his feet, gave the Mountain Leader a quick 'Cheers Royal' under his breath, and joined the back of the queue for the button lifts.

The courses culminated in the survival phases – above and below the snow line – including a brief dip through an ice hole, which I found a lot colder than I had hoped. As an officer, the Mountain Leader kept me in the water far longer than he should have, asking me to recite the Commando Qualities forwards and backwards, along with a number of other mantras. I was in a pretty bad way when I got out.

Survival above the snow line was great fun – simply dig a snow hole and get in it. There would be four of you digging a deep trench, and then at a suitable depth you'd dig a shelf that you could all fit along like sardines, and then huddle up for some warmth.

Survival training below the snow line was a little different. You had to build a structure resembling a wigwam from tree branches, pad out the holes with snow for insulation, and build a fire in the middle. You would then catch some fish and fry them on a shovel. After not eating for some time, they were delicious – bones, eyes and all.

It was important to leave a small hole in the top of the wigwam so that the smoke and heat from the fire could escape without melting the snow insulation. This is something Goose forgot to do. After an emotional night, with melted snow soaking and then re-freezing the men in his shelter, his entire section – bar himself – reported sick the following morning with varying degrees of frostbite and frost-nip. They looked, to me, a broken bunch, and I felt sorry for them. Goose thought they were all a 'little weak'.

With no overnight kit or sleeping bags, my blokes also got cold very quickly that night, and I remember getting a bit fed up with them as I built our shelter almost single-handedly. Sleep can be a much-needed escape during survival exercises, but in the Arctic it is inevitably in short supply because it's freezing. As the nights wore on, the blokes – who would be all on top of each other for warmth – would often joke that the end was nigh, as the temperatures dropped below minus twenty.

One character I was given to look after during the survival phase was another regimental legend – Norman Fox. Norm had passed the Commando Course at the age of fifty-four

– still the oldest ever. Not content with this, he wanted to sample some survival training in the Arctic. So when Norm woke me up in the night telling me he thought he was about to die, I thought he actually might. So I spent most of those nights awake, talking to him and trying to keep our pathetic fire going. Often in my haste I hadn't built it with a firm enough base, and it kept disappearing into the snow.

Jimmy was breezing through these courses without pausing for breath. He made me look very average. On a rare evening off in camp, while everyone else headed up to the bar to drink £11 pints of strong Norwegian lager, Jimmy and I went skiing around the civilian cross-country course opposite. He was an athlete. I was not. I think he got bored of waiting for me on the course, but he covered it up well. He won the regimental ski race at his first attempt. I did enjoy the odd night down in the local town, too. Never before or since have I paid so much for alcohol; never before or since have I had a hangover like it. Something about the altitude, apparently.

Towards the end of the deployment the weather started to warm, and the nightmare temperatures of just above freezing during the day (water everywhere as the snow melted), combined with plummeting temperatures at night (freezing said water) meant that soldiers started dropping like flies. Jimmy and I were accustomed to the place now, and worked hard to keep the lads going.

Towards the end of that Norwegian winter I seemed to be spending most of my time completing forced marches across the mountains as the rear marker, pulling a pulk (a sledge used to carry equipment). A 300lb sledge is simply unstoppable on some slopes, which is a bit of a nightmare if you're attached to the front of it. It could, on occasion, be extremely funny to watch an individual driven down the side of a mountain by the sled he is pulling, unable to stop. I did hope the Russians weren't watching.

We returned to the UK in late April. I arrived home on the RFA *Sir Galahad*, enduring a good North Sea storm on the way back around the south of the UK to Plymouth. When I arrived at the Citadel ready for Easter leave, my CO informed me that I was to supplement manpower in another battery in the regiment – 79 Battery – on a trip to the US to practise interoperability with the US Marines. I'd be leaving just ten days later. I was rather upset, having recently acquired a new girlfriend, but unfortunately the Army is not an optional service.

As it turned out, there were a couple of silver linings. Firstly, Jim Philippson was in 79 Battery, so I knew it would be fun. Secondly, by the time we were ready to set sail it looked as if we would, in fact, be off to Iraq, taking the place of some Spanish troops in the north of the country. The Spanish had decided that enough was enough following the Madrid bombings of 2004; the enormous political pressure at home meant they were pulling out of Iraq.

At the time, 79 Battery was the Lead Commando Group. This is a sub-unit formation of 3 Commando Brigade which, along with 16 Air Assault Brigade, forms the United Kingdom's high readiness response for the strategic military require-ments of the Government. 'High readiness' was a loose term; it did not prevent the blokes from drinking heavily on Union Street in Plymouth, but it precluded foreign holidays. Usually a battery could expect to be the Lead Commando Group for one year, in a three-year cycle. The upside was that you could expect to be deployed to fairly interesting places; ours would be Najaf, near Fallujah in northern Iraq.

The day before we left I went to see my new girlfriend in London, meeting her on the Millennium Bridge during rush hour. I remember watching all the commuters dashing about, most on their way home after another ordinary day, and thinking that tomorrow I was off to Iraq. I had to remind myself that I had chosen this path, and that this day was always going to come. The following day my girlfriend gave me a lift to Southampton to board the RFA *Sir Tristram*; part of a small fleet of ships, headed up by HMS *Ocean*, heading for the Gulf. It was a bright, clear and crisp early summer's morning as I kissed her goodbye on the dock.

It remained a challenging time inside my head. I had become a bit of a machine, passing arduous military courses at a canter. I drank with the best of them and seemed relatively well-liked amongst my fellow officers and the men of the regiment. Yet some nights inside me the battles returned, only ending when I collapsed into much-needed sleep. My 'hardwiring' from home still had a hold over me. I spoke to my parents less often by then, but I was often reminded that 'God could see everything that I was doing'. I thought I had put all this stuff to bed, but the truth was that it still haunted me. The others saw it, too. Jim Philippson laughed at me, telling me it was all a load of bollocks. He did seem to understand the grip it held on me though. Jimmy just thought I was weird, and spent too much time in the bathroom washing my hands.

RFA *Sir Tristram* had been extensively rebuilt after suffering a direct hit in the Falklands War. Consequently, speed was not her thing. She could cruise at nine knots, but no faster. We pushed out from Plymouth into the Atlantic waiting for the final call to start heading to the Middle East, and then sailed in a five-mile box shape for four days before we were told to revert to our original mission and head to the US. It appeared the UK Government was not prepared to commit any more forces to Iraq.

It takes two weeks to get to the US on a ship going nine knots. I found it hard to retain my sanity and my cabin mates did not help. I was sharing with Philippson and yet another Jim, who was senior to me but junior to Philippson. It would be fair to say that these two Jims did not get on; I, as the junior rank, simply observed their stand-off.

The new Jim declared on the first day that he 'did not believe in deodorant' – which on a ship heading through the tropics was always going to be a problem. He had also brought a guitar with him; he thought he possessed a talent for music, but was sorely mistaken. Philippson had a short tolerance for most things, but by his own admission this particular set up was a challenge for him.

Philippson and I became very close during this trip. Our days would be similar; getting up together, doing some strenuous physical exercise, reading (I think Jim was trying to read the entire Bible at the time, cover to cover) and a lot of smoking off the back of the ship after dinner, watching the sun go down, chatting. Philippson had also started a book about his life, which I am sure would have been a terrific read; I don't know what happened to it in the end.

We docked in Virginia at Naval Station Norfolk – the biggest naval base in the world. Soldiers who had been cooped up for two weeks were released into the city at 1900 hours on a Friday night, and warned against being absent when the ship headed further south in three days' time. Carnage was inevitable.

Philippson and I stuck together, ending up spending the night with a couple of girls at a house they shared in Virginia. These girls entertained us for a good couple of days, showing us around the place before we had to return to the ship, where I promptly wrote a letter to my girlfriend at home telling her how much I was missing her. The following day we headed further south (again at nine knots) to conduct exercises and ship-to-shore manoeuvres with the US Marines, using an array of helicopters and landing craft.

Once we got ashore for the main part of the exercise, we spent the long, sweaty days firing and moving the 105mm Light Gun Howitzers that were the mainstay of the regiment. When we weren't firing the 105s, we conducted some basic jungle training in the swamps. Each evening we would take a run to the nearest beach to cool off in the Atlantic Ocean. Life was good.

After a month or so in the field, the exercise finished and we embarked on another short period of R&R. Jim Philippson, myself and a couple of others hired a car and drove down the eastern seaboard of the United States. We spent a particularly memorable weekend in a hotel that was hosting a cheerleader convention, and I was offered a job in the Abercrombie & Fitch shop in Jacksonville by a very attractive girl, which I seriously considered. When I told Philippson, he informed me I was a wimp for not taking it and absconding service.

R&R trips abroad were one of the reasons you joined the Army in those days. In a world of increasing commitment and declining resource, I fear they are often the first items on the agenda of any cost-cutting exercise; a sore mistake. In some parts of the British Army, R&R is a very controlled science. Blokes are given specific packages of accommodation and activities, are usually escorted by officers and bussed to and from specific locations rather than given a free rein. In 3 Commando Brigade, we were told when the ship was leaving, and precisely how much shit we would get in if we were not aboard. Many commandos have, in the past, been seen running towards a retreating gang-plank in last night's clothes; one story involved one of the Senior NCOs conducting a boat-to-ship transfer using a local police boat in New York. Happy times.

6

While I had been earning my dollars (or not) with Jim Philippson, my best mate in the regiment, Jimmy Goddard, had been rather jiffed by the system and didn't come to the US. I'm not sure how, because he was a very popular bloke, but Jimmy had ended up with a sequence of indifferent junior staff jobs. After our courses in Norway, instead of going on exercise Jimmy was tasked to host visits to Norway from British dignitaries and ministers, including the regimental chaplain, who was to become a great friend to both of us. Karl Freeman still enthusiastically runs his church in Plymouth; we became such friends that he married my wife and me a decade later.

Jimmy did manage to benefit personally from his time pushing papers in regimental HQ. We had both assumed that, as neither of us had been to university, we would have a slower rise to the rank of captain than our fellow officers. This was the norm for non-graduates back then. You can imagine my disdain when, one morning shortly after my return, he burst into my room, took off his second lieutenant rank slide and threw it on my floor, proclaiming, 'I won't be needing this shit any more.' He had managed to convince 'the system' that his NVQ in bricklaying was the equivalent of a degree, and was to be promoted.

After his stint in regimental headquarters, Jimmy was to be

posted to 7 (Sphinx) Commando Battery; a sub-unit of 29 Commando located in Arbroath, some 600 miles from Plymouth. Soon afterwards, I was completing another twenty-four-hour orderly officer duty on Tuesday, 3 August 2004, when I received a call from Jimmy's brother Andrew. Andrew informed me that Jimmy – along with Claire Stickler, a friend of ours from Sandhurst – had suffered a horrendous climbing accident that afternoon on the Gower Peninsula. The fall had killed Claire and, amongst multiple other injuries, had snapped Jimmy's spinal column, leaving him paralysed. Jimmy wanted to see me.

I rushed up to the Morrison Hospital in Swansea, where I found Jimmy's family. I was taken up to see him and, looking through the glass window of his room, I could see the severity of his injuries for myself. I opened the door, and Jimmy sat up as best he could, stretched out his arms – ripping out the multiple cannulas – and gave me a bear hug. He was beside himself with grief for Claire, completely disregarding his own situation, as ever.

Desperate and dark days followed. I committed myself to spending my summer leave in the hospital with Jimmy, his mum and his sister. We took turns sleeping on the floor in the family room. I would shave him in the mornings and make sure, led by his family, that visitors were both available and wanted. I went to see Claire in the mortuary. Jimmy had asked me to say goodbye for him; at this stage we didn't know if Jimmy was going to be able to do it himself. She looked peaceful and happy. I kissed her forehead – the first of my friends to die.

There were some very long nights during the hot August of 2004, as we all struggled to comprehend the horror of the accident which Jimmy relayed to me a number of times.

During our darkest nights he wanted to join Claire, and I struggled for words. This deeply impressive and strong young man would now be wheelchair-bound for the rest of his days, and I resolved that I would always be there for him, regardless of our separate journeys from here on.

Jimmy was in hospital for thirteen long months following the accident. After the initial summer leave period I managed to get up and see him perhaps twice a month, as I returned to my duties in the Army. He'd been moved to Stoke Mandeville, where he undertook strenuous rehabilitation. This involved working hard on his balance while learning the basics of self-reliance in a wheelchair, including transferring in and out of the chair into car seats, sofas and toilets. Adapting to life in a wheelchair, while emotionally and psychologically demanding, is also a huge physical challenge, as the most basic of human functions must be re-learnt. I found his determination to progress inspiring. At Stoke Mandeville, an institution where many in his position did not work as hard as him to adapt, it was a privilege to go and see him on Christmas Day, Saturday evenings and other potentially lonely times.

We resolved that once he had finished at Stoke Mandeville hospital we would go away for a while. He loathed the fussing over him; everybody helping him to do the smallest of tasks. We got him a Motability car, packed it out and decided to drive it as far as we could without falling out with the vehicle or each other.

We departed from Bracknell early one morning and headed to the Channel. We drove through France that first night, straight to San Sebastian in northern Spain, where we pulled up in a layby, blew up the roll-mats and got a bit of sleep. We spent some long and hot days in and around San

Sebastian before heading further south through Madrid to an apartment in southern Spain that was owned by a member of Jimmy's family. During the days, we would often head to a swimming pool or the beach and lounge around. In the evenings, we would inevitably head into the nearest town and put away a few beers, as Jimmy enjoyed discovering how much he could now drink.

Jimmy had always been an extremely fit man, and he was determined his injury would not put an end to that. We had managed to strap his hand-cycle to the top of the car for our holiday, and he got in it at every opportunity. He drove it on the roads like he was at the wheel of a lorry, commanding other drivers to get out of the way and scaring the life out of me. We engineered a contraption that meant we could hook his wheelchair onto the back of the bike, so that when in town he could transfer into that and get about a bit easier. With me on a clapped-out mountain bike we looked like a travelling circus, but neither of us cared. The Spanish police stopped us on our way home most evenings, assuming we were thieves with a penchant for wheelchairs and hand-cycles. I won't forget the time we had to prove Jimmy was unable to use his legs.

The holiday gave Jimmy time to get used to his new life. It was rigged with challenges that can be overcome with close friends – personal hygiene was dealt with by the fire-hose at the apartment we used; the sea provided a well-needed bath. Maintaining dignity was a big thing for me, and an even more important thing for Jimmy. I didn't want to fuss over him, and it can't be easy having things done for you by mates who you used to look after yourself. But we both just got on with it; laughing as I occasionally collapsed into the sand under the strain of carrying him hundreds of metres to and from the sea; often letting him struggle and work things out for himself. It was just what both of us wanted – a chance to get away from life in the UK and spend some quality 'tramp time' abroad.

7

During the winter of 2005 I was dispatched to run the regimental ski team, competing at a series of events across Norway and Europe for four months. It sounds rather idyllic, until I tell you that it was cross-country skiing (not downhill) and I had to wear a Lycra all-in-one gimp suit for the races.

When I returned to the UK a decorated athlete (not), I was sent to the jungle warfare training school in Belize, probably to warm up a bit.

Belize was another formative experience for me. I was put in command of a troop of Royal Marines, with two sections made up of marines from 45 Commando, and one of soldiers from 29 Commando Regiment. We spent thirty-two days in the jungle without respite – initially on a course and then on a three-week exercise. I didn't know any of the personalities before I left the UK, but gelled fast with my troop sergeant, 'Doddy', who was a rough, tough but brilliant soldier. And a Scouser.

The whole experience shaped me further as a young officer. The jungle was a terrific environment to operate in as an infantry troop commander. It was claustrophobically wet and hot, and the days were long and physically exhausting. I learnt how to live, survive and fight in both primary (untouched) and secondary (re-grown, after deforestation or similar) jungle.

There was plenty of wildlife to keep you amused as well. The nearest watering hole for a wash was also home to some crocodiles, who peered at us through weeds on the opposite side of the lagoon as we swam. To wash we would all strip naked, lather up and then dive in. The soap was sucked off us by hundreds of tiny fish; an exhilarating clean! Living like an animal amongst the jungle wildlife and my brother soldiers, cut off from the outside world, was a very happy time for me.

This stint in the jungle was followed by a short but memorable period of R&R, where I took the opportunity to go diving off the stunning St George's Caye in Belize. Upon returning to camp to begin our transit back to the UK, we discovered that our plane had been delayed by three days. The CO addressed us all in the camp. In his apologetic speech, he included the instruction that under no circumstances were we to head into Belize City, and certainly not to a place down the road called Raul's Rose Garden.

As soon as darkness had fallen we were all on our way to Raul's Rose Garden in downtown Belize City. I went with my troop sergeant. We walked into what looked like a scene from *Apocalypse Now*. Prostitutes were everywhere; fights were sporadically breaking out; chairs were flying; and all in this warehouse, shed-type structure that was meant to be a bar. Doddy and I got a drink and observed. Blokes were engaged in sexual acts all over the place. The Army unit we had been supporting for the exercise finally saw their chance to throw a few fists at my marines, after we had mercilessly taken the piss out of their soldiering skills for the last six weeks. It was carnage. We stayed for a bit to make sure that the lads were sticking together and were OK, before getting a tip-off about an impending police raid. We left by the back door and headed to a quieter bar for the rest of the night.

Back in the UK in the autumn of 2005, regimental life continued its unstoppable rhythm in Plymouth. Like I said before, one of the deep privileges of serving in 29 Commando was the characters you shared your experiences with. One of the men in the regiment who had a big influence on me at this time was Justin Barber, who had served in almost every officer position in 29 Commando. He was now second-in-command (2IC) of the regiment. He was, in every sense, Mr 29; indeed, his father's ashes had been spread on the battlements of the Citadel.

Justin was feared, and rightly so. Six foot three and nineteen stone, with a grin as wide as his face and hands like a bear, we developed an affectionate if slightly discomforting relationship. I got to know him better after a particularly stupid escapade with my driver on the M5, coming back from a regimental exercise during which one of our soldiers had been killed in a road accident. We were cruising well beyond the speed limit in our Land Rover Wolf reconnaissance vehicle when we unexpectedly overtook the CO and Justin, as we passed Exeter. Realizing my fate was sealed as soon as they saw me, but hoping to avoid execution, I gave them both a courteous wave as we sped past. I knew I was deeply in the shit the moment I saw Justin's face. I was in command of the vehicle, and vehicle safety and adherence to speed limits had been reinforced after the accident only a week before. It was monumentally stupid.

Predictably, a few moments later, my mobile phone rang. It was my battery captain, and he didn't sound best pleased.

'Mercer?' he said. 'Is that you?'

'Yes, sir,' I said.

'You need to report to Justin's office immediately on your return,' he said. 'And take your gumshield.'

The line went dead with an ominous click.

I arrived at the Citadel and, after taking a few deep breaths, set off to find Justin. He was outside the officers' mess, surveying the seventeenth-century guns that are placed all around the parade ground as a mark of our heritage. They had all been slightly moved off their placements while we were away, after a 'do' in the sergeants' mess. Justin was not happy; he took his heritage very seriously.

I approached him as smartly as I could and threw up a salute. I called him '2IC', not Justin. He was ordinarily fairly relaxed and we were on first name terms; I did not feel now was the time to trade on that. He turned slowly towards me as I stood rigidly to attention. I felt this Exocet of a fist strike my upper chest and my right shoulder simultaneously, knocking me back a few steps. He could see I was devastated at having been so stupid and letting him down.

'I cannot tell you how disappointed I am in you,' he said. 'How fucking stupid are you?'

'Very.'

'By sunset I want every single one of these guns back on their placements. If I see you asking someone to help you or using a vehicle, I'll fucking destroy you. You're lucky – times have changed in the Army; sometimes I wish it was not so.'

Even back then I knew that sometimes you can fuck up; sometimes you simply can't. Racing down the motorway, when one soldier has already been killed in a road traffic accident on the same exercise, exposed an immaturity I was still trying to shake off at the time. I spent that afternoon and evening straining under the weight of these massive seventeenth-century guns, trying to lever them back onto their placements. I can still feel the pain in my back to this day. I got them on, and with blistered hands and a humiliated ego I put the incident behind me. Another valuable life lesson learnt in the Citadel.

8

The following Easter of 2006, the battlegroup of 3rd Battalion, Parachute Regiment was deployed to Helmand province, southern Afghanistan. Instead of the uneventful tour they were promised by ministers and MI6, 3 PARA walked into a hornets' nest, immediately coming under sustained attack from the Taliban. They'd been caught out by a lack of reliable intelligence (after Iraq, even I could see this was now becoming a theme). Jim Philippson's time at 29 Commando had come to an end, and he was now with 3 PARA, helping to train the Afghan National Army (ANA). I wasn't particularly 'plugged-in' strategically, but in the back of my mind was the thought that, in a few months, I might be going too.

Meanwhile, Jimmy Goddard wanted a challenge, and decided that he was going to attempt the first arm-powered ascent of Mount Kilimanjaro, Africa's highest peak, in June 2006. He asked me to be in his support team, which was going to consist of myself, Goose, Jimmy's dad and his physio, and a team of native porters, to ensure we didn't get lost.

The climb was another happy period. The team would rise with the sun and eat a small breakfast, before packing up our tents and associated equipment and getting on our way. Lunch would be a twenty-minute break, before we were on the move again. It was a slow slog through the lower reaches of the mountain, and a hot slog at that. Day after day Jimmy powered away on his arm-bike, with Goose and I laying track for him from some metal rails we built before we left. The metal rails were not heavy, but were cumbersome to carry. The heat was sticky and clung to you; warm air trapped by the African canopy. But this was a small issue in comparison to the demands placed on Jimmy, so we were loath to do the one thing that always makes it easier – moan.

It was during our expedition to Kilimanjaro that the conflict in Afghanistan first touched our lives in a very personal and devastating way. One sunny evening on the north-western foothills of Kilimanjaro, we finally broke the tree line and set up camp for a particularly picturesque dinner. The view was stunning. The sweaty, humid jungle, with its thick canopy and muddy tracks was below us, replaced by an open, almost barren stone wilderness that allowed us the perspective on how far we had climbed. We tucked into a hearty dinner of a nondescript stew and vegetables, made extremely tasty by the combined effects of altitude and fatigue. Dinner had just finished, and I was recording our diary over the satellite phone with Jimmy's brother Paul, who was filling in our online blog (by now, Jimmy had a considerable following). Paul said he had something important to tell me, for which I should be out of earshot of the rest of the group.

'Sure, mate,' I said, getting up and walking to the edge of the ridge to stare out into the vastness of Africa. 'What is it?'

'I've had a call from Jim Philippson's brother. It's bad news I'm afraid,' said Paul. 'Jim was killed this morning. I don't have many details but I understand he was shot.'

'Jim Philippson?' I said, my mind reeling, making sure I was hearing the news correctly. The satellite phone line was extremely crackly.

'Yes, I'm afraid so, Johnny', said Paul.

I ended the phone call quickly and took a couple of minutes to collect myself before breaking the news to Jimmy and Goose, who were in tears.

Life as a young officer in a commando regiment was an intoxicating if wild existence at the time. There was no man more suited to this than Jim Philippson. He was a good man. He had his edges, but he was very much a product of the regiment, and proudly so. The stories surrounding him are rightly legendary, from packing only a Superman outfit for a sky-diving holiday in the US, to turning up to an Oscars party in only his pants and a layer of gold paint. Often on nights out on Union Street in Plymouth, as we ascended the hill back to the Citadel, he would insist on a fight with one of us other junior officers to 'get it out of my system before bed'. It's thanks to him that there was a complete redesign (at a cost of hundreds of thousands of pounds) of the security arrangements in the Citadel; he was refused entry at the front gate and managed to successfully break into camp. The man was a true commando.

His finest hour was undoubtedly in 2003, onboard HMS *Ark Royal* on the way to war in Iraq, when the sea air and some contraband alcohol got to his head one warm evening. He struggled to find his way back to his room and ended bursting through the door into the cabin of the Commander, Amphibious Task Group (only the most senior UK official in the war).

'What the hell!' shouted Commodore Jamie Miller, who had been preparing for the invasion by watching the film *Zulu*, and was startled to be confronted by a large and erratic intruder.

'Who are you and why are you in my cabin?' Jim demanded.

'Why are you in mine?' Miller asked, bravely pushing Jim out into the passageway. 'Who are you?'

Sobering up slightly under the bright lights, Jim wisely held his tongue. He realised he was in the shit when the Commodore pointed silently at the brass name plate on his door. When asked for his unit, Jim replied that he was with the Brigade Recce Force (he wasn't).

'You're drunk!' accused the Commodore.

'If you say so, sir,' replied Philippson, unconvinced.

Jim was transferred off HMS *Ark Royal* to an RFA support ship, where he saw out the rest of the journey before landing in Iraq and taking part in the invasion. He was suitably admonished with some sort of 'official displeasure' from somebody, but as ever, it bothered him not. A full, official account of this incident hangs on the wall of the officers' mess in Plymouth, as a tribute to the quintessential commando junior officer.

Somehow, Jim got away with it, and his wonderful career was allowed to continue. But beneath that aggressive and macho exterior was a huge heart and a forgiving soul. He was by my side when I made all those Junior Officer mistakes, and he never repeated them to anyone. He laughed at me when I tried to beat him on a run and nearly passed out from the heat not long after we docked in Virginia; I was totally unaccustomed to the blistering and clinging humidity. He cared deeply for his family, particularly his brother, and was fiercely loyal to his friends. He was very much my older brother in the regiment, and I was deeply affected by his loss.

As I always maintained until I left the services: it's all good fun until someone gets shot.

On Mount Kilimanjaro, we set off again the next day, with

Jim never far from our minds. Jimmy progressed well up to the start of the crater, where the lack of oxygen began making life more challenging. His fatigued body became more susceptible to infections and illnesses, and the ascent became extremely tough on him.

In the years since, I have seldom seen strength to match that displayed by Jimmy. After a night on a fifty degree slope with no sleep, he would simply re-mount his bike and head for the summit. He bared his soul on that mountain, and we found it exactly as we all knew it to be; dedicated, courageous, committed and strong. An exceptional human being.

After two weeks, we arrived at the crater floor, where camping is usually not allowed due to the lack of oxygen, but we were granted permission. Jimmy lay up for two days, but it was clear that he was not going to improve without a proper oxygen supply, and with the summit just 270 feet above us (less than a day's climb), we had to call it a day.

Jimmy hadn't failed; he had succeeded beyond all expectations. The summit was irrelevant to me; his resilience and sheer physical effort was something I hadn't seen before or since, and all as a paraplegic. In a world where you can be deemed a hero for the most insignificant of accomplishments, I found those three weeks in Africa watching Jimmy deeply humbling.

On returning from Africa I went to see Justin Barber immediately, not only to catch up (as our relationship had healed by now), but to find out what my next tasking was likely to be.

The regiment was deploying to Afghanistan, as expected. I was going too, but not as an artilleryman. I was to take on the task of running an Operational Mentoring and Liaison

Team (OMLT) with a kandak (company) of the newly formed Afghan National Army. Specifically, I was to shadow the Afghan company commander through training and fighting, as part of the UK commitment to rebuilding the Afghan Army.

'You need life insurance,' giggled Justin as I started to leave his office.

'What?' I replied.

'Here's the stats of all the OMLT that have been injured this summer.'

I can't remember the number now, but it was very considerable.

'You are going to get shot,' he continued to laugh. 'Have a good weekend!'

If Jim Philippson was my brother in the regiment, Justin Barber was certainly my father. We maintained our relationship when we both went our separate ways at the end of our time at 29 Commando, and I would go and visit him in High Wycombe where he had a terrible job – something to do with chemical warfare.

I was devastated when I received a call from his brother one evening in 2009, telling me Justin had been out on a run that morning and had suffered a massive, fatal heart attack. His father's ashes were on the battlements; Justin's joined them. The man was the regiment, and the regiment was the man. There are very few like him around.

9

The summer of 2006 was a brutal and bloody one for the British Army. For months, 3 PARA Battlegroup fought valiantly to stay in Helmand, waging battle after battle against an enemy determined to drive them out. 3 Commando Brigade started replacing them in August, with an official handover date in mid-September.

Troops from my regiment had deployed in 2001 as part of the initial efforts against the Taliban and Al Qaeda after 9/11, and again in 2005 to provide security cover for the construction of the main British camp, Bastion. As a regiment, we therefore knew Afghanistan was a rough place, but did not expect some of the stories being relayed back in 'lessons identified' documents in June and July 2006. Outposts were running out of ammunition, were unable to communicate with each other and had been stealing equipment from other nations to survive. We hoped these were teething problems that we would not have to cope with. It was clear, even from the UK, that something was not right in either our force-laydown, or the intelligence understanding of the problem we were facing in Afghanistan.

As Justin Barber had told me, my small role in this huge operation was to work as part of the OMLTs and mentor an Afghan kandak commander. A kandak is a mirror image of a company of men in the UK Armed Forces; about ninety soldiers split into three platoons and a company headquarters. The kandak commander was the equivalent of the rank of major; I was therefore promoted to captain earlier than I was due, in order to narrow the difference in our ranks and fill my post. I had three Royal Marines to help me train the kandak, who would mentor the company's three platoon commanders. Between us we had one interpreter. The four of us were essentially injected into the Afghan Army at the beginning of their operational training cycle, to train them in British tactics, techniques and procedures, and to ride along with them on operations. I was doing this job as part of 7 Battery – the sub-unit within 29 Commando that Jimmy Goddard had been posted to before his accident. Here I was serving under a new battery commander – a bizarre individual. He, in turn, was embedded into 45 Commando Group, thus making my CO for the operation the commanding officer of 45 Commando Royal Marines.

The soldiers and officers that we were replacing were clearly dispirited after some extremely high-intensity warfare. This concerned me – British soldiers moan and whinge; they do not get dispirited. They had endured some horrendous experiences. I got on particularly well with a lieutenant from the Light Infantry Regiment – I will call him Tom – who had been doing my new job so far that summer. I was anxious to pick his brains without prying too much, but he gave me a good brief as to what to expect. It was clearly unbridled chaos across the British area of responsibility.

Tom related to me in some detail how it was impossible to tell how the Afghan National Army would react day to day, whether you were training or on operations. He had, on many occasions, been left to fend for himself in contact with the enemy, and I could tell the experiences had had an effect on him.

When you are training in the Army you are only ever part of a team. You could be part of a small group of four as a fire team or fire support team, you could be part of a larger formation such as a platoon of thirty men, a company of ninety, and so on. Nothing prepares you for the moment when you realize that all around you have exited the stage, the enemy are close and aware that you are on your own, and there is no one to be brave for but yourself. In theory, it should never happen. It would happen to me some four years later.

It had happened to Tom on that tour. Winning a Conspicuous Gallantry Cross for his efforts that summer, Tom was an extremely bright, robust and salt of the earth bloke. I would bump into him a few years later on a course, and find a changed man. He was withdrawn from that course and I never saw him again. He was put in a place by his country that we should never accept – under-equipped, under-prepared and out on a limb – and he paid a heavy personal price that he did not owe.

Afghan soldiers would be recruited in Kabul, vetted and brought down to us at Camp Shorabak, which was a small camp about a mile from Camp Bastion. Once with us, they would generally follow a fairly crude cycle of two months of training, then two months of operations followed by a month of leave. Seventy per cent of them did not return from leave, and so building up a skill base and capability amongst them was very difficult. Getting the soldiers on parade at 8.30 a.m. each day for some basic lessons in first aid, contact drills or how to search a car, was a major achievement. The training was extremely basic, and given the language barrier it was very difficult to work out how much was actually being assimilated.

Afghanistan was – and regrettably remains now – a place of extreme terror blended with supreme beauty; it must sound strange when I say I found it intoxicating.

At certain times of the day, Afghanistan has a special beauty about it. Just before the sunrise, and just before the sun sets, it appears like no other place on earth. I don't know if it was the contrast between the beauty and the vicious and brutal nature of close combat that drew me in; I don't know if it was the family of soldiers and marines that I was with, engaged in a primal struggle for civilization in a very uncivilized part of the world; I don't know if it was the contrast of high-tech military equipment in a land where electricity and running water were far from common. The blend of all of it got me, and still does. Even now, some years later, I have never seen sunsets like the ones that sink behind the mountains of southern Afghanistan.

The daytime is brutal. The dust gets everywhere – fine, caster-sugar like dust has a permanent place in your ears, on the back of your neck and in your eyes. The heat is oppressive, destructive and draining – usually in the forties, but it can reach the fifties. In those temperatures it requires real effort to just complete the basics, like going to the toilet in the 'sweat box'. At the time, it was not a problem for me; looking back now I do not know how I survived, let alone thrived, in that environment. And yet, come sunset, for a brief moment the place looked almost serene. The sun takes on hues of amber for the last hour of daylight, bathing the mountains, the water and the faces of the people in a warm glow. It was without doubt my favourite time of day. I would often pause in whatever I was doing to take it in. If I could,

I would pull out a cigarette and think about how a stunningly beautiful country had been universally devastated by man's inhumanity to man.

The native smells of Afghanistan are unique. A Brit will smell like a Brit. No matter how long he has been on a patrol, when you come to ripping off his body armour to deal with a wound, he will still smell faintly familiar. An Afghan is like something you haven't smelt before. It was not that they were dirty – they rigorously washed their hands before food, and their accommodation was usually very neat and tidy – but I think it would be fair to say that everything below the belt line was disregarded. Toilet roll is not an 'in demand' product in Afghanistan. We gave the ANA part of Camp Shorabak a toilet block to help with their sanitation, some-time in mid-September of 2006. When I went to use it on a rare occasion in October, they had destroyed it. There was shit everywhere. Imagine *Trainspotting*'s 'worst toilet in Scotland' then multiply it a hundred times. There was even shit in the apex of the roof. It was impressive, if a little rank.

So there is, I'm afraid, a bit of an enduring smell of poor sanitation that hangs over the urban areas of Afghanistan. This was sometimes masked by the delicious aromas of the local bread – similar to Indian naan – baking in clay ovens. On later tours I'd find it almost overwhelming, after eating 'Menu A' from a British ration pack for six months, to get my hands on some of this bread. In some compounds, usually where women were present, there was a distinct effort to make the place smell better, and oils and incense were burned which could linger in the structure for days.

All these ingredients led to a heady mix of smells in Afghanistan, which were completely alien to me before I went there. The first time the aircraft doors opened in Kabul and the air and the smell hit me, I found it a little discomforting. On return visits, though, these smells became enticing, framing good memories and bad, and were an integral part of any Afghanistan experience.

The accommodation in the British half of Camp Shorabak was a purpose-built, pre-fabricated Nissen-type hut that housed about thirty of us. I was on a top bunk, and the previous incumbent had kindly left some pictures of semi-clad females on the walls for me. The accommodation had a hard PVC floor that seemed to absorb some of the sand that we brought in every day. There was no air-conditioning; during the day it became like an oven, but at night-time we could open the windows and get some fresh air into the place. This almost – but not quite – helped mask the odours of some of my comrades who, struggling in the heat, let their personal administration slide somewhat.

Life could be very chaotic on that first tour. One evening, minding my own business and taking in the sunset as I strolled across the camp in my flip-flops and towel, I was surprised by a commotion coming from over the wall in the ANA compound. There was much shouting and starting of vehicles; it appeared that there were competing voices, some urging restraint and some encouraging others into some sort of action. My interpreter came running over to me and told me that there was an attack on a nearby town by some Taliban. For some reason, this rather ordinary occurrence had hit a nerve with one of the kandak commanders (not mine) and he was ordering the entire battalion to line up their vehicles behind his, ready to lead a charge to the village and fight back.

This all sounded fine, except that the idea of heavily armed ANA soldiers roaming around the desert looking for a town (they could not map-read) without talking to any of the NATO forces in the area (they had no tactical radios, and didn't believe they were useful anyway) meant that the potential for carnage was great. I went into the Ops room and told my CO what was happening. He frantically tried to get his counterpart to intervene, but it was too late, and the vehicles were already leaving the camp gates with soldiers hanging on to the sides and the backs, high on vengeance.

The battalion returned that night. How they found their way back in the dark I'll never know. They had lost 'a few', but felt theirs had been a worthy cause. I wondered how many of my own kandak would be on parade in the morning. The Afghan National Army had no concept of war-fighting beyond gang violence. Teaching them how to look after each other, about fire and movement and about command and control, was futile; they were a group that had diminishing respect for life, whether their own or the enemy's. The size of the strategic task – building up an army that was capable of bringing some degree of security to Afghanistan for the next fifty years – was beyond most of our comprehension, even at this early stage.

This first tour of mine was, on the whole, tedious. I spent endless sweaty days on the range, firstly training the ANA and then staying behind and trying to master the array of weaponry we Brits had suddenly had given to us in theatre, most of which we'd never seen before in the UK. Back then, even Minimi machine guns – now commonplace in the British infantry – were new. Underslung grenade launchers required some practice if you were ever going to be able to employ them effectively in combat. In later years, pre-deployment training for an Afghanistan tour became almost a greater test of endurance than the tour itself. This was probably an over-reaction to these early days, where preparation, cultural understanding and – crucially – equipment were simply woeful.

It's hard to believe it now, but on that first tour we deployed in Cold War-era stab vests, with a plate inserted over the heart, to conduct high-intensity war-fighting operations. These vests were generally worn because they would keep your body in one piece following an explosion, rather than keep anything out. They also kept you rather warm at night-time, when the temperatures dropped, but were otherwise useless. Another piece of equipment, the Snatch Land Rover, was already considered a coffin on wheels after the Iraq War, yet we were still travelling around in what was effectively a barely armoured Jeep, getting in the back each time thinking this may be our last journey.

That was the general state of affairs, but things were even worse for the OMLTs. We used stripped-down Land Rovers known as WMIKs – short for Weapons Mount Installation Kit. These are barely modernized hangovers from the 'Desert Rat' operations in the Second World War – and they were our primary weapons platforms. 'Stripped down' not only meant no roof, but no doors either. Consequently, there was little to hide behind, and you had to hope an incoming bullet would hit one of the struts in the vehicle. Great for mobility; did nothing for protection. I remember spending a bizarre afternoon taping and strapping some Kevlar plates we stole from the Americans onto the side of a WMIK for doors, so the crew could at least duck if they got stuck during contact.

This approach contrasted with the other nations in theatre. When they talked about 'up-armouring vehicles', they meant a complete re-fit by the vehicle's original manufacturers – a professional job involving upgrades to the original panels with armour plating and, sometimes, explosive reactive armour. We Brits taped misshapen Kevlar plates to the driver's door. The contrast was a little dispiriting.

The .50 calibre was the most powerful machine gun we had. It was simply devastating – firing a .50 calibre round at roughly 900 metres per second will destroy the engine of a vehicle, or cut through concrete walls. A really relentless pounding from this weapon system is enough to take down buildings and, as such, it is vital for suppressing, outgunning and killing a numerically superior enemy. Unfortunately, we had very little of the ammunition required for it, and were forced to ask convoys from other nations using our base for a night's stop if they could relinquish any of their stocks to help us out. I remember going to the range one day, cock-a hoop that we had managed to acquire some for practice from some very friendly Estonians. We got to the range, set up three guns and prepared a range practice. I was the Range Controlling Officer, even though I had only recently passed my weapons handling test for this gun.

We then endured a frustrating hour as we tried to figure out why the guns were only firing two or three rounds before stopping. We were pulling them apart, examining firing pins and case extractors, changing gas-settings and everything else, before we realized that the case of the rounds was ever-so-slightly too small to create a seal and thus feed the gun correctly. The ammunition was of a lower quality than it should have been, and now instead of machine guns that could chew up everything in their way, we had very large, very bulky .50 single-shot rifles.

When I reported this to the adjutant, he desperately searched the entire Task Force Helmand for some ammunition for us, but was told that, unfortunately, 3 PARA

Battlegroup had fired nearly all of it that summer, and we were to take a crateload off the Estonians for operations as it was 'better than nothing'.

Yes – the proud British Army of 2006.

We would make significant cross-cultural efforts with our Afghan friends, regularly having dinner with them after a hard day's training. It was clear from being around them that there were a lot of tribal feuds being silenced to accommodate the new fighting force that was the Afghan National Army. The feuds were always simmering just below the surface, and violence in their ranks was a daily occurrence. I witnessed a particularly brutal attack quite early on in my tour, when there was a disagreement on parade just after we had handed out the weapons for that day's training. Fortunately, the ammunition was still safely in the shipping container, and so these two Afghans were forced to trade blows with the stocks of their weapons. The beating did not stop when one was knocked unconscious, at which point I decided my respect for 'cultural disagreements' had reached its limit. Eventually I persuaded the kandak commander to step in to stop the violence.

It was clear just looking at the soldiers, as I was training them or even just on parade in the morning, that their ranks were festering with the enemy. They looked at me in that way, studied my movements, spoke Pashto under their breath to their friends as I passed them. I could not even fathom how you would 'vet' these guys before they came to me, and I had to assume that I was in a little personal danger, and act accordingly. It was not customary to take long-barrelled weapons into tents and meetings with the Afghans – it kind of ruined the atmosphere if you just sat there in your helmet and body armour with your safety catch off. The few pistols the British had were safely strapped to the expanding waist-lines of the staff officers in Camp Bastion and elsewhere. When I raised my personal security with my CO, he smiled wryly at me and told me to make sure I had my knife on me at all times when in the Afghan camp.

These evening meetings were always fairly banal, but crucial to building relationships between us. There had been no serious ANA-on-Brit violence at the time, and much of the evening was spent sharing stories about our different cultures rather than talking about how we would operate in the field. I do remember being asked to celebrate Eid, which marks the end of Ramadan, with our Afghan colleagues. They had somehow come across two goats on the firing range, had killed them and spit-roasted them over a fire. Despite our strong reservations, we joined in and had some of the meat, along with other delicacies. The following day our camp was a sight, with more than sixty soldiers and marines laid out side by side on the ground, each with a drip in them to rehydrate after a particularly violent episode of diarrhoea and vomiting.

Regrettably I became disillusioned with the experience on my first tour of Afghanistan. It should have been a period of real excitement and opportunity, but the chaos and disorganization really affected me. Jim Philippson had been killed in a piece of epic disorganization before I'd even arrived, yet many were treating the war like a game. The truth was that just three years after the Iraq invasion we had wandered into yet another conflict entirely unprepared for what was coming. I wasn't sure it was worth the sacrifice.

Before my first tour, I was at the stage in my career where I was 'corps-pissed', as they say in the US; I was totally committed to the military, to my regiment and to the concept of fighting in foreign fields for a safer homeland for my loved ones. I saw the military as this great institution, constantly evolving after hundreds of years to defend this great nation of ours. I believed that after years in Northern Ireland and experience of other insurgencies, such as Malaya, we were a more intelligent, more effective fighting force than other countries, including the US.

But my experience was turning out to be quite different, and I found that challenging. We were gaffer-taping armour to our Land Rovers; we were asking the Estonians for ammo that did not fit our guns. We had no idea what we were doing and people were dying because of it. My immediate commander, who seemed to think this was some sort of jaunt from the days of the Raj, appeared to be more interested in building a fucking concrete cricket pitch in the base to play cricket with 'the natives' than ensuring we had the equipment for our primary role.

The picture of the enemy that had been painted for us was nothing short of fiction; I suspect the author of these government and MI6 assessments now has a successful career writing children's books. Patrols were getting involved in epic, all-night firefights, like the one in which Jim Philippson had been killed. Training and mentoring my arse; more like hang on until your six months are up and some other poor bugger can 'stag on'.

A couple of years later, while working with a Special Forces (SF) unit and having high security clearance as a result, I became aware that the CIA felt that the British, in 2006, had set Helmand back thirty years. Initially when I learnt this I was perturbed; friends had been killed or injured in this war, I had seen the sacrifices we had made to secure our mission in that period. But on reflection, the CIA was absolutely right. Commentators the world over have also since examined that period, and sometimes denigrated the British effort.

But the ground truth – and what the CIA was actually saying – was rather simpler. Our intelligence was so poor, and our foresight so woeful, that we were placing our people in desperate situations. No one seemed to think that the hornets' nest that is southern Afghanistan would react so violently to international interventionism. This, despite the almost constant war that had been going on over the previous thirty years; this, despite the fact we'd been entirely caught out by an under-estimation of the problem in Iraq. It seemed madness to everyone but us to put a handful of soldiers in an isolated, exposed compound, and ask them to hold off the enemy while simultaneously making friends with them. When our troops were inevitably attacked, the only way to avoid a massacre was for them to shoot their way out with small arms and overwhelm the enemy with violence. It was kill or be killed. But the 'thinkers' – the strategists, the generals and the politicians – were quick to decry our violence, both then and as the war drew on. The louder they shouted, the more disconnected we felt. The more doctrinal and idealistic the missives, the more comically out of touch they looked. You can't bring peace if you are focused purely on survival. We didn't want to die, and it led to some showdowns.

The scale of the violence served to turn a population against us from a very early stage. The harsh truth is that they came to prefer the Taliban, and they knew that this beautiful country, raped by years of war, was being criminally violated again. The first time British troops went into Sangin, in the summer of 2006, they drove straight up the high street in berets. By the end of the war, Sangin was infamous in living rooms up and down the UK as a result of the number of British soldiers killed there.

I met one individual who provided me with the role model I was looking for as a young officer ready to be formed, but struggling to deal with an organization in disarray over its core business. Joe was a company sergeant major in 45 Commando, and I became very close to him. He was extremely professional, and I took it upon myself to learn as much as I could from him. He taught me how to use a sniper rifle, how to fire the 51mm mortar with great accuracy and drummed into me the importance of the marksmanship principles – all good stuff for a gunner officer who had let his infantry skills diminish somewhat.

One incident summed up the experience of that tour for me. I was in the Ops room one day when a young bombardier came through. He was on a patrol with a friend of mine called Al, and had stopped by to rest for the night before pushing further south. Al was a captain in the Royal Marines, operating as a Fire Support Team Commander, coordinating joint fires. Al was cutting around with a sniper rifle as well as his SA80 assault rifle. Some thought he was mad; I thought it was rather sensible.

The bombardier was someone I still have loose contact with now. That day, in a contact, he had called-in an air strike from a jet which killed some women and children in a compound. He was devastated. He was no macho, wannabe soldier; he was cerebral, dedicated, committed. But at the point of his position being overrun, he had requested the drop from a British Harrier and in doing so had killed some civilians.

My battery commander went for him. I cannot recall the conversation verbatim so I will not attempt to reproduce it here; suffice to say the bombardier left the Ops room almost tearful. Not for the first time, I wanted to use the cover of 'war-time stress' to flatten my battery commander. As far as I was concerned he was a classic product of a disconnected and over-privileged elite. While some admired his almost colonial approach, when it came to war-fighting I struggled to find it amusing.

I followed the bombardier; I told him I was ashamed of the way my fellow officer had spoken to him and that he should ignore him. I thought his team, with Al, was doing a bloody good job and I could only imagine the pressure they were under.

'I'm glad you followed me out,' he said. 'I've a present for you.'

He went into his backpack and dug out a bottle of cider. It was surreal.

'This is from Captain Ivy over in Bastion; he says you might need it.'

I had left earlier than most of 29 Commando for Op Herrick 6, as that Afghan deployment had been called. My officer mates from the regiment had been to a cider festival after I'd left the UK, and had brought me a bottle so I didn't totally miss out. That evening, I sat on the HESCO bastion protective wall around our camp and drank my warm West Country cider, watching the explosions and tracer fire from an attack taking place miles to our south against the darkening sky. It was a funny old war.

One evening in early November, I was heading over to the mess hall from my grot when I saw the regimental sergeant major (RSM) from 29 Commando speaking in hushed tones with my battery commander. They called me over.

'Johnny, I've got some bad news,' said the battery commander.

From this fool, this could mean anything from the delay of his order of wicket-keeper gloves from Amazon to the death of a close relative.

'You're doing a great job, and we've done absolutely everything we can to keep you here. But for some reason the Manning and Career Management Division of the Army has sent through your posting order for your next tour, and you are going to have to leave us.'

'Are you serious?' I said, thinking there must be some mistake. I always knew this was a possibility – as an officer one must move on from units in the military after a defined period of time – but surely this would not happen during an operational tour?

'I'm afraid so,' the RSM said. He was a good man whom I had known for some time, and he was behaving in an extremely odd and uncomfortable way. 'The CO has phoned everyone, including the CO of your next regiment, but there's nothing to be done for it; you have to go.'

'The CO told me that he'd ensure this did not happen,' I protested to the RSM.

'He's tried everything, Johnny, I promise,' said the RSM.

'Okay,' I said. 'How long have I got?'

'You'll be heading home in two weeks,' said the battery commander.

I knew something, was not right. I was under the operational command of the Royal Marine commanding 45 Commando, so I asked him over a coffee if I was being removed for struggling with the battery commander. To my surprise, he told me he struggled equally, had been impressed with me thus far and had worked me into his seven-month plan.

Given my posting order, I knew who my new CO was going to be. He was a lovely man who I had worked for previously.

Once back in the UK, I spoke to him about this particular posting process, while re-affirming my commitment to my new job. He said he hadn't heard anything from 29 Commando, and that if he had then of course I could have stayed with 45 Commando for the remainder of the tour; 29 just couldn't bring themselves to do the requisite administration.

Anyway, back in Afghanistan I had two weeks to push. I had been training my kandak, ready to go on operations in a fortnight. This meant I was going to miss out on any real combat. The CO of 45 Commando kindly gave me the option of going up to Sangin for a couple of weeks of action before I flew home. In Camp Shorabak, where I was, there was a beautiful memorial to my friend Jim Philippson, carved from wood and attached to the side of the mess hall. He had been operating from this camp when he went out on the patrol that was to claim his life. Having seen his brother and parents at his funeral, I had promised myself before I came on this operation that I would not chase 'the action' as hard as he had, so I declined. I was happy to accept that he was braver than me.

In those two weeks, I became deeply disillusioned with the whole thing. The mission, the Army and the commanders who were supposed to be coordinating this madness. In a moment of childish nonsense, I decided that I was not prepared to commit my professional life to the Army as a whole, and wrote a letter to my 29 Commando CO resigning my commission.

I deeply regret this. It was not a clever move and was the result of an almost childish sulk. The truth is that I suspected I had not done enough to mask my growing misgivings about the operation as a whole, and I had a fear within me that my CO in Afghanistan had not fought as hard to keep me as he claimed. My reaction was pathetic, and one I took a life lesson from. Almost immediately after I handed in my letter, I regretted it. Thankfully, my commanding officer told me to not be such a child, and put my letter in the bin where it belonged.

I left theatre in November 2006, to take up my new role of training fresh recruits, and tried to put the experience of my first tour of duty behind me. At the age of twenty-five, it was clear that I still had some growing up to do.

10

Following my return from Afghanistan, I embarked on a tour of duty at the Royal School of Artillery in Larkhill, on the rolling hills of Salisbury Plain. I was given the opportunity to bring my recent operational experience to a rather gentrified training programme. My boss was an experienced, late-entry commissioned soldier who was precisely the sort of individual under whom I would thrive. He encourages me to this day.

I re-wrote the way we trained our soldiers for operations in the Royal Artillery and implemented it – a significant feat in a military system that is resistant to change. I refocused efforts away from conventional vehicle and equipment maintenance; retaining its importance but ensuring that every soldier was capable of sustaining themselves in the field for extended periods of time. Royal Artillery soldiers in Afghanistan were being used to conduct a wide range of tasks, so I wanted to ensure that they had the core qualities of discipline, fitness and resilience required for operations in a harsh environment.

Being an instructor in the Army is an immense privilege, and provided me with some of the most satisfying experiences of my time in service. I'd met some truly inspirational instructors and I took a little bit from each one.

In truth, though, there wasn't any single instructor who had the complete package. Perhaps Pete Simmons from the pre-commando course at Okehampton was the closest. Or the instructors on Rowallan Company, who I imagined murdering at times. On Rowallan they did everything with us – from crawling through cow shit to yomping from the top to the bottom of Dartmoor without a break. Remarkably, they would let us get lost, despite being on the hoof for forty-plus hours, and patiently wait for us to figure out how to get back on track ourselves. Crucially, this let us learn from some pretty emotional and painful self-generated mistakes.

One of the main reasons that the instructor job was one of the most rewarding periods of my early career was that I could see myself in many of the soldiers who came through the training regiment. Young, away from home, in a challenging environment. They were making immature decisions both at home and in the Army – much like the one I had recently made in Afghanistan. The difference between me and them was that I was now aware how immature I had the capacity to be, and they were not.

I had a good team around me and I worked the same long hours as I had in Afghanistan. There was one soldier in particular who summed up the entire experience for me. He had decided to leave Parachute Regiment training because he wanted to come to the Royal Artillery; not a popular move at the time. I knew there must be more to the story, but I did not pry.

He was asked to turn-to in 'smart casual' attire for the first day. Smart casual to him meant a matching Ellesse tracksuit. He didn't immediately come to my attention, until I caught him telling a female corporal to 'fuck off' during one of her field lessons. I took him to one side. I never shouted in anger, and wasn't going to start now. I simply told him that this behaviour was not acceptable in the Army. I may have used the C-word.

He was a big strong lad, and loved a physical challenge, so from then on I always paired myself with him on PT – I did every session with the troops – and made a point of rubbing his nose in it, in a nice way. I could tell he had serious potential, and he was beginning to like me and, crucially, respect me.

One day he came into the office and asked how he could become a specialist soldier like me – they knew I was from a commando regiment. I gave him a completely unachievable training programme and told him I would be paying even more attention to him. I found out about his home life; no father, just avoided being taken into care, from a family of 'tough' criminals and drug dealers in Manchester.

On the last day of his course I heard a confident knock at the door. He was standing there in his No.2 Dress uniform, as smart as a button. He marched in and banged his feet into the ground as he came to attention and gave me a salute.

'What's up, Cooper?' I asked wryly. 'Come in for a hug, have we? Getting all emotional now you're leaving us.'

He didn't react to my stupid piss-taking. In silence, he pulled out a box of Celebrations chocolates and put them on the desk in front of me. He wasn't smiling. He tried to say something – I think it was a thank you. Nothing came out and he coughed. He threw up another salute, turned smartly to his right and marched out and off to his regiment.

I was later informed by his troop mates that he had never said thank you for anything in his life before, but he wanted to say thank you to me. He'd had no male role models whatsoever, and we had provided that for the first time. He finally believed he had a future outside of Manchester and all of the problems with his home life; we had given him a chance and he was determined to take it. (I say 'we' because my training team were far better than me, and did all the work.) It wasn't the fact that I had made him a soldier that I found so intensely satisfying; it was the fact that I had invested something of myself in him, and inspired him to make something of himself.

In 2008, at the completion of my tour at the training regiment, I expressed an interest in taking part in Special Forces operations. My reports from senior officers were very good at the time and I had personally come a long way from the rather sulky child who had turned up two years earlier. I don't know if it was because I had endured a little bit of bad luck with my last move between regiments, but this time things went my way and I was offered the opportunity to deploy with a Special Forces group. I would be a non-qualified Operations Officer with a unit charged with man-hunting tier one targets in Afghanistan, and along the border with Pakistan.

I would be in civilian clothes for the duration of this tour; testament to the entirely different experience it would provide me with. I joined a team of dedicated professionals at the top of their trade – in stark contrast to the OMLT mission in 2006 – and I felt that I might have finally found my niche. It was blisteringly hot as I arrived back in Afghanistan in the summer of 2008. I was to be based in Kandahar – scene of the Taliban's last stand in 2001. They had been conquered by US and UK forces back then, but now it was the seat of the major insurgent commanders in the area.

I was housed in the very comfortable SF compound, named after an operator who had been killed the summer before on a counter-terrorist operation. It is always difficult joining a close-knit team, particularly on operations, but this group of individuals made me feel entirely welcome. My role was to be very fluid. The guy before me had seemingly got the pizzas and coffees in when an operation went into the early hours; I was keen to play a far more active part, and early on it was made clear to me that the opportunity was there to do so.

Al Qaeda and the Taliban were very much an interchangeable title at the time, although the AQ influence in Afghanistan was nowhere near what it was in Iraq. These terrorist networks establish themselves very much like any other organizations that have a hierarchy of power and pursue their aims ruthlessly. The task force's specific job was to kill or capture as many of the Taliban/AQ leadership within the country as possible. They were directing a campaign of terror and intimidation on the local populations, and hounding the International Security Assistance Force (ISAF) operating on behalf of the NATO mission with a daily wave of bombings and shootings.

We would spend most of our days trying to find the targets, before deciding on a time and place for an attempted detention. In almost all cases these individuals resisted strongly, and attempted detentions became killings. It would be inappropriate to outline the methods employed, but I can relate some non-specific personal experiences.

Finding an individual target in the complex human and physical environment of Afghanistan is an enormous challenge, but we had some powerful tools and friends to help us. My role would often be to take part in the surveillance of a target, looking for a specific person leaving a house or advising on target viability for prosecution. We would sometimes use traditional methods, such as a kinetic strike using drones, but would more often than not deploy the blokes forward and interdict targets using helicopters.

Al – my friend from 29 – was working in the same unit. Al is a dour Scotsman, almost impenetrable without a beer. But we became very close as we both grew into our new roles.

Even operating at the strategic level, innovation is key. After some young Apache pilots started missing High Value targets that we had tracked for days without sleep, we sat down with Al and others and worked out a different way for the helicopters to interdict vehicles at speed. I was made to feel very much part of the team and I relished the opportunities they gave me.

It was an intensely rewarding period. As a task force we were up against some of the very worst evil in mankind. We would sometimes capture individuals with paedophilic material on their phones, or personally filmed beheading videos. We would conduct operations with a relentless pursuit of the enemy, slowly working our way through the Taliban and Al Qaeda leadership networks on intelligence-led, violent night-time visits. It made me want to operate with these teams for the rest of my career, but I was 'non-badged', and would be returning to the regular army after this tour.

Because we were conducting high-level, strategic man-hunting operations that fell outside of the Army's Task Force Helmand mission, our plans often required ministerial sign-off. Government ministers – including the Prime Minister – and other political decision makers would regularly visit our compound, and I was part of the 'visits team' when they came. We would all put on our uniforms for the day and try and tidy up a violent and messy operation into a neat PowerPoint slideshow that indicated clinical strategic progress. I was impressed by then Shadow Foreign Secretary William Hague's capacity to absorb information. He was very sharp and asked the questions you would expect from someone with his intellectual and strategic horsepower. David Cameron was also good, if very tired. I fear we sent him to sleep at one point. He spent time with, and clearly got on with, the blokes. Gordon Brown's visit just before I arrived apparently didn't go so well. He asked the team to fast-forward some Predator drone video footage of the blokes 'on target' because he didn't want to see it.

During December I was briefly CASEVAC'd (casualty evacuated) back to the UK for a scan on one of my testicles, which had become inflamed from washing in dirty water and was showing the characteristics of testicular cancer. It was all fine in the end, but I'll never forget the simply bewildering emotions I felt on arriving at hospital in Birmingham just six hours after leaving Afghanistan.

It is very difficult to put into words how it feels to extract from the sort of operations I was conducting and be entirely on your own in a civilian environment, especially a hospital. I was put on a ward with all the other sick and lame from Birmingham. As the nurse left, drawing the curtains behind her, my head felt like a washing machine. Should I be getting so much professional pride from what I'm doing? Do these people in Britain know what we do to keep them safe? Would they care or object?

I couldn't phone anyone. I couldn't talk about what I was doing with anyone. In any case, my family didn't want to know. When I had returned from my first tour in Afghanistan my mother had barely raised her eyes when I walked into the room, calling me a 'coward' for returning home early; she had clearly not grasped the inexorable methods of the Army posting system. My older brothers wavered from being outright war-haters to mildly protective, but were thoroughly disinterested in my life. I did not want to appear weak to my friends and telephone them. I'd felt completely alone in what I had experienced on my first tour, but even more so in what I was experiencing now; I had never felt so isolated from the world before or since.

I could feel my character bending, maturing and being forged for life during that summer, autumn and winter in Kandahar. For a start, as a task force we killed a lot of people, and I had a role in that. It would be fair to say that there was a grinding of the wheels in my mind between my Strict Baptist upbringing, a fairly sheltered first tour, and then the industrial pursuit of targets on this tour.

Perhaps because I felt increasingly distant to and different from my family, my mind settled considerably. Something dropped into place and I knew I had to trust myself and the way I figured life out, as opposed to following what I was led to believe was the truth by some hardwiring I had received as a kid. Our targets were fucking bad people, and there was nothing wrong with ending their lives. I felt myself become, finally, entirely self-assured – my own being.

This may sound odd, but if you've had an upbringing like mine, the reason it is so pervasive and doesn't let you go is that you have so many moments when you think you might have got it wrong. That perhaps you *were* bloody naughty and deserved the discipline you endured. That perhaps 'God' does have it in for you, and you can do no good. Finally having a mind of my own meant I could accept that while some people – including my parents – felt that way about life, I didn't have to.

A lot of this had to do with the people I was with. Al became a bit of a brother to me, and it was easy to respect those around me. The friends I made on that tour helped me define myself. Like them, I became obsessed with the gym.

I particularly enjoyed a Tuesday night, when the machines were removed, thin gym mats placed on the walls and floor, and 'fight night' would begin. For me, this was a chastening experience. Inevitably paired with the bigger man, I would get used to suffering a humiliating defeat. Being an officer and being 'non-badged' were both perfectly sound reasons to hand my arse to me on a plate on a weekly basis.

My favourite fights were with Al, when he tried to teach me a thing or two. He would resist my aggression with skill, and then place me in holds from which there was no escape. I would lose my temper, and he would just be talking to me calmly, telling me to control myself. I became strong, fit and resilient, and was committed to doing the six-month course required to be a permanent operator within the United Kingdom Special Forces Group upon my return from the tour.

It didn't work out quite like that. I got back to the UK in 2009 to discover that the Army had other plans. I was part of a larger regiment that was committed to providing Terminal Controllers for the ongoing field army operations in Afghanistan, and I was to do that course instead, before deploying again for a third time in four summers to Afghanistan.

11

During these years, around my tours in Afghanistan and my stint with the training regiment, my personal life seemed to blend seamlessly into my professional life, and girlfriends took a back seat as a result. Leave was often planned well in advance with old mates, and some epic holidays were enjoyed.

The summer of 2007 was spent with Dave – a long-time close friend of mine, who had returned from a tour in Afghanistan just in time to find out his girlfriend had sought comfort elsewhere while he was away. This coincided roughly with the time our 'operational bonus' was being introduced – a financial reward for war-fighting service. I hadn't spent mine yet, and Dave was on a mission to run through his money as fast as possible and forget the loss of his childhood sweetheart, so we booked tickets to fly to Los Angeles for three weeks. Without any set plans, we hired a convertible Chevrolet and headed off on a round trip that took in San Diego and San Francisco. We went skydiving in Perris. And, of course, we went to Vegas.

We spent more time drunk than sober. We were banned from the Piano Bar on the Strip for insisting that I could play better than the professional musician they'd paid for that evening (demonstration included). We stayed in pricey hotels with infinity swimming pools where it seemed that the mandatory order of dress for females was topless. We met Jenna Jameson's manager, who invited us to a house party which we were too drunk to attend. (If you don't know who she is, neither did I. I do now.)

One baking west-coast evening, we were befriended by a group of women in Los Angeles' famous Sky Bar, as we watched the sun sink down over the city. Some rather large, rather aggressive and very rich Asian men were trying to move in on them; the girls were more interested in us. The Asian chaps were flooding the table with expensive alcohol; Dave and I were helping ourselves. The Asian guys were acting very shady, as if they were part of some crime cartel, and invited the girls to a party with Lindsay Lohan, which the girls refused to attend without us.

Reluctantly, the blokes invited me and Dave, and when I indicated I was not willing to contribute to the $3,000 table price, they ended up paying for us too. They sped off down the strip in two Lamborghinis while Dave, myself and a couple of the girls followed in a taxi.

In the early hours, the man who seemed to be their leader had had enough of us taking the piss.

'Come on, you two, you've been freeloading all night; let's do some shots!'

'OK,' said Dave, before I could intervene.

We followed them to the bar, where I was able to lean over and get the attention of the barmaid.

'These guys are cocks. Water for us, vodka for them, put it on the table tab, OK?' I shouted at her over the music.

As they sunk glass after glass, beating their chests and bouncing off each other, Dave and I tucked away our waters, glad for the respite. After a few, I cannot remember how many, one of them clicked, and they were very angry indeed.

Dave and I couldn't match their aggression, and collapsed in fits of giggles. They were ejected from the club and we returned to their $3,000 table without them.

The rest of the evening passed in a blur until Dave, while speaking to the party organizer, asked, 'Who the fuck is Lindsay Lohan anyway?' He had a point – I didn't know who she was either – but from the woman's expression, it seemed like a good time to leave.

When one is young, without ties and either training for or recovering from an on-going military operation such as Afghanistan, one can be rather fatalistic, and life can become quite chaotic. Looking back, I feel rather embarrassed by my lifestyle back then; but no one got hurt. Sort of.

I was very close to my fiercely loyal friends, who were all experiencing the same process, and found it very difficult to talk to anyone outside that circle. I did not like to think too hard about the war while I was in the UK, but it was difficult not to be moved by the constant churn of news from theatre, and wonder what personal fate lay ahead. The war was not ending any time soon, and I knew that I must endure more of it at some point. I found my answers were usually at the bottom of the glass.

One of my dearest friends was called Charlie Fisher. Charlie and I had met over tea and toast one afternoon while at 29 Commando in Plymouth. The rain was beating against the window as another storm blew in across the Atlantic, slamming against the Royal Citadel.

'Good day for a sea-swim,' he had said to me, with a glint in his eye.

Ten minutes later we were off the Plymouth foreshore and swimming out around a buoy and back, before returning to the mess to finish off our tea and toast. We became friends for life.

Charlie, who left the Army in 2008, had a girlfriend I could not stand. His group of friends all worried that she wasn't right for him. Halfway through my 2008–09 tour, Charlie wrote to me to say that he and his girlfriend were now engaged, so of course I wrote him some hearty congratulations back. When I returned in early 2009, the wedding was just a couple of months away, planned for April that year.

After months in Afghanistan, I was more than ready to enjoy myself. Charlie and I seemed to spend much of the spring together, as I used up my post-tour leave and operational bonus on the streets of west London. It became apparent that all was not well with his impending wedding, and after some very long, very drunk conversations, the pair of us the last drinkers in the bar, the wedding was called off three weeks before the big day.

Charlie had made the correct decision, but being determined not to miss out on a holiday, he went on the honeymoon by himself, seeing the funny side of it all. When he returned, the bank he was working for asked him, with almost perfect timing, to go to their New York office for a year.

I went out to see Charlie in the summer of 2009. By now I knew I was returning to Afghanistan the following year, and regrettably my fatalistic behaviour had not improved. I was definitely in a challenging place in my mind, still recovering from returning from my last tour, and knowing the risks I'd be taking when I deployed again. Charlie, meanwhile, had a new girlfriend – a friend of his ex-fiancée who was supposed to have been the 'Maid of Honour' at their wedding. It would be fair to say that both of us needed a stiff drink or two, and New York seemed as good a place as any. At the end of one particular evening, for some unknown reason, we tried to swim across the Hudson River.

The current was very strong, and so we turned back and got ourselves out of the water. Inevitably, the NYPD had turned up. One of the cops was cool; I told him I was an idiot and was so sorry. The other was a twat and wanted to taser me. Again for some unknown reason, I wanted to be tasered to 'know what it felt like'; I reckoned I could 'take it', and the twat cop was gearing himself up to do it. At this point more police turned up, Charlie played peacemaker and we promised to return to his apartment.

Standing in my pants on the New York foreshore, I could not find my clothes. I was convinced – in that drunk way where one can never be wrong – that a tramp sleeping on a bench nearby had stolen them. I gently woke him up and asked him if he had my clothes – he didn't. During this whole charade I had managed to cut the back of my head quite badly, and blood was running down my back. As I started walking back to the apartment through the financial district of New York in just my pants, pissed, wet through and bleeding, I thought it might be time to grow up a bit.

12

Back in England, I tried to get my head into gear as I was officially warned off for operations again. The following March I would deploy on Op Herrick 12 as part of 3 Regiment Royal Horse Artillery (3 RHA), in a ground-holding operation in northern Nad-e Ali.

I met my new unit at their base in Germany. The key individuals within my particular sub-unit – D Battery – made every effort to welcome me. The battery commander, Adam Wilson, was to become a dear friend. This friendship, however, did not start right away. I didn't want to be there – I wanted to be given a go at passing United Kingdom Special Forces Selection; I was done with all this Regular Army stuff. But the Army, understandably, had other plans. The war in Afghanistan was intensifying; jobs with my skill-set needed to be filled out there, and they wanted another tour out of me as a Fire Support Team Commander.

Adam made it clear to me that I was there to get this group of men ready for war, and that is why I would not be released to go and pursue my own career ambitions. I don't know if this was just said to make me feel better, but I came to realize that he had no time for my selfish ambitions, and rightly so. He was charged with taking his battery on operations and that was his focus, not me. It took me a few months, but it was a classic case of him killing me with kindness.

The challenge was huge. Germany-based units had a very different composition and ethos to either a commando unit or an SF unit, where physical fitness and discipline were characteristics to be achieved and admired. From day one, I encountered significant resistance as I set up a training programme that would drive the unit towards the kind of professional standards that I knew they would need if they were to be able to perform on operations in Afghanistan.

The soldiers were rough. They smoked a lot, they drank a lot and they fought a lot. I wasn't really one to judge on this score, but my behaviour was a by-product of hard, professional soldiering, which always came first. It was an escape, a letting-off of steam; I felt their behaviour was their *raison d'être*, and I had no time for it. They were entirely disinterested in the campaign in Afghanistan, and I felt slightly put-out that while some of us had been involved in this conflict for a few years now, this lot seemed isolated from it.

An artillery battery is the same size as an infantry company – about eighty men when fully manned. The battery is usually split into four composite parts: the gun line, the fire support teams (FSTs), the logistics support group and the command posts. Each one of these composite sub-groups will be commanded, generally by an officer but sometimes by a senior NCO. The gun line was where the soldiers manned the guns; in this case 105mm L118 Light Gun howitzers. The guns will be told where to fire and where to move by a small command post group which is split into two positions, duplicates of each other. The logistics group will generally be commanded by the quartermaster sergeant. The FSTs are commanded by an officer.

There is generally a divide in the modern artillery battery

between the FSTs and the rest of the men. The rest will often act as one sub-unit; fire support teams will be working on their own with whichever forward ground unit they are tasked to support. The general idea is that the small FSTs work in close proximity to the enemy, and bring the guns, which are further back, on to target to achieve the effect required. Modern British FSTs have developed into something like the ANGLICOs (Air Naval Gunfire Liaison Companies) from the US Marine Corps. They are now multi-skilled teams that are designed to be able to control any indirect weapon system, launched from any platform in the air, on land or at sea. It requires a lot of training.

The process of achieving a joint fires effect on the ground – i.e., bringing a bomb, shell or missile into a collision with the target – is more complicated than it first seems. The target can be big (a building) or very small (a person). In an operation like Afghanistan there are multiple ground operations going on at any one time. There may well be Troops in Contact (TiCs) elsewhere who have a first call on air support; there may well be a 'kill box' (an area on the ground where a sensitive operation may be taking place) set up, waiting for a trigger, like we used on my 2008–09 Special Forces tour.

You cannot engage a target with a longer distance weapon such as field artillery without ensuring that there are no helicopters or other air assets on the imaginary line between the target and the gun line – for obvious reasons. Separating these assets is called 'de-confliction', and you can de-conflict by either space or time.

Once you have decided which method to use, you must work out the precise effect you wish to have on the target. Too small, and the individual might get away; too large and you risk casualties to your own side, or to civilians. Furthermore, if you create more mayhem than you need to, you are inevitably firing up the jihadists and creating more Taliban – which was not in line with the overall mission. This part is called the weapon-to-target match, and is ideally done before you select a platform to use, but inevitably you have to strike a balance between the available resources, the need for speed and the tactical situation.

The responsibility of dealing in extreme violence, while in close proximity to friend and foe, is like little else in life. Inevitably it draws those whose responsibility it is together as a tight team. Some resent this – rank structures become informal, standards of dress may relax – but in my experience, in any unit the joint fires guys are usually the last to bed at night and first up in the morning. They become specialists in all forms of radio and data communication equipment, without which no one leaves camp. They become expert battlespace managers; always aware of their precise location on the ground, listening for other engagements on radio systems, forewarning of any asset shortage. They spend endless hours staring at a TV screen watching for 'pattern of life' in a Predator drone feed, while simultaneously submitting requests for support for future operations. And yet the moment the enemy is sighted or attacks the patrol or the patrol base itself, the withdrawal and safety of the group under attack largely depends upon the ability of the joint fires guy to bring down fire and end the engagement.

Within these teams, one soldier might be a Joint Terminal Air Controller (JTAC); another might be a mortar fire control; another might be a specialist with radio equipment. This team should be commanded by a junior officer who is qualified in each of these roles. He is the interface between the ground commander and the joint fires community, and it is his responsibility to produce the required effect on the ground, however he chooses to do it. He ultimately assumes responsibility for both the successes and the failures. Many, many things can go wrong; he manages the risk. While a ground commander gives ultimate authority to engage, when it goes wrong it is clear where culpability lies.

The battery commander's job is to select his FSTs and manage them. As an FST Commander you do not have control over who you select; soldiers can, however, ask to be in your team. My team in the summer of 2010 was to be built around three of us; myself, Corporal Shaun Barrowcliff and Lance Bombardier Mark Chandler.

Shaun, known as Baz, was a junior NCO from the Queen's Royal Lancers who had re-roled as a JTAC. He was the same age as me, northern, and nowhere near as stupid as he would pretend to be. He had a family at home – with a wife and newborn child – and was a veteran of the Iraq War. He was meticulous in his approach to his soldiering, but particularly to his air and aviation control. This was to be his primary role. He was charged with ensuring that every weapon delivered from the air was safe, and that those airframes operating above us were safe as well. He had to seamlessly manage and understand the capabilities of Apache and Cobra attack helicopters, and the array of fast-air jets that were available for coalition operations in Afghanistan at the time. He had to de-conflict by time and space on the move, usually in contact with the enemy, as well as identifying targets and, if required, lighting those targets for the airframes to see using handheld equipment. He had a sense of humour that was drier than an Afghan's flip-flop, but he was rigidly professional in all that he did and kept me well and truly on my toes.

Mark Chandler – known as Bing – was a junior NCO from my D Battery. I wanted him to be my Ack – my closest assistant, with me every step I took – and it was my luck that he had asked to be in my team. He was older than me and Baz, but was just one of life's really good blokes. He had courage and resilience in spades, and I had been impressed with him throughout the process of pre-deployment training. He was tough without showing it, he was humble; he was perfect for me. Mark was a trained specialist in the terminal control of artillery fire, and he was also qualified to control attack helicopters in a close-combat role.

Myself, him and another junior NCO called JT had first become close after an exercise on pre-deployment training in the Arizona desert, where we qualified ourselves in the use of the Apache helicopter. We had to do multiple 'controls' – correctly identifying and locating targets for missiles from the helicopters – in order to qualify ourselves to do it on operations. Time on the range was not hectic, and the three of us took it upon ourselves to explore the delights of Phoenix and the surrounding areas of an evening. It was a thoroughly enjoyable time.

We would rise early each day and conduct some tough physical training while it was still cool, then make the two-hour drive up to the range. After long hours in the sun, we would drive back to our base, get changed and cement our friendship in a local bar, often with unintended results. Although my general behaviour was rather poor in between tours in those days, it did, I am ashamed to say, take another nosedive in those weeks in 2010 leading up to my third tour, and I suggest that the Arizona desert was probably the best place for me.

One night I inadvertently committed a crime by consuming

alcohol ever-so-slightly over the threshold of a bar in down-town Phoenix – alcohol is strictly forbidden off licensed premises in Arizona. An off-duty cop attempted an arrest, which did not go quite as he planned. I thought he was assaulting me, JT and Bing came to my defence, and a quite serious street brawl broke out. Eventually, some cop cars turned up. By then Bing, JT and I were in well over our heads, having been swamped by angry locals. The irate local police chief rescued us. Having been given the details of my trespass, the chief told me he was going to inform my CO. He wanted his telephone number.

Drunkenness affects different people in different ways. Some fight, some chase girls endlessly. I act like I am eleven years old before falling asleep. I *was* my Commanding Officer in the country at the time, so when I gave the chief the number of my CO and my phone went off in my pocket, he was unimpressed.

'*You* are an officer?' he exclaimed.

'Yes – believe it or not,' I replied.

'You, sir, are a fucking disgrace.'

'I know.'

He told me to go and sit in the back of his police car, like a naughty schoolboy. JT was cuffed in the vehicle next to me, and we couldn't stop giggling like kids. After about twenty minutes they realized we were no threat, and we were summoned over to the off-duty cop who had started the whole thing. I explained my ignorance of the local drinking laws, and that I hadn't realized he was trying to make an arrest. We agreed on some significant cultural differences before heading back inside the bar to all have a beer together. Admittedly, I found it hard to chat to a guy who had kicked me in the face on the floor while I was unable to defend myself, but we all pretended we were now best friends for the police chief's benefit. Once he left, we quickly went our separate ways.

Most of the pre-deployment training for Afghanistan was, however, done in the UK. If I could skip it I did – ducking out of some very basic lectures about Afghan culture (don't swear at the kids, etc.), myself and another officer would take off to Leeds for the day, the nearest city to our temporary base.

It was while en route to one of these UK-based training serials – at perhaps my most unstable both personally and professionally – that I decided to visit an old schoolfriend of mine. I was driving to Lydd Ranges in Kent – miles from my temporary base in Yorkshire – and I wanted to break up the journey.

We had lost contact, as I had with almost all of my childhood friends, and I hadn't seen her in years. I knew as soon as she opened the door that I was in trouble.

It was the worst possible time to meet Felicity. I was a very rough individual, caught in a seemingly endless cycle of military training and war – a rather 'loose' domestic life to say the least – and about to deploy to Afghanistan for the third time. But you can't control the timing of these things.

She was small, petite even, as the hall lights silhouetted her body in the doorway that Sunday. We got a takeaway and chatted all evening. She was warm and engaging, and tanned, with a beaming smile and a gorgeous figure. Living on her own in a little converted barn miles from anywhere, seemingly relaxed with a simple life, she was perhaps the opposite of me; happy, contented, stable and secure.

As I returned to training I tried extremely hard to focus

on the impending tour, managing to remain professional at work as I continued the relentless build-up to what was going to be a bloody summer. But I now had other things on my mind. I found I had to become incredibly mentally disciplined, desensitizing myself to anything outside of my mission, and becoming quite a hurtful person in the process, particularly towards Felicity. I could not entertain the idea of falling too hard for her and letting the fear of not returning from Afghanistan stop me from taking the risks I knew I would be asked, and expected, to take. I was truly torn, and it was not an easy period. I guess I knew I had just met my wife, but I was determined to fight it until a more convenient time.

Looking back, I'm embarrassed by the way I treated her. But there was a reason I was so rough; it kept the thoughts at bay. I didn't want to look too closely at what I was hiding from. Perhaps it was fear of what lay ahead; perhaps it was the way I'd learned to deal with the obsessions and compulsions that lay dormant in my mind, waiting for the chance to rise again. I just knew that it all faded if I did not engage my brain too heavily. I had a ruthless commitment to fitness and the resilience of me and my men. I did everything hard – running, soldiering, socializing. Fitter men lasted longer on the battlefield, and I knew resilience was not in healthy supply in some of the men, so I kept at them. They needed it; I knew what was coming that summer. I developed a total disregard for the wider strategic situation in Afghanistan; the place was becoming horrific – a trap of IEDs and gunfights that I just needed to survive.

Some of it was undoubtedly fear.

When I returned I could think a bit more about our future.

13

It felt familiar now to be putting on my body armour and helmet as the RAF Tristar commenced its final approach into Camp Bastion. There is something very 'British Army' about wearing a helmet and stab vest while on a passenger aeroplane, as if they would do any good at all if you were shot out of the sky on approach. From the air, I could see that the camp was five times the size it was when I was there in 2006.

When the aircraft doors opened, I was hit by the dryness and the scorching heat and the smell, which brought memories both good and bad. As alluded to before, it is not unpleasant, but you are left in no doubt that you have landed in an environment that's entirely different from your home, and you can't escape by ducking into an air-conditioned hotel. I had to ignore any personal discomfort as I surveyed the blokes waiting to pick up their baggage as we moved towards the holding pen for new arrivals.

For some reason, that first night in theatre on 23 March 2010, I felt very strange. I felt suffocated, as if I knew something terrible was about to happen, but I was unable to do anything about it. I remember getting out of bed, walking past the stinking toilets and the swarms of flies that didn't disappear when it got dark, and stopping by the NAAFI to have a cigarette. By now I was a committed smoker.

I don't know what it is about war that makes one smoke. For some it is the diet, with food so tasteless that one wants the cardboard flavour gone straight away. For me it gave me time to catch my breath. It gave me an enforced five minutes to collect my thoughts and try and remain on an even keel.

I was struggling, because the truth is I didn't want to be here at all. Afghanistan was an interesting experience once, maybe twice at a push. But this, my third time, was getting a bit repetitive. And back in England, try as I might to 'swim the other way', the effect of meeting Felicity had been rather profound. Despite my best efforts, I was feeling real fear, because I had something to lose. I had been frightened before of course, but the conflict had changed remarkably since I was last in Afghanistan. The stories that we had listened to and tried to learn from, particularly from the previous summer of 2009, were simply horrific. The bloodiest day for the British Army in Helmand had been 10 July 2009, with five killed and ten wounded in one incident alone. The insurgency was ramping up again. I was aware of the risks and what this life entailed, but this time, for some inexplicable reason, I was convinced that I would be lucky to return home. Very hard to explain. I put it to the back of my mind and didn't share it with anyone.

The first few days of an operational tour are always the worst for me. No matter if you have been to the theatre before, there's no escaping the 'in-theatre pre-deployment training' for those who are going to be outside of Camp Bastion. We were herded around like cows from one training serial to the next. On top of the boredom, I was getting annoyed by the rigid atmosphere in the camp. When I first came to Afghanistan in 2006, there was a very deliberate focus on survival and soldiering. While in camp, the blokes could relax and essentially cut around in whatever gear they felt comfortable in. They must, at all times, retain the highest levels of professionalism with regards to servicing kit, physical conditioning and operational capabilities, but dress and camp routine were rightly allowed to be relaxed. It was a bloody hard war.

But in the intervening years the culture had completely changed. The blokes were not permitted to leave their tents unless they wore full uniform and beret. There seemed to be an attitude of 'everyone before me was shit, so I'm going to do things differently', across the rank spectrum. Senior officers were specifically requesting to come to Afghanistan so they could get 'combat' on their annual reports. Almost to a man, they thought that they had the answer to an almost insurmountable problem, and the Afghanistan war had only been going as badly as it had because they were yet to have their turn at the wheel. Blokes like me, who were returning for a second or third time, were left in no doubt that all we had done before was wrong, we were now fighting in the 'right way' and we should get on board with the programme. The effects of a long-term war, I suppose.

It was Sunday, 28 March when I went into the Ops room in the joint fires area of the camp to receive my forward deployment orders. As I sat there, I thought of my parents going to chapel. By now, I had command of a seven-man team – augmented in theatre from elsewhere, including reserve forces, to fit the area I was to deploy to. Three of the team were going to support two patrol bases (PBs) that were satellites for the main camp in the area – PB Khaamar – where the rest of the company and the core team of myself, Baz and Bing would be located.

PB Khaamar had been set up after Operation Moshtarak

– the largest operation of the entire Afghanistan war in February 2010. This operation was an effort to strike at the Taliban heartlands – the hardest core of a no-go area for the Afghan government in Helmand. There were plenty of 'Tier One' Taliban commanders in the area – those who liaised regularly with Al Qaeda in Pakistan and drove the waves of violence across the province, which seemed to be getting worse. Led by the Americans just further south in Marjeh, the coalition was determined to strike a decisive blow against the insurgency in Helmand with this operation.

PB Khaamar was set up just south of Showal – a place General Stanley McChrystal had labelled as the 'insurgent capital' the previous month, just before it was cleared by British forces. The operation was largely a success, although inevitably a great deal of the Taliban simply downed their weapons or left the area. Those who ran had generally congregated immediately to the south of Showal and to the east of PB Khaamar, in an area on the map known as 31 West. One of the three PBs established in this area during Op Moshtarak had been overrun the previous month, and the resident ANA soldiers had had their throats slit.

Completing Op Moshtarak in the winter was a smart move by the coalition – fighting is significantly lighter in the colder months, when the opium poppy harvest is growing. But the coalition were yet to hold this ground for a summer, by which time the poppies were safely harvested and Taliban commanders could turn their attention towards UK Forces in PB Khaamar.

We passed from the pre-deployment training at Camp Bastion to Forward Operating Base (FOB) Shawqat – the main base in the Nad-e Ali district, which was still relatively secure. From there I would fly further forward to PB Khaamar.

At Shawqat I briefed my team on their own for the first time. I assured them that there were worse places to go. I told them about another team leader who, upon finding out how dangerous his patrol base was, went back into the Ops room in Camp Bastion and told them he wasn't going. I must confess I found this extremely amusing. Amusing primarily because I wasn't going there, but also because this guy had rather fancied himself throughout the pre-deployment training.

I had met him as he was walking back to the Ops tent again, this time to reconsider his decision. He asked me what to do. I laughed and told him to get on with it, and never tell anyone he nearly bottled it.

To be fair, he pulled himself together – unlike one of my own team in Shawqat. There are multiple challenges associated with commanding small teams in difficult and stressful environments, especially when the individuals are not brought together by friendship but simply because of their skills. I began to feel that one of my soldiers had lost his nerve and was going to ask to leave our team. Sure enough, he came to me and told me he had a back problem. Maybe he did but he was one of the fittest and strongest of my soldiers, and I felt the likelihood of him having a genuine back problem was pretty remote.

I gave him an easy way out. I could have taken it personally and charged him – something I had never done before. But deep down I knew that one day he would grow up, and he would have to carry this with him for the rest of his life. He was a loud character, one who would consider himself quite 'hard'. However, when faced with a challenge slightly greater than sinking a pint, or lifting some weights in the gym in front of his mates, his will to fight collapsed.

I called him over for a chat the day before we left to deploy forward. I told him I was disappointed. That I had worked hard to train him, not because I liked him as an individual, but because we all had a role to play in keeping each other alive in this place. I told him he should not approach me again once our helicopter had left Shawqat. I then found the rest of the team back at their accommodation testing some comms kit, and addressed the situation honestly with them. Unbeknown to me, they didn't like him anyway and were relatively happy he was staying behind, if slightly embarrassed on his behalf. I never spoke to the soldier again. We were all undoubtedly anxious, but quitting before it had even begun?

We were due to fly out the following day at dawn. The final few hours before leaving the relative comfort of FOB Shawqat were not much fun. You knew that you would be shitting in a bag for the next seven months; you knew you would not have any internet or shower block. Some tried to drain their intestines in a last 'porcelain poo'; some spent the time on the phone to their other halves; some spent the time mingling with mates from other units who were returning from the line, and worrying themselves stupid about what may or may not occur.

My routine in times like this was always the same. I made sure my kit was in A1 condition. No broken straps; full functionality on the radio and optical kit I had. Once this was done I made myself not look at it again. The endless checking can send you insane very fast. I called Felicity for a quick chat. You never know if there will be phones at these outposts, and so you warn your loved ones that it may be your last chat for a bit. The welfare package had come on a long way since 2006, however, and I was hopeful there would be telephones in my new PB.

Once this was done I would keep myself to myself. I would build my Bergan, webbing and body armour into an extremely comfortable recliner and sit on it, cradling my weapon and contemplating. On this particular night people came over for a chat – officers from other teams and some of the blokes. They seemed to think I knew what I was doing, and congregated around me, pulling up their Bergans. I felt a bit of a fraud – even then I didn't have any real experience of war-fighting, but I wasn't about to tell them that. There was a furtive, restrained but hard-edged atmosphere. Everything changed once you left this place, and we all knew it.

We were flying that night and we slept beside the helicopter, waiting for our 2 a.m. lift. It was 30 March 2010.

14

The Merlin helicopter touched down and Baz, Mark and I leapt off the back. We performed an 'Arctic Huddle' on our kit, to make sure it didn't blow away in the enormous down-draught as the helicopter lifted-off back into the night sky.

It was pitch black as we arrived at PB Khaamar, our home for the next six or seven months. We were met by the company commander – very decent of him at this hour – from 1 Battalion Royal Welch, who had been here since Op Moshtarak in February. After six weeks in the small patrol base with his men, the company commander was pleased to see some fresh faces.

We were shown to our accommodation. The Army still segregated officers and ranks when it came to accommo-dation, something I was uneasy with but recognized was probably what the ranks wanted more than anything else. However, this was not going to work for our team, and I managed to get us all in the back end of a spare tent together, and we set about sorting ourselves out.

It is remarkable how quickly one can adapt to austere conditions. I always found it best to completely surrender myself to the scenario, and adopt a survive or die attitude. Someone who tells you that they enjoy shitting in a sack and eating boil-in-the-bag sausage and beans for thirty days straight is, I'm afraid, lying. But it is possible to find a measure of comfort in the routine of it all, and this is what we began to do.

During our first week, the Royal Welch lost a man in a firefight just outside of the PB. Fusilier Jonathan Burgess died of a sucking chest wound – a gunshot wound that allows air into the chest cavity – and the company were in clear shock. He was an extremely popular soldier and his death affected the men, especially so close to the end of their tour.

The Royal Welch had just gone through a challenging winter, but the pace of operations was clearly changing as the season started to warm. TiCs were a twice or thrice daily occurrence, and with this uptick came the inevitable casualty list.

Set on a piece of land commandeered from the local population, the patrol base was essentially a modern fort built using blocks of HESCO bastion, or HESCO for short. A HESCO block is a wire cage lined with a brown felt bag that in turn is filled with sand and rocks. These blocks can be fixed together vertically and horizontally to create a perimeter wall around a base. They can also be stacked up into watchtowers and sentry positions. They are an ingenious invention that allowed ISAF forces to build a PB in the best tactical location, rather than making do with a prebuilt structure.

PB Khaamar had separate areas for accommodation, cooking and washing. Toilet seats were cut out of plywood, below which one could hang a bag. The bag was then thrown into the nearby 'burns pit', which was subsequently burnt once a day. The shower block was a 9 x 9 military tent into which you took a bag of water, hung it over a strut and then stood under it. It was important to have clear lines of delineation between these various activities to stave off the very clear threat of diarrhoea and vomiting, which could wipe out a company quite easily. While there were no central cooking facilities to speak of, it was good practice to ensure we ate together in the cooking area, to avoid the risk of both fire to the tents and decomposing food lying around. All very basic stuff that ensured good personal hygiene – and by extension operational effectiveness – could be maintained for long periods of time in an austere environment.

Baz, Mark and I started our familiarization patrols, and over the course of a week we accompanied the company commander to every corner of our area of operations (AO) to get a feel for the place. Our AO was almost triangular in shape and surrounded 31 West, with the main feature being the Nahr-e Bughra (NEB) Canal running along the northern edge. Built in the sixties by the Americans, the NEB Canal irrigated large parts of the Nad-e Ali district. There were three main roads dominating the three outer edges of the triangle, and it was along each of these three main routes that we had a patrol base, the main one (Khaamar) being on the western edge. The further one moved from these routes, the more dangerous things got. Indeed, despite Op Moshtarak, UK forces were yet to penetrate the centre of the triangle and reach the heart of 31 West. It was so riddled with enemy that it was known as the Jungle.

There are two schools of thought when it comes to commanding a fire support team. Some like to remain in the operations room, where they can fully assess the big picture and make decisions on weapon-to-target matches, de-confliction between the various air spaces and conduct the battle on the radio in a relatively calm environment. Some prefer to go out in the field. My primary role was to save coalition life and – if required – to kill the enemy with overwhelming firepower as quickly as possible. Being closest to the violence that I was imposing also meant I did not take any silly risks with weapon effects, and it gave me a quick eye-to-eye with the enemy to check my weapon-to-target match without relying on other people. I felt this could be best achieved by being on every patrol that might come into contact with the enemy.

This meant being on every single patrol from PB Khaamar.

There was a nasty air around theatre at the time concerning the use of joint fires. It was shit on the ground trying to coordinate fires – bloody scary too at times – while armchair Ops room staff down the other end of the radio were telling you what you could and could not do. I wanted the soldiers around me to have confidence in what they were doing, know we would never lose an engagement, could stay out longer, be bolder and fight harder while someone else (me) took care of all those awkward questions from the higher-ups.

The most enormous pressure was being put on our young field commanders and soldiers. Their actions were subject to an almost constant overwatch and second guessing – usually by someone who had yet to experience their first proper gun-fight. The rules of engagement were there to protect our troops as much as anything else, but commanders became obsessed with analysing secondary and tertiary effects of almost every engagement. This had the effect of both paralysing ground troops and commanders, and bringing some friction to the relationship between those of us on the ground and those commanding from PBs. In close contact with the enemy, this could prove fatal.

I did not want a situation to materialize where British soldiers in my area of operations were not giving themselves the best chance of success because they were perplexed by the rules of engagement, or restricted their use of joint fires for fear of getting it wrong. By now, I knew both of these two subjects inside out, and I was pleased to be able to deploy my knowledge on the ground. It was unfair to place this overwhelming strategic pressure on our Junior NCOs just to please the Americans and atone for previous tours by painting ourselves as whiter than white.

A degree of constraint was understandable. As ever though, it went too far. There had been escalating civilian casualties in the war, and admittedly some erroneous use of firepower from some. As a result, from 2009 onwards there were significant efforts to address the British Army's use of heavier firepower. General Stanley McChrystal – a legend of the Iraq campaign – took over ISAF in-country and introduced the term 'courageous restraint'. The concept was good – should I, could I, must I engage this target, with the emphasis on the last one. This, however, is a very easy process while sat in a headquarters watching the action unfold on TV; it is a great deal harder to assess what 'must' be done if it is you that is involved in the mortal combat.

But given General Stan's stature and reputation, British commanders – seemingly unable to think for themselves and now heavily deferent to the Americans after our early exit from Iraq – were falling over themselves to be the one who instigated his directive to the strictest degree. If I could use my knowledge and skill to ensure my NCOs could act unconstrained by a chain of command with one eye on promotion, and one eye on the General, then I would.

Bing, Baz and I would operate as a bolt-on to every patrol that went out in the 31 West AO. We worked as a three – reluctant to go out without one part of the team. If we were operating from one of the other satellite patrol bases, we would always work with our team member there. The actual rank of the patrol commander I was supporting varied according to the size of the unit that I was accompanying. Sometimes it would be a corporal, sometimes a sergeant and sometimes the company commander himself.

The end of our familiarization of the area of operations also marked the end of the tour for the Royal Welch, who were replaced in Nad-e Ali by 1st Battalion The Duke of Lancaster's Regiment, or 1 LANCS.

Following the troop changeover, Mark, Baz and I dropped into some semblance of a routine as we accompanied all of the changeover patrols, themselves getting familiar with the area. The alarm would go off at 2.30 a.m. and I would stumble in my pants to the end of the tent and get the stove fired up for some coffee. I would sit there and have a cigarette in the pitch dark.

The cigarettes were bloody awful. Just before we left Camp Bastion, the public health team flew over from the UK and for some unfathomable reason, decided that the local cigarettes that were being sold to UK soldiers inside the camp were not fit for our consumption. The rumour was that they contained human faeces. My team ran down to the bazaar and bought enough to get us through the first few months before they were collectively burned.

After years of early starts, my body had developed a routine of going for a shit first thing. The cigarette helped in this process and ensured that when I was at the gate going out on patrol in about an hour's time and I needed the loo, I could be sure it was nerves and not a genuine need. All good personal admin that had to be squared away.

Mark would come and join me as I sat there in the darkness, watching the flames lick around the pot we used to boil water. Baz was always last up, and usually in a bad mood. We would say nothing as we drank coffee and tried to waken from another very short night's sleep, before eventually giving in and getting dressed in our battle fatigues. We had to wash our clothes by hand so we wore them for a three-day period, unless they had too much mud or blood on them. After a patrol they would be hung over the guy ropes on the tent so as not to create a hygiene problem inside, and putting them on for the second and third days sometimes felt like trying to get into a crisp packet.

All the preparation was done the night before. My webbing and my helmet were stowed at the end of my camp cot; my rifle within arm's reach, loaded but not made ready. I would then sit around before bed with Bing and Baz, and brief them on the patrol commander's orders; I usually attended his briefing on my own. A set of orders is essentially a speech given by the patrol commander to tell his men what is going on, or at least what he plans to go on, during his patrol the following day. From inexperienced commanders, 'orders' can be a truly painful process. I always went to make sure I didn't miss anything vital, but I was not prepared to put Baz and Bing through them on a regular basis.

After having fired up the lungs with a cigarette and the brains with a coffee, I emptied the bowels and made sure our radio was working with a quick comms check to some sleepy radio operator in Camp Bastion. We would then make our way over to the back gate as a threesome, where we would meet the particular patrol we were supporting that morning. It was always still dark. And miserable.

This routine was the same almost every single day during the tour. For seven months.

15

General, ground-dominating patrolling was a twice-daily activity. Longer, more adventurous, more complex and larger patrols as a two-platoon or company group were conducted perhaps twice weekly. Our first one of these was about one week into 1 LANCS's deployment, some time in early May 2010. This time it was a 'company sweep' into the Jungle, which local intelligence had told us was not just riddled with Taliban but also provided shelter for some of their key commanders, who were coordinating the laying of IEDs on the main route in and out of our PB Khaamar. The Taliban often surged out of this area as well; to intimidate and harass the local population, to spread fear and to collect money for so-called protection. There was evidence they were trying to impose sharia law on the locals. They also made a practice of hiding their weapons in various innocent civilians' compounds, so that if we were ever to do a helicopter assault into the Jungle it would be difficult to find the evidence required to arrest them. The idea that some people back home seemed to hold – that the Taliban were a rag-tag bunch of misunderstood freedom fighters – was bullshit.

Our job as a ground-holding unit was to spread Afghan government control into these civilian areas, in order to give time and space for some sort of peace or political agreement to take place. It would be fair to say that we never expected to hold the terrain we ventured into, but merely to create an opportunity for the Afghan National Army – who accompanied us on every patrol – to engage with the local population. The hope was that some kind of intelligence or assistance would be given to the ANA if, and it was a big if, the locals wanted to stop being controlled by the Taliban.

There was another reason we went into the Jungle daily, rather than stay in the PB and let the ANA go out alone and hope for the best. The truth was that at PB Khaamar, the enemy really were at the gates, and if we did not make the effort to keep them from our door with regular patrolling, we would be setting ourselves up for disaster.

On that dark May morning, on our first serious company-level patrol, we pushed south and east of our PB, leaving it manned by the doctor, the company 2IC and a handful of men in the watchtowers.

We were on foot, moving in a standard formation: two platoons forward, one back and the company command group in the centre. The ground was a series of fields separated by irrigation ditches and dirt tracks. The area had been irrigated by the Americans in the late seventies as part of a huge infrastructure project in the region – another external attempt to get the country on its feet. The American engineers had laid tracks out in blocks about 350m apart and criss-crossed at ninety degrees by tracks running the other way, which neatly divided the area into rectangles. This layout provided convenient pause-points as patrols progressed across the fields, giving us a chance to draw breath, and consider our next move.

There were little groups of dwellings spaced 500–1,000m apart along these paths. One could easily use these as 'hand-off' points for navigation, and also head for them if no other cover presented itself. Inevitably the IED risk was high, so it was best to avoid obvious crossing points on tracks and between fields. Generally, the irrigation ditches were good paths of navigation – unlikely to be mined and providing a bit of cover if the patrol came under fire.

The first two platoons had pushed east over a north–south running track, and the company commander's group – which included me, Mark and Baz – were pausing. I'd just looked down to see where I was going to place my knee when we came under sustained and close small-arms fire.

The first thing you notice is the sound, as bullets split the air around your ears. What you hear is not a 'bang' as such, but a 'crack'. The bangs come when you and your men start firing back.

This was my first experience of close-quarter combat. I grew disturbingly familiar with it after a while, but I was certainly not at that point yet.

I immediately returned fire at the property where the shots had come from, directly into the window.

'Fucking hell, Johnny, careful, we have troops over there,' the company commander said in a panicky voice.

I saw the flash of a muzzle.

'That's the fucking firing point!' I shouted back at him. 'Just there. Baz, that window on the far right of that compound.'

'Roger, boss,' said Baz. 'I'll send a contact report and request air.'

Baz and I ducked into the ditch and started on our respective jobs. I gave a 'Contact. Wait-out' on my radio too, so that I had first shout on any joint fires asset in the area (assuming there were other patrols out who might be competing with me for assets). I could see Bing on the other side of Baz, emptying his rifle into the window that had engaged us. The enemy position stopped firing. Either one of us had killed the firer in that particular window, or the enemy's attention had switched from our position to one of the forward platoons.

We were in a very shallow irrigation ditch. The company commander started talking into his radio, asking for a situational report (SITREP) from one of his forward platoon commanders. This always annoyed me. The blokes would send a SITREP as soon as they could; first they had to win the firefight. Best let them get on with it. I didn't say anything.

We moved location only slightly, to get into cover from the compound that had engaged us. By now I had stopped firing my weapon and was talking on the radio handset to the gun line.

The company commander asked me for some 105mm smoke shells to screen our withdrawal. Mark retreated into the ditch with us, and we independently ascertained our own position before identifying exactly where we wanted the smoke to fall. We took account of the wind, the spread of the guns that we would be using some 12km away, and the nature of the ground into which these rounds would fall (wooded, in this case). This process took about fifteen seconds.

Mark and I breathed in relief as the shells landed, but the effect was not what we were hoping for. The wind was almost non-existent, and a good smoke screen between the enemy and our forward platoon did not build up. I wanted to switch to high explosive (HE) and shift the point of impact closer to the compound from where the fire continued to pour. We had still not been allocated any air support, and I wanted to end this firefight as quickly as possible before someone got shot.

Finally, I could hear Baz chatting away to an American B-1 bomber that we had been allocated, giving the pilot our current SITREP. I informed the company commander that I now had a jet on station as well. The company commander paused for a moment, and then decided that he wanted to show that he was doing what he had been taught in his extensive pre-deployment lessons, and 'escalating force correctly', before letting me loose with some HE. He wanted a 'show of force' from the B-1 bomber, which was now two minutes from our location.

A 'show of force' is essentially an effort to frighten the enemy into submission with a low, loud and fast fly-by from a jet directly over their position. In some cases, this had proved to be successful, but by now the Taliban were beginning to get the hang of it. The jet did not drop during this process, but it was seen as a good 'non kinetic' effect to use. I was at pains to explain to the company commander that a B-1 was not the optimum airframe to make a show of force with. It was, generally speaking, a slow flying, high altitude stealth bomber that was unlikely to have the effect we wanted. He insisted that he wanted the B-1.

Almost simultaneously, an Apache crackled into my secondary handset, which was listening in to a different radio frequency. The pilot requested an update and informed me he was available for work. Bing was next to me by now, and I gave him the handset for the gun line and started speaking to the Apache pilot to confirm his position. At the same time, I told my company commander that I had an Apache available for use. Baz was delivering a 9-liner to the B-1 Bomber.

(Commands are given in force-wide conventions, usually in lines to ensure information does not get missed, and in conformity between nations. Combat attack helicopters can be controlled using a five-line brief; fast-air jets by a nine-line brief. Guns are given fire control orders in a broadly similar way. Each line contains vital information, such as the position of the observer, the position of the enemy, a weapons-to-target match and other details.)

The company commander still wanted to hold off the Apache and use a show of force by the B-1 bomber. I told him that my formal advice was that this was the wrong option and as soon as the Apache was overhead, the enemy fire would most probably stop before it engaged. He overruled me.

I explained this to the Apache pilot, who was getting understandably frustrated by us going through this process of de-escalation. Remaining loyal to my company commander, I ignored his comments and told him to hold off while we conducted this show of force. I could tell he thought I was doing the wrong thing.

'Boss, am I clear? Thirty seconds out,' Baz called over to me.

I checkfired the guns, and cleared Baz to bring in the jet.

'Fifteen seconds!' I shouted to the company commander.

It was hideously embarrassing, but not altogether unexpected, when the B-1 flew over the target at 500ft as opposed to 50ft. It felt like we were at a bloody air show and I could hear the Apache pilot laughing into his radio.

I immediately ordered the Apache to come into the overhead and talked it onto the target compound, from where we were still taking fire. The fire stopped as soon as the Apache came on the scene, and being unable to see any enemy meant I couldn't engage. It had the desired effect though, and we conducted an orderly withdrawal back to the PB, having achieved, in my view, absolutely nothing.

16

The smaller patrols were where the action really happened. As a company group we were never really going to get taken on by the Taliban and be given the opportunity to kill them. We were also unlikely to get any really useful information from the locals because it was so obvious we were there, and none of them would talk to us for fear of retribution from the Taliban.

We worked out pretty quickly that the best way to understand what was really going on was to send out small patrols, leaving every day before dawn so we could be in place in a dangerous area as the sun came up and could watch pattern of life. These patrols nearly always came under contact from the enemy, who were never particularly pleased to discover us in their backyard.

A few days after the company operation that achieved precisely nothing, my team were tasked to support a patrol that was due to push into a particularly contested area that locals had told us they were prohibited from visiting. Bing, Baz and I were tacked on to this patrol, which consisted of seven Brits and four ANA personnel. They also had a terrific interpreter called Frank, who was in his thirties, educated and hated the Taliban. The feeling was mutual. They goaded him on their radios because they knew we were intercepting their traffic, and Frank was interpreting it for us.

Patrols into enemy occupied areas generally always went the same way. An uneventful push into the target area in darkness followed by a watch of the morning routine of the enemy – including their sentry routines – before leaving around 8 a.m. On the way back to the base we'd spot the key combat indicators, which always give you a good idea about how long you have before you are engaged by the enemy. These would start with some frantic driving around on motorbikes by young, fighting-age males, usually followed by women gathering the children into the nearby compounds. Then the chatter on ICOM – the Taliban's handheld radio system – would start to liven up, and we'd know what was coming. ICOM handsets are press to talk, walkie-talkie type devices which we easily intercepted using a similar device tuned in to their radio frequency. As your time went on in Afghanistan you could understand key words and phrases the Taliban used.

Knowing what was coming, we would try to avoid obvious ambush spots on the way back to the PB, but avoiding all of them was not possible. The patrol order we adopted was usually the same: Afghans on point (you don't want them behind you), the British section in the middle and then my FST in the rear. The trouble with this set-up, though, was that whenever we were returning to our patrol base we inevitably got hit from the rear, and so the fire support team ended up being first in contact – not how we had intended it to work.

On this particular morning, as soon as it was time to head back to the PB and we deliberately revealed our presence, the ICOM radios bubbled into life. We had barely left the target area when we were engaged, but this time were still some considerable distance from the safety of the PB. The fire was particularly heavy as well – they were clearly using a mounted machine gun, firing in accurate and regular bursts, and there seemed to be multiple firing points, although all in the same general area.

'Contact rear!' I shouted as we turned around and engaged in the general direction of the enemy fire.

The section engaged the enemy, and between us we formed a fairly solid baseline before conducting 'fire and manoeuvre' towards the enemy and into an irrigation ditch, which was the nearest decent bit of cover.

A Minimi machine gunner was next to me – I think the section commander had sent him over so that he could protect me while I worked out what to do. I called a contact report into my radio to the gun line, then had a conversation with the section commander.

'What do you reckon, boss?' he said.

'I don't know,' I replied. 'That was pretty heavy, but I don't know how many of them there are.'

As I said this, a Taliban fighter stood up in the long grass about twenty metres away. The Minimi gunner fired a burst into him. He fell immediately. I could see movement about 120 yards to my front in another irrigation ditch. I also saw movement to our south, and ICOM chatter suggested they were going to try and encircle us. This was not in itself unusual but it was disturbing on this occasion, given how far we were from the PB.

Baz was talking into his radio and seemed to be getting frustrated. I asked what was up.

'Nothing available at this time. I've put in an ECAS request,' he replied. (ECAS – Emergency Close Air Support.)

I had been talking to the gun line throughout our patrol, updating them as to our progress, and I knew that they were good to go. I could not take the risk of just getting up and moving the section – the Taliban were clearly all over us, and probably a bit fucked off with one dead already. I was going to use the guns, and I wasn't going to mess around with any smoke or similar – I needed to neutralize this enemy position, and re-seize the initiative so we could disengage and get back to the PB.

The trouble was that HE had not been used in Helmand for months by this stage, and certainly not on this tour. We believed there might have been a ban on it, although this was never confirmed. General McChrystal's 'courageous restraint' policy was dominating every conversation, and the first casualty of that 'progress' was inevitably unguided high explosive munitions, like our 105mm guns. But, used properly, I was convinced there was no better weapon in this environment.

Artillery is by no means perfect. It can go wrong, and clearly precision weapons conducting precision strikes are far more effective. But in the fields of Helmand, much like the fields in Normandy or Vietnam, some things never change. If you are constantly being ambushed by the enemy – being engaged in a time and place of their choosing, inevitably pinning you down – getting a joint fires effect on the ground can be the critical factor in reducing the chances of casualties in your patrol. This was not Special Forces – there wasn't an abundance of precision assets at our disposal; we had to wait. And there was no point waiting ten or fifteen minutes in the hope that a precision weapon might become available in time, with the enemy persistently taking pot-shots at your men in poor cover. Clearly if you are in a compound or a PB, this is not an issue; but being pinned down in a ditch is not the same. You need to act to reassert your authority and reclaim the initiative from an enemy who have chosen both the ground and a time to engage you that gives them the most advantage.

So artillery is known as the 'god of war' for good reason; it is bloody quick, it's bloody frightening and it works. Even if you cannot land the round directly on the target for fear of hitting civilians, the splinter distance and the sheer effect of 105mm HE going off near you – perhaps just outside your compound, or the shrapnel piercing the trees around your head – means you are far more likely to keep your head down and stop shooting at me than if I just sit there and wait for a better asset to turn up.

Using it is a skill. You cannot be stupid and level buildings to flush out a single fighter, or indeed try and hit a precise target by endlessly engaging an area – that is dumb use of dumb munitions. But it is fast to use, it can change the momentum of a battle even if it doesn't precisely kill the enemy and it gives you time and space to either get out of there or get somewhere more secure. It gives you a break to improve your situation, and sometimes that is all you need when you have been ambushed and caught out in the open. It remains the god of war.

It is indeed a skill. The 105mm howitzer is not a precision instrument – you set the direction and angle of the gun and then simply use gravity to hit the targets. There are multiple factors that go into working out where an unguided artillery shell is likely to land – wind speeds at different altitudes, the different muzzle velocity of each gun (which varies due to wear and tear and how many rounds each individual gun has fired), temperature, distance, weather, terrain, where the gun is in relation to your target. But without doubt the best way to ensure accuracy was to practise and practise and practise with the gun line to achieve speed of response and accuracy to the target. Actually, one of the first things that I had done on this tour, when it was clear that the company was going to require artillery on an almost daily basis, was to drive some 25km north of PB Khaamar during the hand-over between 1 LANCS and the Royal Welch and spend a couple of days taking time to make sure that I could land artillery shells where I wanted them to go. I patiently 'fired out the error' in each of the six guns in the battery that were supporting me. This meant that with good operators on the gun line, following the correct drills, I could be *almost* certain where each round would fall. There were so many factors to consider if you wanted to become good at it that some thought it was a bit of an art. My formula was practice, a cool head and attention to detail.

When the patrol commander called over to me, 'Can you do anything?' I was ready.

I scanned around. There were no compounds for at least 300m. 'Yep – I'm going to use HE,' I replied.

Bing's eyes lit up.

I gave my orders to the guns. The company commander came on the net, to confirm my use of HE. I gave no reason, simply confirmed my weapon-to-target match. The fires net went very quiet. The artillery CO came onto the net and again asked me to confirm my weapon-to-target match.

'Witchcraft four-three, this is Witchcraft zero-alpha. Confirm ammunition – HE?'

'Roger. We are a good distance from the PB, engaging multiple firing points, ambush continuing, I confirm HE.'

I wasn't asked again.

I had been by far and away the best at this job in my cohort for some time, and my CO knew this, having told me previously. My experiences on previous Afghanistan tours had helped enormously with my understanding of joint fires, too. It wasn't natural ability; I had received a huge head start on my Special Forces tour.

The trouble is that no matter how many times you practise, doing it for real inevitably brings a distinct nervousness with it. I remember looking at Bing, who clearly didn't give a shit about any of that and was wondering why I was taking so long.

I asked him to check my grid reference, and saw out of the corner of my eye that he was looking at his map.

'Yeah, that's good, boss, good grid,' he said.

The intensity of the incoming gunfire had increased as the enemy had worked out that we were essentially pinned down and not going anywhere, but the pressure of dropping artillery shells in close proximity to friendly forces as quickly as possible drowned out any fear for my own safety.

I ordered the guns to fire, and we then had a fourteen-second wait to see where the rounds fell. There is no opportunity to recall them; your fate lies with your workings out (worrying, if you consider how bad at maths I was at school).

I ordered the patrol to take cover while I peered above the berm to observe fall of shot. Bing didn't bother to pretend to take cover – he was grinning with excitement.

As soon as I'd given the order to fire I had that inevitable second thought, and asked Bing again what he thought of the grid I gave, only to notice his map was upside down.

'You haven't even fucking checked it,' I said, unimpressed.

'Yeah, sorry, boss. Just can't wait to see it go off,' he grinned.

'That's not really how it works, mate.' They were the first cross words I had spoken to him.

Boom!

I'd ducked down for the impact, but immediately the shrapnel had passed over my head I looked up and saw from the smoke and falling undergrowth that the round had landed exactly where I had wanted it. The thunder of close range artillery is louder than anything you can imagine – it's got a real bass resonance to it, and can be somewhat addictive. The ground shudders, the world stops.

The contact from the enemy stopped immediately.

I got on the radio. 'Delta two zero, that is a delta hotel [direct hit] on the target area. Smoke clearing. Extracting now. Stand by for BDA [Battle Damage Assessment].'

'See – you don't need me to check.'

'Not cool, Bing. That never happens again.'

'OK. I'll get the wets on when we get back. Don't tell Baz.'

Over ICOM the enemy were screaming that there had been two fatalities.

The truth was that they had begun to take the piss out of us Brits and became lazy, because they thought we were so hesitant to use heavy weapons and would just extract using fire and movement.

As a patrol, we had a brief wash-up when we got back to base. In my head, I wanted to reinforce my view in a professional, officer-type manner that we needed to carry on in this vein if we were to make a difference in the nightmare that was the Jungle, and not be scared to use joint fires. That we needed to back ourselves, that I would always take the responsibility if required, but that we could not let ourselves be constrained by others' interpretation of our situation and what we were doing.

I think it came out more like 'If we don't kill these fuckers, they'll keep trying to kill us, and I'm not spending the next six months tiptoeing around the Jungle trying not to piss people off while finding locations for a school or something. This place is riddled with Talibs. If they want to fight, let's kill them.'

I could see the blokes thought I was bit mad, but nothing wrong with that. Keeps them on their toes, I thought.

I was glad to have disappointed the 'radio generals' around the theatre, who listen all day and all night in their tents to the radios, trying to second-guess commanders and pick up on any cock-ups. Clearly I was feeling over-sensitive; not everyone listening in was like that at all. Some, like my friend Steve the quartermaster, really got it. Steve only listened in to see how he could help, and check we were OK. He worked seventeen-hour days for me and my team, making sure we had the right kit and equipment. He would often go down to the pan in Camp Bastion at 3 a.m. to get some mission-critical equipment onto a helicopter just before it was going to take off. Often that mission-critical equipment came with some sweets, magazines or coffee. He was the embodiment of a team player – he was all that is good in the late-entry commissioned officer community in the Army. That comforting hand, the dogged loyalty and the experienced wise head.

17

With the end of the poppy harvest in mid-May, the real summer had arrived, bringing with it temperatures in the forties and daily firefights with the enemy. Some of these would require the use of joint fires to end them, some did not. I was reluctant to engage unnecessarily, and thereby get a name for myself, but I was not prepared to see a British casualty because I had been slow off the mark. It was a balance, and I felt I was striking it.

When we weren't patrolling, Bing, Baz and I had established a sort of 'prison gym' in the yard, and combined with patrolling twice a day with radios and equipment in excess of 80lb, it meant we were supremely fit. My smoking must have brought this down somewhat, and was beginning to get out of hand, but there was no other way to ameliorate eating the same food from the same ration packs day after day. Baz taught me boxing. I was not great, but I think he quite enjoyed hitting me in the face (who wouldn't?).

The average morning or sunset patrol would only last 3–4 hours; longer, deliberate operations could last anything up to two weeks. A patrol in the Jungle generally moved very slowly indeed. The front man will often be using a Vallon metal detector, constantly scanning the ground in front of him for IEDs. With any disturbance of the topsoil – or as we liked to say 'the absence of the normal, and the presence of the abnormal' – the patrol would halt to ascertain what lay beneath. This stop-start nature of the patrol, combined with a persistent shuffling of fire positions, going down on one knee and crawling around, required the sort of fitness it is simply impossible to train for. The aches and pains associated with constantly going down on one knee are something no soldier forgets quickly. Resilience is key.

On patrol one could easily slip into a slight sense of complacency and boredom, but that was a dangerous road to go down. To avoid it, I would be constantly looking for ditches and trees and other areas that would provide me with cover. I would also be scanning for potential firing points, and working out what I would do if we were to come under contact from a set point. I would be quietly chattering away continually to whomever was providing cover for us – either the gun line or an attack helicopter – commentating on what we were doing. These regular SITREPs often get forgotten about, but by now I had learnt that with a good series of SITREPs behind you, as soon as you came under contact it was far quicker and easier to engage the enemy using whichever platform you had at the end of the radio.

All these patrols were accompanied, of course, by a monkey on your shoulder called Fear. Some days you would be fine, and would saunter off up the track on your way to the bazaar to chat to some of the locals with violence far from your mind.

But some days the fear was suffocating. This was usually after someone had been hit and suffered an injury, or worse. The agility of fear was such that it could creep up and fill your veins with what feels like aerated blood, tingling into your fingertips, with no apparent change in your physical situation. All of a sudden, with the thoughts completely uninvited, you can vividly recall seeing that lad get shot and the bullet tearing into his arm, breaking the bone in an instant and releasing a jet of sticky warm blood. You remember the taste of it hitting your face and a drop resting on your bottom lip as you shouted at him that he would be OK. It tasted like iron, and if you didn't lick it off quickly it became congealed and sticky. You remember how your hands felt as you tried to stem the flow of blood, often inflicting more pain on the casualty. You remembered what the inside of someone's arm felt like; what the inside of someone's head felt like. And you worried how much it was going to fucking hurt when it came to your turn, which seemed a matter of when, not if. About how it was going to feel fighting the fog clouding your vision as you looked down at some bloody stumps where your legs used to be, knowing that you only had a few more minutes of breath, of feeling the air on your face. And 'the test' – would you pass the test? Would you die like a man, or crying into the dust, beating the ground in pain. Would you fight hard enough to get your own tourniquet on to stem the blood before you passed out, or lie back and accept the inevitable theft of your life.

But then I would grit my teeth. Because the truth was if you could park those thoughts – put them in that part of your brain that doesn't get opened except in extreme moments – you could control fear, or at least keep a lid on it. How others did it I do not know, but for me it was all about compartmentalizing. And keeping busy.

Our morning and evening patrols followed a regular routine. We often got a bit of sleep in the afternoons – the heat of the day was a challenge for locals and ISAF forces alike – but this was almost always short, and always interrupted by the searing heat and waking up in a pool of sweat.

I was responsible for joint fires throughout the '31West' area of operations, regardless of who was the terminal controller on the ground. This meant that whenever there was a TiC situation, I was summoned to the patrol base's operations room to oversee the employment of joint fires, and if necessary conduct the engagement myself.

I wanted to empower the blokes both in my close team (Baz and Bing) and in the satellite patrol bases. I liked to let them get on with it themselves rather than leaning on me, while keeping a guiding hand on the tiller so they did not make any mistakes that would make life difficult for them further down the line. Ultimately, every engagement was my responsibility, and any joint fires accident would always be followed with the question: 'Who was the FST Commander?'

There was no doubt that 31 West was a particularly dangerous part of Helmand that summer. Patrols from other units who were passing through the AO were regularly caught out in complex ambushes, where IEDs would strike vehicles and be followed up with small-arms fire from the Taliban. Were it not for the resilience of the new vehicle fleet – Huskies and Mastiffs – there would have been even more casualties.

The Mastiff in particular saved countless lives. A vehicle being struck by an improvised explosive device in my AO was probably a weekly occurrence, and although casualties were taken, the injuries were limited to severe shock and compressed spines rather than fatalities. However, a vehicle that had been hit was often unable to move and could not be left behind, meaning that the patrol was alive but fixed in a place of the enemy's choosing, and would often be exposed to one of these complex ambushes.

One afternoon, I was slumbering in my sweat pit in the

heat of the day when I heard gunfire from outside the compound, but at least a couple of kilometres away. It would be an exaggeration to say that I woke to gunfire every day that summer, but it wasn't far off. I ran to the Ops room in my shorts and T-shirt to hear a familiar voice on the radio attempting to employ joint fires right on the boundary of my AO. De-confliction of forces around boundary lines was always difficult, because neighbouring units use different code words and frequencies to talk to each other. All that is generally needed is someone with a clear battlespace view (i.e. back in camp) to take over, de-conflict forces, battlespace and airspace in the coolness of an Ops room, cue up the assets to strike and then allow the ground controller to control the engagement through you. Emma was one of the few female Joint Fires Controllers in the Army, and the only one in Afghanistan at the time. I liked her; she was a good soldier and very capable. On this occasion, she was simply unlucky to get hit, and had become bogged down in thick mud, having been ambushed on Route Nike, somewhere 1 LANCS patrols did not go, because it was riddled with Talibs. The lead vehicle had been disabled with an IED strike, and the enemy were employing a 12.7mm Dushka against her. A Dushka is usually a vehicle-mounted, but always fixed, rapid-fire weapons system. It can be extremely dangerous.

I knew people would be queuing up to knock Emma down. Some of the officers I was with in PB Khaamar and across the task force considered themselves far superior to her simply because she was a woman. Coming from a specialist background myself, I had more perspective on the situation – there was a huge gap that existed between these guys and the Commando units in which I had previously served. They weren't bad soldiers, but were not of the standard I expected in my own men, and certainly not in a position to cast aspersions on others' abilities in this environment.

I listened in to see if I could help, as I would have done for anyone. On the main net, I asked Emma some obvious questions that would give me an insight into how concerned she was, conscious that probably a hundred commanders around theatre were listening in, willing her to fail. They did not want her to fail to the extent that casualties would be taken; they wanted her to struggle enough to validate their ongoing arguments in the Army at the time against women in frontline service. I told her to switch to another net that I had set up in the area, so I could chat to her in private.

She agreed that, being bogged down in a complex ambush on a tactical boundary with no visibility, she could do with some help. I established an operational box around her and proceeded to sort her out with a combination of artillery smoke and a couple of runs from an Apache. She completed the strikes and her troops were able to limp their vehicles back to their PB. She had proved what I had always known; that, like any bloke, a woman will remember her training and perform in combat. Whether they should train specifically as infanteers is another matter, but there was nothing mentally weak or inferior about females in combat.

Sexism in the British Army in 2010 was rife, and this was a good day for it.

18

Bing always stuck to me like glue. Despite our rather awkward start with that HE round, he obviously knew and completely understood the brainwork required to employ joint fires quickly, accurately and safely in close-quarter combat. He was a brilliant sounding board, very meticulous and gave me confidence when I needed it.

But the fighting was so close and so intense that summer that by early June we had worked out it was quicker if I just did the radio work myself and Bing kept us alive, providing my protection and making sure I didn't wander out into a field of fire as I struggled with the myriad of mental challenges involved in delivering joint fires in close proximity to a determined enemy. Bing would keep me safe if I was exposing myself unnecessarily or losing ground awareness while controlling multiple weapons platforms over two radios – one to the gun line and one on the air net should I need it for controlling attack helicopters. I always checked everything with Bing though – a two-man check is vital. The cock-up, when it happened, was entirely my fault.

By now I had become increasingly skilled in the use of 105mm high explosive artillery, having been forced to use it frequently in the extremely demanding environment of the Jungle. In the very specific role my unit was tasked with – effectively walking into enemy territory and fighting it out every day – speed and effect were crucial to win back initiative. As mentioned before, the effect of 105mm dropping, if only in an open field, dominated any firefight, and more often than not stopped that engagement without reverting to a more precise weapon put straight into someone's house. My red line was that we would not take a UK casualty because I was reluctant to use the firepower at my disposal for fear of pissing off the chain of command. If it was safe, proportionate and 'good practice', I did it. I had the inevitable successes against the enemy that confidence and a good team bring you.

One day, we were in a slower-time firefight as part of a more deliberate operation rather than a regular patrol. I don't know how it happened, but while I was on the radio I transposed two digits and relayed the wrong grid to the guns – a potentially fatal error, and one from which it is hard to recover confidence. A completely unacceptable mistake.

The guns fired on the reference I'd given them and the round landed about 30m away from me, Baz and Bing; not 300m. I was fuming at the guns, convinced they had cocked it up, and was badly shaken. We were only still alive because the round landed in a ditch and the blast and shrapnel went skywards, not towards us.

We got back to the PB and I spoke to the officer in charge at the gun line on the phone.

'What the fuck happened there?' I said, exasperated.

'I'm sorry, Johnny, but I've gone over this three times now with the lads and I fired on the grid that was written down in the signaller's note book, direct from your radio call.'

'Impossible!' I retorted. 'It was a slow-time engagement – we were in cover and I wasn't under pressure, I wouldn't have done that.'

At that point Bing came running in. 'Boss, I've got something you need to see.'

Bing had taken his headcam that day. These were banned in theatre by now, but I actually found them a good way to recall events that would otherwise be confused by the noise and smoke of the battle. Their footage enabled me to conduct good after-action reviews amongst our small team so I chose not to enforce this ban – it was not in my gift, and not right, but that's what I did.

Bing played me the footage from before the near miss, and I *had* given the wrong grid to the gun line. A very small mistake that can sometimes have catastrophic consequences. Baz looked at me with sympathy on his face. He knew how I felt: transposing digits was every terminal controller's nightmare. I started out for the Ops room to telephone the officer in charge and own up to my mistake.

'Boss, boss, you can't do that,' Baz said, while Bing ran past me.

'I can't cover it up, mate, it's a matter of integrity. I'd take responsibility for you guys and take the hit. Just because it's me doesn't matter – I've got to own up.'

'There's other factors at play here. We're at fucking war. It's not just about you.'

I didn't listen and kept going, trailed by an exasperated Baz. We got to the operations room in time to hear the back end of a bollocking being delivered by Bing to the brand-new signaller in the command post on the gun line – for writing down the grid wrong.

I turned on my heel and left the Ops room to head back to our tent, where I sat down and had a cigarette by myself. I was pretty cross, and felt my authority over the situation waning. But, truth be told, I learnt a lot from this little incident.

Firstly, my team's loyalty to me was obviously absolute. I had made a serious mistake, and yet Bing was prepared to bollock one of his mates and lie to everyone up and down the chain of command so that my mistake did not get out.

Bing and Baz joined me. Bing felt that we simply couldn't afford for the gun line, or more importantly our commanders, to think that we had made a mistake as a team. We were by far the busiest – and the most effective – of the twenty-two joint fires teams in Helmand at the time, and he felt that to acknowledge an error would destroy confidence in our abilities. The blokes on the gun line were getting up early every time we were going out on patrol because they knew they would probably be used. There was a bit of buzz going around about us.

A patrol from the Brigade Reconnaissance Force (a composite group of soldiers who could be assigned to single tasks) had come to our PB the night before and their commander had sought me out, wanting to meet me. As we stood around in a circle, he said that at HQ I had become known as the '105mm Sniper'. Everyone laughed, but I was embarrassed. His blokes destroyed him, taking the mickey out of him, and rightfully so.

The truth is, I was overwhelmingly uncomfortable with any kudos, because deep down I knew that so much out here was luck. You see, it was physically impossible to control the exact landing point of a 105mm shell. You can get it very close, but it is not a precision weapon relying on GPS or the like. So every time I hit the target, I was very lucky. I couldn't have been a '105mm sniper' even if I'd tried.

But I am human, and to be known for your capability in

killing the enemy during war was something I suppose I liked in a way. Perhaps a bit of arrogance did creep in, and I made a mistake as a result.

I told Bing and Baz about a very good Royal Marines company commander on my 2006 tour, called Oliver Lee. His company became renowned across 3 Commando Brigade for their standards, fitness, capability on operations and morale. But he had a clear message throughout: 'The precise moment you start to believe your own hype, is the precise moment it all starts to go badly wrong.'

I never did quite believe my own hype, but I was obviously leaning that way before this incident, which my team covered up. It's embarrassing to recall it now. I resolved to never even think like leaning that way again, whatever I did in life.

Bing saw no value in destroying confidence in our ability to protect patrols and kill the enemy, and eventually neither did I. In this game, lives were saved by our ability to deliver joint fires onto targets in close proximity to the enemy, daily. We could not afford to give either the troops we were supporting or the platforms we were using reason to question their confidence in us.

I found it a major challenge to my integrity, but Baz's words rang in my ears: 'It's not all about you, you know.' I was poor at many things, but when I made a mistake I was the first to own up. Yet I was not going to sink the team with a vanity gesture. I went along with it, resolving to correct the situation and ease my conscience at the end of the tour, if I was still alive. Life is not black and white. And it certainly wasn't out here.

After we returned home I sought out the soldier who had been blamed for my error and confessed. He said everyone in the command post had heard Bing's bollocking. They all knew the mistake was mine and that he was just protecting me. They had played the game too, and kept their wounded pride to themselves.

This incident taught me a very good lesson in humility – one that I was extremely grateful for. War can be the ultimate challenge for mankind, the ultimate arena, where you live or die. It was going to my head a bit. I should have had an accident; I got away with it. I would learn and move on. I would never again have much time for people who 'dined out' on their medals or battlefield escapades, but I would always respect them – it takes courage to operate under fire, no doubt about it.

I believe that if you hone your skills and use your drills correctly, as you have been taught, you significantly increase your chances of survival on the battlefield. But I remain convinced that those fickle bastards – fate and luck – always play the deciding hand. Always.

That lesson was about to be brutally reinforced to me.

Clockwise from top left On exercise on Salisbury Plain, in my early days as a commando officer. On the rope over the regain tank on my Commando Course at Lympstone, winter 2003. Jungle training in Belize, 2005. I ate, shat and fought like an animal and loved it.

Top left Jim Philippson, who was rather like a big brother to me.
Top right Jimmy Goddard and me in Norway, 2004.
Above Jimmy's peerless efforts on Mount Kilimanjaro in June 2006.

Top Trying to brush up on my mortar skills on my first tour to Afghanistan in 2006.
Above With Bing (left) and Baz (right) at PB Khaamar, 2010.

Above left Bing (standing), Baz and me in our tent.
Above right Bing takes a knee and looks over at me. My favourite picture of him.
Below On patrol, finding time for a cigarette.

Top left Dawn in Afghanistan. *Top right* In the Ops room with Baz.
Above left I always felt drawn to the children in Afghanistan, and what
they had to endure. *Above right* I respected my men as individuals
and as soldiers, and always felt they respected me in return.

Above The memorial we had built for Bing at PB Khaamar.

Left With Bing's parents, spring 2011.

Right Amalie and I spent much time together on the moor in Cornwall near our home, as I struggled to readjust after my 2010 tour. She was my rock.

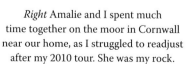

Top The River Tamar is one of the most beautiful river valleys in the UK; it was another source of comfort to me as the scars began to fade.

Above left Felicity's and my wedding day, 19 July 2014.

Above right Campaigning in St Budeaux with Joey on my back, January 2015.

Left On my campaign bike in some terrible weather, as I knocked on voters' doors, Plymouth March 2015.

At the count when Felicity and I first realized I was to be an MP for Plymouth.

© Paul Slater Images Ltd

At home, Cornwall, autumn 2015.

© Penny Cross/Plymouth Herald

19

8 June 2010 dawned like any other day for Bing, Baz and myself. We sat silently outside our tent in the cool pre-dawn darkness watching the yellow flames lick around the bottom of my metal mug which was full to the brim with water – precisely the amount we needed to serve three of us coffee in the smaller mugs we had commandeered from the mess hall in FOB Shawqat. I drew hard at the foul cigarette that fired up my lungs after a few hours of rest.

This morning we were going to patrol west, directly into the Jungle to a compound about three and a half kilometres away that looked very interesting. It seemed to have three storeys – a rarity in these parts – and we heard that the man who lived there regularly left the country. The smaller satellite PB that we would be leaving from, PB Shawaal, was coming under persistent and prolonged attack; as ever, if we were to keep the enemy from the gates we would need to go out and dominate some of the ground that lay to the west. No one wants to wake up with a Talib at the end of their camp cot! (This did happen to some.)

A few days earlier the Brigade Reconnaissance Force had attempted to land in the area we were going to patrol into, to conduct a three-day operation with the same aims as us, but on a much larger scale. However, upon 'flaring' in their CH-47 Chinooks before landing, the ground below them had seemed to open, peel back if you like, in three places. The Taliban trained their 12.7mm Dushka heavy machine guns against the three CH-47s, firing with such ferocity that the landing and operation were aborted. This was unusual for a number of reasons. Firstly, the Taliban knew that operating heavy weapons made them a clear priority target, and so they were rarely seen or used. Secondly, it was also unusual because these weapons were placed in almost-professional gun emplacements that were concealed below ground, and only revealed when the enemy knew an operation was striking into the heart of their territory. It was game changing for my company in terms of the threat we were up against. It also indicated the enemy were serious about protecting something in that area.

We had an idea of this threat before this incident, but not the extent of it. Earlier that summer, in the same area just south of PB Shawaal, we were returning from a vehicle move when we patrolled straight into a complex ambush– a combination of an IED and fire from a Dushka poured onto the immobilized patrol. We were lucky to escape with no serious casualties. It was only the quality of the new vehicle fleet and the skill of Baz in controlling two Apache helicopters that enabled us to return the vehicle to camp.

As a result of this more complex threat, my joint fires team was attracting more strategic focus across the task force. What this meant in practice was that we were allocated more assets – such as Predator drones, fast attack aircraft and our own dedicated gun battery. By now I was being given almost complete freedom to employ these assets as I saw fit to allow me to mitigate the threat and protect the men as best I could, and I felt in no way as inhibited as others certainly did, or indeed as I had done at the beginning of the tour.

That morning we were expecting a fight. After linking up with the men from PB Shawaal just outside PB Khaamar, I had a quick check to confirm we were still on for the plan that the patrol commander and I had discussed the night before. The only change was that the particular focus on this area from the broader task force had spawned an additional team of Afghan Special Forces for this operation. They were in the area and had travelled under the cover of darkness to link up with PB Shawaal for this morning's patrol.

While clearly dangerous, this patrol was planned like any other – careful, gentle, slow movement into the area, go firm, watch pattern of life around dawn before dominating the area as we patrolled back to PB Shawaal. A standard, ground-dominating patrol.

There was a brief problem with the radios when I tested them before we left. The security setting that was designed to encrypt our radios had been changed after someone somewhere else in Helmand had left behind a radio on patrol. Just to be extra safe, all patrols across Helmand changed their settings to ensure our communications were still encrypted. Baz and I had a good wrestle with the radios and after some heavy swearing, switching them on and off again a few times and eventually changing the settings, we left about fifteen minutes after our planned time to head east into the Jungle. We were eleven soldiers from 1 LANCS, a female medic, four ANA, Frank the translator, my team of Baz and Bing, and a Tiger Team of Afghan Special Forces. We all pushed east.

It is a strange feeling, advancing into a certain firefight. The truth is that mentally you do attain a sense of invincibility – 'it won't happen to me' – and this weighted the balance between fear and excitement towards the latter. I didn't mind coming into contact with the enemy; I just wanted to ensure that we won the fight and that I used our overwhelming firepower advantage carefully, but with skill, on those who were trying to trap and kill us. It was a challenge, I suppose, and I was up for it. Did I get scared back then? Yes, but only on a superficial level. As the bullets cracked overhead, or an RPG whizzed past sucking the air out of my surroundings, I just thought about how much it would hurt if one of those hit me. Not the finality of that result. There was none of this head-banging rubbish you see in films; psyching myself up or any such nonsense. Just calm, clear professionalism.

I could hear Bing walking about five yards behind me in silence. Behind him Baz was talking quietly into his radio. There was a familiarity about the noises that made me feel comfortable. The patrol commander was two in front of me. He would often refer to me for advice or use me as a sounding board for ideas. I gave it when asked, but I always made it clear that I was not an infantry officer and that he was in command. I was entirely content with the operation – he was a good team leader and I simply focused on joint fires options for the firefight that was coming.

As we patrolled along I quietly chatted away into my handset. As soon as we left the PB, I had laid three guns onto a tree line where I thought fire might come from. I moved this 'shadow' target constantly as we moved across the ground, so that the moment we came under fire I could engage if required. I never laid the shadow target onto compounds – that was exactly what the Taliban wanted, with the inevitable civilian casualties, and was not consistent with surgical counter insurgency operations. Instead, I laid targets in a safe area nearby to what I assessed were likely firing points; the firing points themselves would therefore hopefully be within the 40m splinter range of the 105mm HE shell, and the enemy would be forced to stop shooting and duck for cover.

This was unconventional use of artillery, but it genuinely saved lives daily in this environment. It meant that in those chaotic first few moments of a proper ambush (when the patrol came under accurate, heavy fire; not a 'shoot and scoot') if requested I could provide a significant effect on the ground some fourteen seconds (the time of shell flight) after being asked. Bing and I had come up with this practice together. He would ID the likely firing points, discuss them with Baz and then relay them to me. Baz would ensure that the gun–target line (the imaginary line between the gun line and the target) was kept free of air or aviation. I gave the orders to the guns.

This tactic was perhaps not to be found in any textbook, but it was a result of walking into ambushes and fighting our way out, day after day that summer. For me, Army doctrine was there to enable the fight, not inhibit the fight. If it required changing, I would think outside the box and change it. In a small way, I was quite proud of the successes it brought; in ambushes like this the deck is so stacked against you that to continually get away without taking UK casualties was some sort of success.

As we pushed further east into the Jungle that morning, the locals started to wake up. The ICOM chatter had started by now. We paused regularly as it was translated for us by Frank. By analysing the intercepts and matching them to the ground picture as we moved through the area, an hour into the patrol Frank and the team commander were reasonably confident that they knew where the enemy were preparing a present for us. It was not an exact science, but sometimes you can almost pinpoint where the enemy are before they reveal themselves. On this occasion, it was clear that they were observing us from a compound about 400m to our front, while encouraging more Taliban to move behind us to seal off the way we had come and trap our patrol.

We paused. We had a number of options. We could have moved north, away from our objective, and taken the long route back to the patrol base. Some of us – me included – were getting a little tired of simply extracting every time there was sniff of the Taliban, letting them chase us back to the safety of the PB.

After a bit of a Chinese Parliament, which I stayed out of, the team commander decided that we would close with this enemy position and destroy it before returning to the PB. I was in absolute agreement. I worked hard to retain our fighting edge and counteract the effects of constant with-drawals and ambushes on the morale and spirit of our men. I could not fault the commander's intent.

'We're going to go for it, Johnny,' he said calmly.

'Roger,' I replied.

I was about five metres from the patrol commander and turned around to briefly relay the plan to Baz and Bing. Bing said something like, 'It sounds good.' We had paused next to a compound, which gave us cover from the assessed enemy position. I tried to speak to the gun line to give them an update of our intentions, but was struggling with intermit-tent communications.

Despite never having paid attention to any radio training lessons in all my career, I was now becoming a bit of an expert. I could change angles of tactical satellite receivers to point towards a satellite in the sky; I could tell if the weather was going to be good or bad for communications that day; I could piss on the ground and put a ground-spike in the wet patch to improve the refraction of the radio waves in the extremely dry conditions of an Afghan summer.

Eventually, I got through to the guns. I briefed the control post on the tactical situation and gave them a target, 50m away from the compound where the patrol commander believed the enemy to be hiding. Shrapnel would hit the side of the compound and, although it would not hurt anyone, it would shock the enemy and perhaps buy us time to bring a more precise asset to bear if required, or to extract if we were in trouble.

Hopefully none of this would be necessary, because the plan would put us in the enemy's compound before he knew it. The patrol was going to split into three parts. The Tiger Team would patrol north to act as bait for the enemy position. Once engaged, they could go firm in the drainage ditch they were handrailing, and we would be close enough to the enemy to get in there and kill them from the flank, at close range, while they were looking elsewhere. A small, simple plan that offered a very good chance of success.

My part of the patrol (less the Tiger Team) would again split in two. One group – comprising most of the Afghan soldiers and the medic – would stay in our current position in cover, ready to act as a 'reserve' and provide some rear protection. My group would assault the enemy position.

There was no air or aviation immediately available. I paused, debating whether we should go for this without these assets on station. It was always a balance – bring an Apache into the overhead and the enemy usually scattered;

nothing achieved. Hold a platform off and the time it will then take to bring it to bear increases, and thus your exposure in an ambush can be longer. It is all a balance – there is no right or wrong answer. I assessed that, on the face of it, this plan was not bad; it was tactically sound, with good use of the ground and a reserve in place. Doctrinally it worked.

As the reserve group set up the strongpoint and Tiger Team headed off north, our small assault group monkey-walked (walking in a crouched position) further east, using a small wall for cover. We were heading for a medium-sized compound just to our front that would provide us with cover directly south of the assessed target compound. From there we could launch the final assault on the enemy position. We moved slowly, carefully and methodically.

As we moved forward, I did not at the time grasp the significance of a very small gap in the wall that would have exposed us to the compound where the enemy was. Instead I was focused straight ahead on a small figure running from one side of the road to the other, eighty metres away.

'What's that?' I asked as I raised my weapon to look through my scope. I thought it was a Talib moving position. I was hoping to see a long-barrelled weapon and drop him. I was still very calm at this point.

'Just a kid, I think, boss,' said Bing from immediately behind me as he looked too. 'Yeah, it's just kids.'

Kids running away is one of the last signs.

20

The patrol rounded the south-east corner of the compound and reset our course from heading east to heading north, handrailing the side of a muddy track that passed for a road in this part of the world. I thought the enemy was now about 120m away in a compound straight up this road. My head started to pulse with excitement.

The team commander could see better cover on the other side of the track and crossed over; we began to follow in a single line. Looking north I could see the Tiger Team moving between some compounds 400m away – they were far too obvious for the enemy to miss.

We crossed the track one at a time, quietly. I was the fourth patrol member to head over, with Bing directly behind me. He was my protection and we did everything together. Baz would follow up last.

I got to the second tyre rut in the road when we were engaged from very close range by a burst of heavy automatic weapon fire.

The fuckers were in the nearer building right next to us, closer than we anticipated. A second passed as I took two steps forward up against a muddy wall. There was no cover from the firing position available to me. I knew Bing and I were the target – we had been caught in the open. The enemy had clear line of sight and fire to me, and carried on firing. I anxiously scanned in front and either side of me for somewhere to head to. It was just a wall. There was no cover available. The worst possible place to get caught out.

The remainder of the patrol had taken cover in irrigation ditches on either side of the track.

While I was panicking, I heard Baz yell out in a tone I'd never heard from him before.

'Man down, boss, fucking man down!' he shouted.

I spun around. I looked between me and Baz, who was in the ditch on the other side of the road, to see Bing face down on the first tyre track, arms flailed towards the enemy, motionless.

It took a couple of seconds for the image to compute in my head. Time stood still, even as the enemy fire continued. There was still nowhere for me to go without wandering straight in front of the firing point. Forward, back, back into the road – no cover anywhere. I was pinned up against the wall, just waiting to die. I was very frightened. My mouth went dry and I could not feel my body.

Then something flicked in my head. I saw the desperation in Baz. I remembered who I was and where I was. Somehow I told myself to die 'properly', without fear. Like a man. That was it, nothing more. No glory, no patriotism. Just die properly. Don't embarrass yourself.

Baz was staring at me, repeating, 'Man down'. If I shut my eyes I can still picture his face now. The shock, the tears starting to well. It sounds strange, because people get shot in war all the time – we should expect this. But Bing was instantly killed; literally like a switch being turned off. He was talking to me seconds earlier. Our friend.

Seeing Baz made me snap into action. If I was nothing else, I was a belligerent little fucker, and I was going to fight like a bastard to stay alive and keep the others alive. I forced myself to stop thinking about being shot. I wasn't going to die today as well. I shouted at the three members of the patrol in front of me who were in a ditch, attempting to locate the firing point.

'Man down. Fucking man down!' I shouted, getting confidence the louder I shouted. The message went up the patrol towards the patrol commander.

The enemy were still firing in bursts at me from about thirty yards away. It was so loud compared to previous engagements because they were so close. I could not see a person with a gun, but I could see an area behind some vegetation where the fire was coming from. I attempted to bring my weapon to bear on their position. But it was a right-handed weapon and engaging the target would have further exposed me. I was getting frustrated at my helplessness and I backed into the wall again. Baz started to reach out to Bing.

The enemy saw Baz do this and the rate of fire increased. It seemed as though another firing point from the same direction had opened up on us. I could see the rounds ripping through the vegetation just above Baz's head. Another couple of inches, and he would have taken a round in his skull too. I shouted at him to be careful.

I made myself as small as possible against the wall and jumped on the radio to bring some HE down into the field that lay to our north west, about 80m away. I had to try to regain the initiative from what was evolving into the most brutal close-quarter contact I'd experienced thus far. All I heard was static, with my radio satellite system unable to work in such close proximity to an obstruction, in this case the compound. I would have to move to use it.

Baz continued to tug on Bing's leg to get him into the ditch with him, but the intensity of the fire around his head increased again. I could see something about to happen, like a slow car crash. At that moment Bing's body turned over and I saw his face and his eyes. There was no life there at all.

'Leave him, Baz!' I shouted. 'Fucking leave him. I will get him. We need to get a weight of fire down and I'll get him.'

Baz ignored me.

'Baz! I'm fucking telling you!'

Baz stopped pulling Bing, and I ordered him to take cover in the ditch and keep an eye to the rear of the patrol. The enemy firing reduced – perhaps they could no longer see me, and Baz was not presenting himself. The section commander was a battle hardened senior NCO, but the sudden brutality of a gunshot wound to the face had affected us all. It was the 'lights out' effect of sudden death. It's very frightening.

There was a man in front of me with a Minimi machine gun – a light but very effective weapon that fires 5.56mm rounds.

'Oi! Oi!' I shouted, unsure of his name.

He looked at me over his shoulder. I will never forget his face; he was young, his helmet was lop-sided, he seemed paralysed.

'Come on, mate, get the fucking rounds down, I need to get Bing,' I said to him.

If he fired bursts down the track towards the firing points I could run out into the track, grab Bing and drag him into cover where I could try and do something.

The Minimi gunner looked at me still.

'Rapid fire up the fucking track!' I ordered him. I thought I might have to take his weapon from him and do it myself.

He faced back up the road and fired two three-round bursts. I was hoping for more. Glancing left I again clocked Baz looking at me; he was observing south of the patrol as I had asked him to. He knew what I was going to do, and I could read his face telling me not to do it.

I had to go, though. I couldn't leave Bing there, lifeless. I had to fucking try. I had no cover where I was anyway – I could get shot at any second. This was as good a chance as I was going to get.

'Right, I'm going, you happy?' I said to the Minimi gunner.

He opened fire again. I didn't think about it, just leapt up. The Minimi machine gun got a stoppage after just one round. But my foot had just touched the tyre track closest to me and it was too late to turn back. It was only six or seven paces, but I thought my time was up.

Convinced I was going to get hit, I adjusted my run into an arc, so that if I was shot my momentum would take my body into the ditch next to Baz, and perhaps he could save my life. All I could think was how much it was going to hurt. There was no bravery, no glory; just childish selfish thoughts about how much it would hurt.

I made it and collapsed into the ditch next to Baz, incandescent with the Minimi gunner. I felt like running back across the track and beating him with the machine gun. I got up immediately and together Baz and I pulled Bing into the ditch next to us.

I started having a look at him. Keeping low in the ditch, I took his kit off him, including his helmet. I felt the back of his neck, where the exit wound was obvious. I heard Baz begin to weep. At that precise moment, we were engaged by further positions to the south-east and south-west.

This was getting out of hand.

Baz started returning fire to the two positions directly south. I could hardly hear him firing in the cacophony of noise.

The patrol commander had done a good job in getting the reserve to close-up to our position, and I could hear them over the radio making their way to the corner of the compound where Baz and I were.

'He's fucking dead, isn't he? He's fucking dead!' I could hear Baz saying to me over the gunfire.

I looked Baz in the eye. 'Yes, mate, he's fucking dead.'

Although the two enemy positions to the south were wildly off target, I could tell by their enthusiasm that they knew they had killed a British soldier and that we were bogged down, unable to move quickly. The Taliban always try to overrun you in this situation.

As soon as the reserve arrived, Baz showed them the enemy positions to the south. The medic was with them and I told her that Bing had no pulse, and had suffered a catastrophic gunshot injury to his head. While she unpacked her rolled up stretcher, took off her rucksack to access her kit and assessed Bing for signs of life, I managed to finally get into communication with the gun line. I slightly adjusted the target I had given them originally, and rechecked the grid to bring the fire closer to the enemy compound. I engaged immediately.

I followed this with a SITREP into the handset. I indicated I was fixed at present, in an ambush with multiple firing points and I required emergency close air support to be allocated to Baz. Ten seconds later I was allocated one of the two emergency Apache attack helicopters that launched in dire situations from Camp Bastion. But they were fifteen minutes out. We were on our own for now. Save for the artillery.

I heard the first two artillery rounds land very close; one seemed to hit just metres from the compound that was firing on us. Confident the rounds were not actually entering the compound, I ordered a repeat.

The artillery fire calmed the enemy from the original firing point to our north somewhat, but briefly glancing south I could see the Taliban moving position. If I'm honest I could not identify who exactly was firing at this point and what direction they were coming from. It was, however, clear that they were coordinating in a deliberate effort to cut us off and overrun our position.

'Have you sent this casualty up your chain on your net?' I shouted at the section commander.

'Yes, boss, I have,' he replied.

I was still on my knees next to Bing's lifeless body. The medic was busy shouting at Bing, trying to get a response to keep him with us, but he was long gone. She wanted to start CPR on him and asked me to help her. I was not comfortable with this. Bing was a goner, and his face would not survive compressions, making a traumatic scene even worse. Similarly, time was not a luxury we had, given the continual movement of the enemy.

However, against my better judgement I let her continue; I felt it was important for her to have control over this situation. She was the medic, I was not. She was brilliant; the sort of individual who let her training just kick in, and away she went.

I heard the 105mm land again, not far from our position. They seemed closer to me this time but were definitely having the effect of keeping the enemy quiet to the north. I quickly worked out in my head where the guns were in relation to my position and whether any error could bring the fall of shot any closer. They were firing over my head; I was happy with the risk.

As the medic started CPR on Mark I ordered a repeat, but didn't have time to listen to the guns repeat my order back to me because I decided to intervene on the CPR. It was clear that Bing's spinal fluid was being forced out of his mouth and the breaths were not inflating his lungs. I ordered the medic to stop but she carried on, ignoring me.

I grabbed her bloodied hands hard in mine and used her rank.

'Corporal! Stop now,' I insisted.

She didn't bat an eyelid and started packing up her stuff. I lifted Mark's lifeless body a couple of inches off the ground and someone else slid the stretcher under him.

I looked around me. For some reason the main patrol reserve had already moved back towards the original position of the strongpoint, leaving five of us on our own. Our group was down to one LANCS soldier (a gristly sergeant who was trying to spot and kill the enemy to the north), me and the medic with Bing, Baz firing east and Frank, who was asking me how to use Bing's rifle. It was entirely unintentional, but we were now dislocated from the main group.

'What the fuck?' said the medic.

'Right, we need to go,' I replied, scared but calm.

I grabbed Baz forcefully by the arm.

'We need to extract now,' I told him. 'These cunts are trying to overrun us. The rest of the patrol has bolted. I'm gonna lead the stretcher party, but it only leaves you to give us some protection as we move, OK?'

'Roger,' he replied.

He immediately snapped into gear, and with professionalism and courage that sometimes brings a tear to my eye when I think of it now, he actually advanced towards the enemy firing his weapon on single shot, to get himself into a covered position in an irrigation ditch. There he could provide our covering fire east and withdraw with us. I threw him a couple of Bing's magazines. If the position to the north started re-engaging us, we were just going to have to ignore it. I needed four of us on the stretcher. The reserve could take care of the south.

Our only option for cover was the small wall that we had followed in. Now I could see that it was risible cover indeed, but beggars can't be choosers.

I got us set to move west with Bing's body. The remaining 1 LANCS sergeant was going to be forward left, the medic back left; Frank back right. On my side, I was going at the front – being fitter I was probably going to have to pull this whole thing along.

We crouched in position around the stretcher, which was still on the ground at this point. I waited for some further 105mm I had ordered, going into the original firing position again. It landed. I should have shifted it onto targets to the south, but it was a task too many. We moved.

Frank started shouting at me that he could see the enemy to our north, but Bing's weapon didn't work. Acutely aware of the risk of him shooting me in the back, I paused the extraction and grabbed Bing's weapon off Frank to check it over. As I did so, I saw it had part of Bing's body on it. I wiped it off on myself and got on with checking the firing mechanism; there was a round in the chamber and a full magazine. I gave the weapon back to Frank. For the first time, he was going to be able to engage the enemy that he hated so much.

I made it very clear where he was to point it (i.e., not at me), and he squeezed the trigger as a test fire in the direction of the enemy position to the north. I briefly explained the concept of the safety catch but Frank just told me to take it off. He promised he wouldn't shoot me so I released the safety catch, and told Baz we were going to move. I heard two more 105mm artillery rounds land to our north. I hadn't ordered them; I assumed my battery commander was somehow able to see my situation and had taken control of the guns. (I later found out we now had a Predator drone watching us, and he had done just that.)

Using this artillery as cover, we again set off as fast as we could with Mark's body. We did it in phases, moving to a position where we could pause in some degree of cover and provide some fire for Baz to catch us up. Basic fire and movement.

Baz was ploughing through his ammunition. The position to the north wasn't letting us go easily; I had clearly not killed with the artillery. As we ran, Frank and I fired into it, our rifles in one hand, stretcher in the other. No doubt we hit nothing, but things were getting desperate.

At least we were making progress over the ground. After about 400m we hit another track junction and, relieved, found the remainder of the patrol. They had been providing us with covering fire onto the positions to the south, which were still engaging us and trying to cut us off. The patrol now set off again, covering our front and south; Baz continued to provide our cover to the rear on his own. Thankfully, Frank had exhausted his one magazine of ammunition. I could now hear the section commander controlling the fire and movement, and was briefly reassured. I slung my weapon and started pulling the stretcher faster out of the area, encouraging the others.

The section commander had simultaneously been busy organizing a rendezvous (RV) with some armoured vehicles that had been dispatched from our PB to come and pick us up. The Medical Evacuation and Response Team (MERT) helicopter was not going to land in such an enemy-riddled area, particularly given the Dushka incident three days before. I suspect if Bing had still been alive this would have been very different – their bravery was astonishing. The armoured vehicles had sped to the RV and I could now hear their comforting heavy fire engaging the enemy back over my head. I hoped they knew Baz was behind me. I shouted to the first vehicle commander to let him know and he nodded in understanding.

I could hear an Apache not too far away now, too. Commanders had seen the enemy's efforts to encircle us from the Predator drone, and were now focused on protecting us. Baz had a radio to speak to the Apache, as did I, but neither of us could get to the radio set on our back to flick onto the correct frequency; him because of the weight of enemy fire, me because I was doing all I could to get Bing out of there. I felt rather helpless and started to get tired; looking at the others, they had clearly reached that point and beyond.

Eventually we made it to the lead Husky vehicle and ran behind it to put Bing down. I looked up and immediately saw the Apache about 3km away out to the west. I took off my rucksack to flick onto the air net and talk to the Apache myself.

'Boss, boss, I'm out,' I heard from Baz.

The firefight had died down somewhat but hadn't entirely finished. The rest of the patrol were busy engaging the enemy to the south while Baz was still under fire from the east, without ammunition, marooned next to a tree about 30m from the Husky.

I reloaded my last magazine and ran forward to draw the fire coming from the positions that were still engaging Baz. I had seen what I thought was some good cover and made for it. Frustratingly it was not a pile of earth, but a pile of dead poppies, and absolutely no use to me at all. It was too late to go back. Standing up I poured a magazine into the enemy position – all twenty-eight rounds of 5.56mm ammunition. Baz bounded back past me. Out of ammunition, I legged it too. We both met at the rear of the Husky next to Bing's lifeless body. The armoured vehicles were still returning some fire to cover the men extracting 100m away, back onto the track.

Baz threw his bag onto the ground and started rummaging around in it while the platoon commander in charge of the armoured vehicles was shouting, organizing our shell-shocked patrol into transport for the journey back to PB Khaamar. Getting his radio out, Baz flicked onto the air net to try to speak with the Apache. As I raised my handset to speak to the guns I heard my Battery Commander give 'check fire' to the gunline.

Now we had the assets I wanted to go back in, I hated running away.

Bing lay dead on the stretcher at my feet. I thought for a moment. I felt sick.

Reluctantly I started to load up too, and get Bing's body in the back of one of the Huskies. He was a big and heavy bloke, and the medic, Baz and I could not get him far enough into the Husky to shut the door. I was not prepared to just fold him in and close it. I took my kit off – body armour, webbing and helmet – and threw them over his body into the far end of the vehicle. I put my rifle under the bench seat and then clambered in and picked up Bing's body with a big bear hug, swung him round and sat down with him on my lap on the bench. I cradled him like a baby.

Baz turned on his heel and headed for the lead vehicle so he could talk to the Apache and engage targets if required on our journey back. The platoon commander jumped down from the gun and shut the door of my Husky, leaving me alone with Bing in the darkened interior of the vehicle. We got moving almost straight away.

'I'm so sorry,' I said to him. 'I'm so sorry, mate. You're a good man. You're a good man,' I kept saying.

I pressed his cheek to mine and gave him a kiss. Staring at his face, for the first time I saw the scorch mark under his left eye where the bullet had entered. I inserted my finger into the hole in the back of his neck, and realized he must have only been hit once. This in-and-out wound had passed straight through his spine, straight through his cerebellar cortex and killed him instantly.

I took off his Help for Heroes band and put it on my wrist. His blood slowly seeped down my breast from the back of his neck; it was noticeably cooler than before.

It took forty minutes to get back to our home PB along the IED-riddled Route Nike. I could hear the Apache overhead and grabbed my radio to listen in to the net, anticipating having to leave Bing, get my kit back on and get back to work. Somehow we didn't get whacked so I cradled Bing the entire way, resting my head on his. It was comparatively quiet, very hot, and deeply affecting to be in the back of that armoured vehicle with Bing. He was neither warm and alive nor dully cold and passed on. During those forty minutes I think his soul left him. He wanted to check we all got out okay before he went.

Finally, the truck stopped. The back of the Husky opened and there was a soldier there with a poncho. I told him to go away and get a proper body bag – Bing wasn't going on the helicopter trussed up like a fucking turkey in a poncho.

The doc came back with a body bag and took Bing's pulse, confirming he was indeed dead. With the doc, I shuffled him into the bag and did up the zip. We grabbed an end each and ran straight out to the HLS (helicopter landing site) where the CH-47 MERT was turning and burning, ready to take Bing back to Bastion. I pulled him up nice and close to the medical team in the middle of the aircraft and hugged his head. The medical team paused and let me have my moment. The officer in charge winked at me. I ran off the back of the aircraft, grabbed my kit from the back of the Husky and walked back to my tent. A crowd of soldiers had now gathered but I had nothing to say. I walked through the tent, straight past Bing's empty and untidy bed and out the back, where Baz was de-servicing his radios.

I pulled his head into my shoulder. We said nothing. We cracked open some cigarettes and sat in silence, working our way through the packet, staring into space, alone in our own thoughts. Baz's eyes were wet; he remained resilient, but in tears. I felt a deep sense of shock.

After some time one of the lads from the patrol we were supporting came around on behalf of his company to offer his condolences. We chatted briefly before he left.

The rest of that morning became a bit of a haze. I

remember there being another contact in the AO, and I was called to the Ops room to coordinate a strike against some insurgents in a tree line who had pinned down a patrol from one of the satellite patrol bases to our north. One of my team from that satellite patrol base was out on this patrol, so I was able to use him as my eyes, and cued him up some 105mm HE. It wasn't a particularly heavy contact; one round broke it and his patrol returned to their base.

At the end of that engagement the company commander called me over. He said that the sight of Bing's blood all over me was putting others off, and asked me to get changed. This seriously irritated me. I turned and left without saying anything. I didn't want to change, to shower or de-service my kit from the patrol. I felt like that would be it then, the patrol would be over and Bing would genuinely be dead. I went back to the tent and joined Baz, who by now was sat on the floor going through Bing's things. A letter had arrived that morning from his mum; he had never had the chance to read it.

I imagined his parents; right at this moment they were probably being given the news. That unexpected knock on the door, too early in the morning to be a friend. As soon as his mum or dad laid eyes on the smartly dressed servicemen they would know.

Whatever pain I felt at that moment, I knew it was nothing compared to theirs.

21

Bing died on a Tuesday morning. Baz and I flew out of the PB together on the Wednesday morning – Bing was being repatriated to the UK at sunset, and there was to be a service at Bastion which we would attend. PB Khaamar would be on 'patrol minimize' – i.e. no patrolling while we were away.

The CO of 4th Regiment Royal Artillery flew in for it. We had a coffee and I told him of life on the line, and he seemed genuinely taken aback at the scale of the fighting. He reminded me that in the Second World War, units would get rotated with relative regularity, but this was not possible in this conflict; thus we were asking some of our men to undertake almost seven months of continuous contact with the enemy. I disagreed with this comparison – some units in the Second World War suffered 100 per cent casualty rates – but I took his point.

He was a very decent guy, and I genuinely felt supported by him. I could not speak of my shock and pain to my men, but I did relay it accurately to Paul. He asked if I would say a few words about Bing at the Service of Repatriation, and form part of the bearer party to put him on the plane.

The day passed in a bit of a blur. Baz and I stuck together, often spending chunks of time in silence. I knew he was struggling with the grief; mine was grief mixed in with a significant dose of guilt. The guilt started small but seemed to grow over time.

It was simple in my head; if Bing had not been in my FST he would probably still be alive. He would have gone on to have a family, get married, build a life for himself.

As we filed towards Bing's repatriation service that warm evening in June 2010, all the reasons for my relentless and almost personal pursuit of the enemy were beginning to seem like nonsense.

The service was deeply moving. I did not expect the whole population of Camp Bastion to be there but there must have been in excess of a thousand men and women in a silent, hollow square. As the sun set in the desert sky, with weak knees banging against the microphone stand as I tried to get a grip on my body, I said, 'Lance Bombardier Mark Chandler was, in my eyes, the perfect soldier. He remained consistent, whether in combat or not. His selfless commitment truly set him apart from his peers. He would just as readily volunteer to empty the bins as go out on a patrol to disrupt the insurgents and protect the people, as on the day he was killed. He was the man that men aspire to be.

'Whenever we were in a dangerous situation, Mark would be sat in the ditch next to me smiling, seemingly without a care in the world. His sanity and calm humour kept our morale up. He was the perfect man to have in a fire support team. It was an absolute privilege to command this example of a man.'

The whole idea of stoical soldiers too hard to cry was another pointless myth about war. I never really cried, but not because I was a soldier. I just didn't feel like it. But as I returned to my place next to Paul I felt the first tear roll down my face since the incident, and I could sense that overwhelming grief and guilt was not too far away. Paul winked at me.

After the service Baz and I made our way down to the pan, where the enormous C-17 transporter plane was going to take Bing home.

By now these repatriation services were a well-oiled machine. We picked Bing up in his Union Jack covered coffin and, in front of the entire Camp Bastion, marched him in slow time across the pan and up the ramp onto the aircraft. He seemed a lot heavier now. I moved on autopilot, unable to think of anything other than Bing's body in my arms in the back of that Husky. I've always been shit at marching. But I tried.

The C-17 roared down the runway and threw itself into the night sky. In the darkness, I walked by myself back to the Royal Artillery part of Camp Bastion and collected my kit before making my way down to the pan for a helicopter flight back out to PB Khaamar. All those there in the support group operating out of Bastion were terrific, but I simply did not want to talk to anyone.

Baz and I flew back to the PB that night. By coincidence, I was going on R&R the next day, so I packed up my belongings ready to fly out again. Baz was going to man the fort for a couple of weeks with a replacement captain from another part of the AO.

Baz came to see me off the next day and we stood with the back gates open onto the HLS, waiting for the helicopter. He knew I felt guilty about Bing. I kept asking him leading questions about decisions I had made and how the patrol had gone, selfishly wanting him to make me feel better. How desperately weak. I needed a break.

I stopped after a bit and we just sat down in the dust near the toilet block and grunted to each other about cigarettes.

22

The Tristar landed at Brize Norton and I was met by Felicity, looking beautiful in a gorgeous blue dress she had worn especially for the occasion. It was always very surreal coming back from 'the front', but this time it was especially acute given what had happened just a day or so earlier.

We stopped at McDonald's at the services in Oxford where I ordered a lot of food, but couldn't even begin to eat a small part of it; my stomach had clearly shrunk. Then we drove back to her little house in Sussex and did what any returning soldier does for a few hours. We had dinner and got an early night. I didn't want a beer; I didn't want to leave the house. I felt overwhelmed, like water was lapping at me; I was being submerged by something but could not figure out what. For some reason, I just wanted to cry, and remember feeling that annoying lump in my throat almost constantly. At one stage I felt like making myself cry and getting it out of the way in the hope that the sadness might shift for a bit. I ignored it.

The following morning, I got up before the sun. I made a cup of coffee and sat outside in my heavy woollen cardigan and my pants. Dawn was different in the UK; wetter, but seemingly swifter as well, as if it knew we didn't need that time to savour before the violence of the day. Same Earth; different country.

I got dressed, jumped in my car before Felicity woke up and drove five hours to see Mike and Ann Chandler – Bing's parents. I had written them a detailed letter about Bing's death which I'd intended to send the day Bing had died, before realizing that I would be back in the UK long before the British Forces Post Office service caught up and could deliver it in person.

I found their house in Nailsworth, Gloucestershire. Mark's parents were not elderly but they had clearly had their struggles. Ann had survived cancer once already; Mike was hardly fleet of foot. Ann opened the door and gave me a big hug. Mike, who was extremely ashen, was in tears in the living room.

'I'm so sorry,' I said to Ann. 'I'm so sorry.'

She was cross with me for apologizing to her. Apparently, Bing had often told her about me, and how he had asked the regiment if he could be in my team because he liked 'the way I did business', although I found this hard to believe.

I recounted in painful detail every second of the patrol that morning, how we repatriated Bing that evening in Bastion, and his service where he was honoured by so many.

I told them how content Bing had seemed in the patrol base with Baz and me, how he was an extremely brave man; in the finest traditions of a British 'Tommy', and humbling to serve alongside. I told them it was a privilege to command him, and that despite the bigger picture and the UK's strategic intentions in Afghanistan, he actually died protecting me, and I would never forget that. I promised my commitment to them would be enduring in the months and years ahead.

His dad wanted to know in detail of the seconds before and after Bing's death, to ensure his son did not suffer. I told the story over and over again during the four hours I was in their house. They were beyond devastated by the loss of the man, who quite clearly was the life and soul of their family.

I left their house that evening. As soon as I got in the car, which was fortunately parked around the corner and out of sight, I broke down for the first time.

It was a long and lonely drive home amid traffic, all those cars driven by people who had little interest in and even less knowledge of what their Army was doing in their name. I couldn't blame them.

That weekend, Felicity and I were supposed to be going to the Maldives for a mid-tour break, which she had booked about a month before. I had a difficult decision to make because Bing's funeral was going to fall precisely in the middle of the holiday. I had a duty to him, but I also had a duty to Felicity, who was enduring all this with me. It was often worse for her, in fact, because she did not know what was going on half the time.

I had talked to Mike and Ann about it and they adamantly told me to go away. I had done my duty to Bing in their eyes, and I personally felt I had said goodbye to him in Afghanistan.

With a heavy heart, Felicity and I flew to the Maldives for a much-needed break. The place was almost celestial in its physical beauty, and I asked Felicity if she would do me the honour of marrying me. She said yes.

Ten days later I flew back out to Afghanistan to complete the remaining four months of my tour without Bing.

23

I passed Baz on the flight pan at Camp Bastion, as he headed off on R&R. Being in separate lines, we could only grab a few words. He seemed OK; he was looking forward to going home for a couple of weeks. I spent a few hours at Camp Bastion before catching a helicopter back to FOB Shawqat, where I would spend ten days as part of Nad-e Ali's quick reaction force (QRF) – a small group of recce platoon soldiers who are used in emergencies. After that I'd return to PB Khaamar for the rest of the tour.

Things in PB Khaamar were continuing to get worse. While I was away on R&R an enemy 'sniper' (I did not believe he was a sniper – in my view he was just a lucky shot who happened to employ his sights properly) had shot three Brits with one round in the PB just north of mine. They all survived. Similarly, another run on the camp had been made, and an RPG had entered the command tent but not detonated, pinging off into the night air.

Patrolling with the QRF was much more relaxed and little happened. I was now deployed as a single FST element – with two radios capable of talking on the fires net and the air net simultaneously. One night we drove to Camp Bastion to pick up a piece of equipment. We slept in the vehicles for a couple of hours before driving back to Nad-e Ali the following morning. The vehicles were Jackals – the new version of the infamous WMIKs that I had used in my first tour. They had a little more protection, but were ultimately designed to be mobile, and as such drivers and operators were exposed to the elements.

On that journey back from Camp Bastion, just as we began to enter the built-up area that stretched down to PB Khaamar, we were engaged by small-arms fire. I was woken by a round pinging off the anti-roll bar just next to me. After some shimmying around we could not identify the firing point and extracted from a heavily urban area without returning fire.

Later that day we were resting back at FOB Shawqat when we were given a shout to move out. A patrol from one of the satellite patrol bases in Khaamar's area had gone out and walked into a complex IED field. Two men had been hit, both losing their lower legs, and two more were now stuck in this field, unable to move. The remainder of the patrol had secured the area, but they were being probed by the enemy. Being fixed in position meant they were very vulnerable. To 'un-fix' them, they would need the specialist counter-IED team to get them out. We were being deployed with this counter-IED team to beef up security.

A CH-47 came to pick us up, as well as two SAS liaison officers who were staying at the base. They were attached to the QRF that had been tasked to secure the area from further attack. There was an SAS squadron conducting strategic man-hunting operations in the area, and these liaison officers were helping coordinate their efforts with our own. Our part of Afghanistan was now becoming very contested, and there were multiple complex threats both from the 'sniper' and heavy built-up gun emplacements, which were apparently not faced elsewhere at the time.

There were about fifteen of us in the QRF, under the command of a junior officer – the recce platoon commander – who was very good. We landed near a compound and headed down to the stricken patrol. We'd just arrived at the scene when we came under contact from about 150m to our south.

It would be honest of me to say that at this point I was very much struggling to readjust to combat post R&R. I felt very, very different on the ground. I had worked hard to put Bing's death behind me, but I could now feel – and even taste – the fear of being back in contact with the enemy. I tried to understand why, and could only think that while I had always considered I might well get shot – which was preferable to being blown up and bleeding out like so many other poor souls – I'd never thought it would just turn my lights off, that my mates wouldn't have a chance to save me. That that would be it. Final. End. I guess I didn't want to die too.

So, when we came under contact I was very very scared. I lost control of my bowels and shit myself a little bit. I was in the middle of the road with one of the SAS soldiers. I wanted to run. Instead, I forced myself to go down on one knee and search for the firing point through my sights. I could feel the fear rising up the back of my neck and my heart trying to jump out of my chest. But I forced my body to comply and stayed there, fruitlessly looking for the enemy.

'Anyone see that?' I shouted.

'No,' the SAS man next to me said. 'Think it was a shoot and scoot. Let's just be careful.' He was Scottish and I struggled to understand him.

'Roger,' I said, after a couple of seconds.

With the small contact over, we made our way down to

where the IED incident had taken place and were met with quite a sight. The incident had actually occurred about thirty minutes earlier, and the two injured blokes had already been evacuated by MERT. I found the section commander.

'What's going on, mate, where do you want us?' I said to him.

'Um – I'm not sure. It was horrific. Two blokes. Fucking hell.' He was looking past me and was not fully engaging with me when I spoke to him.

The SAS guy joined us.

'Where are the blokes cut off?' he asked.

'Just down that alley,' the section commander replied, pointing down the side of a compound to a track that was joined by another compound on the other side. It was not an obvious IED point – he had done nothing wrong in going that way.

The SAS guy spoke to the recce platoon commander and between them they organized some defence. I stayed with the section commander.

'You okay?' I said to him.

'Yeah, yeah. Not really,' he replied.

At this point I recognized it immediately. This guy had gone. I looked above his eye-line for the first time and saw some human remains on his helmet. I wiped them off and told him to come and sit down with me.

'Just chill out here for a minute with me, mate, OK? We've got it from here,' I said to him.

I called the recce platoon commander over.

'He's gone, mate. He's gone. This has been fucking horrific for him.'

'Yeah, roger, Johnny. The counter-IED team are working on it now, I don't reckon this will take too long and we will head back to their PB with them. It's only about twenty minutes north of here', he replied.

The two soldiers who were cut off were uninjured and reasonably calm, and the QRF set about securing a safe area around them. While the counter-IED team did their magic and the two guys were retrieved I chatted to the section commander, trying to get him to chill out. He told me that both casualties had severe lower limb injuries. One realized he had lost his testicles and penis as he was carried out to the helicopter and let out a howl that the section commander was struggling to let go of.

We came under contact another two times while we were there. The recce platoon commander said he knew roughly where the firing point was. We wanted to drop one round of HE in a field just to the north of the shooter, in an attempt to frighten him off. Being fixed in position by the IED field, we had to retain the initiative and control over this scenario. I got on the net and ordered the guns to fire, which seemed to have the desired effect.

Once the counter-IED team's work was complete, the entire group patrolled as a single unit back to the PB under the command of the recce platoon commander. There the QRF waited for onward transition to PB Khaamar, where we were to await further orders.

While we were waiting for the CH-47, I talked some more with the section commander, who remained in a very bad way. Physically he was fine; mentally, something had snapped. It was my first very visceral exposure to battle shock. I walked over to the recce platoon commander to have a quiet word. He agreed that the section commander needed help, so I got the company commander on the radio. He told me that the two guys injured would likely survive, but would be maimed for life.

'You need to think about getting the section commander out,' I told him.

I was no mental health nurse, but this guy needed attention as much as anyone who had a physical injury, and to my mind it was a category A requirement – immediate transfer back to Camp Bastion. The company commander agreed and I put in another discreet call to the MERT on my net, to get them to pick the section commander up. Thirty minutes later he walked onto the back of a CH-47 and flew out of the war, with perhaps his hardest battles about to start. I never knew what happened to him.

The heat of the day was upon us. The QRF, including the SAS liaison team, were sitting outside the Ops room waiting for our lift back to PB Khaamar, sunbathing. I nipped around to the toilet area, where I dug out my wet wipes, wiped my arse and burnt my pants. My shit had not seeped through to my trousers. The company held a daily lunchtime collective call to keep everyone updated on what was going on. In some of the PBs, one could become quite isolated quite quickly, so it was useful to keep everyone up to date. I listened in on most days, although it was all a bit samey. Taking ground, not holding it, extracting under fire, fruitless meetings with elders, locals coming in to claim money for damage we usually hadn't done to their compounds.

If I'm honest I didn't really care about the bigger picture; I was purely focused on looking after each patrol I went on, and then forgetting about the whole bloody mess. The locals hated us, and by now I was beginning to hate them.

The company commander came on the radio. He said that he understood how the lads at this PB must be feeling. That he felt that way too and that we were going to cancel patrols for the rest of the day. He rushed through the agenda for the call, and then signed off. The sadness in his voice was acute.

I was next to one of the SAS guys, and we just looked at each other. We knew the company was getting hammered – I'd been there with them until about two weeks ago. During the few hours I had spent in FOB Shawqat the day before I had spoken to the battalion 2IC. He discreetly outlined to me, officer to officer, that he was beginning to get the impression the company was starting to struggle. The SAS guy confirmed that was his assessment too.

But still, the moment the will to fight is actually snapped is extremely tangible. I felt it was that moment, on that radio call. I felt something suck out the air around the PB. It was clear to me that everyone had had enough for now.

But we looked after each other in the Army – up and down the chain of command. I resolved that I was not going to mention it to battalion headquarters, as I had been asked to do in FOB Shawqat, but would instead raise it face to face with the company commander himself upon my return to PB Khaamar. After all, one could not blame them. They had taken heavy casualties and had been in this area for three unrelenting months now. It was taking an increasingly heavy toll mentally and physically.

I was surprised that the commander was allowing how affected he was to be seen. Maybe his men knew him well enough that there was no point hiding it, but I had always felt that a commander will earn his rank in the heavy moments. The moments that seem to last, where time passes very slowly. The moment when someone gets shot, the weapon jams, the enemy is 20m away, and the radio isn't working. The moment after a death or serious injury like this. The truth is, *it is* fucking scary – we're all fucking scared. Seeing someone lose half their body and scream all the way onto the helicopter is traumatic. Seeing someone shot dead is traumatic. In those moments, you just want to run onto the helicopter, go home and be done with it. That, I feel, is when you earn your rank. It's just a piece of embroidery otherwise. Leadership isn't all about riding your horse at the head of the parade. There are some fucking hard, blood-soaked, dust-encased shaking-with-fear, shit yourself yards you have to find it in yourself to make – you as an individual, not encouraged by others. But everyone has their limit and these guys were being pushed to it and beyond. There were many, many brave young British leaders in Afghanistan. I hoped our nation would be forever proud of them. This guy was one of them. He had just reached his limit.

Ten days after the IED incident Baz returned to PB Khaamar after his R&R. He had been rested, but I could tell something in him had changed, and he had not wanted to come back.

On his first full day back we recommenced patrolling together, with a company operation pushing south and east to secure the eastern side of Shawaal, only a couple of kilometres from PB Khaamar, and seemingly for the umpteenth time. It had to be an ongoing operation, as we were never going to hold the ground and insurgents would simply melt back into Shawaal, and continue to harass us in PB Khaamar.

The patrol itself was uneventful – as usual when there were lots of us out the enemy didn't really fancy it – until we were returning up the main road, a large track beside a river. Suddenly the company commander's tactical group (of which I was a part) were ambushed. We dropped to the ground.

'Baz! Can you see where the fire is coming from?' I shouted in a mild panic. It seemed a little close for comfort.

'It's that fucking compound right there, boss. This one right here!' he shouted. 'What do you want to do?'

I looked over, seeing a compound about 25m away across the river which seemed to be firing at our southern call sign. I thought that if the enemy just popped their heads over the other wall of the house, which was facing us, they would have seen me, Baz, the medic, the company signaller and company commander in the prone position in the middle of the track without any cover between us and them. Easy targets.

Suddenly I felt someone backing into me, like the wife does when she is cold in bed. It was the company commander.

I quietly asked him what the fuck he was doing. I don't think he heard me. I told him that I thought the fire might be coming from the compound just in front of us, and that if the enemy looked over the wall we would all be dead.

There were two or three other soldiers with us – the company signaller and a couple of others I cannot recall.

'Lads, we need to get in hard against that compound wall and have a look inside,' I said.

'Baz, we need to get in there, mate,' I shouted at him.

'I know, I know,' he replied.

'Let's go!' I said and shuffled to my feet, running forward towards the waist-high river.

I moved through the river just to our front, up the other bank, and stacked-up against the wall just down from what appeared to be the main doorway. Fully expecting to encounter armed enemy, I realized I did not have any frag grenades, so I pulled out a smoke. I told Baz to cover to the rear.

That's when I glanced at Baz, and there was a comedy moment when we realized that we were the only two who had crossed the river. The others members of the company commander's group had moved backwards into the ditch, and were now watching us.

A smoke was going to be useless – it would confuse me as much as them. I chucked it back in my webbing and fumbled to do up my strap with my left hand.

The noise I was hearing was either rounds hitting this compound on the other side, or firing from inside the compound. I could not work it out. There was nothing else for it. I quietly slipped my safety catch off and rested my finger on the trigger.

Tight to the wall I peeled around the doorway, weapon on automatic.

A little pair of brown eyes looked up at me, and then another. I can picture them now staring at me over the barrel of my rifle. Two children – a girl and a boy, their eyes so beautiful and dark I couldn't make out their pupils. They were sheltering with their parents in this near corner of their compound.

Initially, I thought that the enemy had commandeered their compound and I crept around the door, weapon raised into the opposite corner, passing their linen hanging in their yard, gently flapping in the wind. It was a small and simple compound, and within a couple of seconds I realized what was going on.

'It's clear,' I said quietly to Baz.

'I think it's the next one over,' said Baz, confirming what I thought.

I called the family over to me and led them to a position outside where they would be better protected from any stray rounds.

'Get in against the wall,' I said in English, I'm not sure why; they would never have understood. Baz gestured to them to come over to him in the shade of a small tree that was against their compound wall.

The little girl started playing with the leaves. She picked one up and gave it to me. I smiled at her, took the leaf and then didn't know what to do with it.

Looking back across the river, I could see the remainder of the company command group in the ditch. Baz was chatting away into his radio. The contact was beginning to die now.

'They've given me an Apache,' Baz said to me. I was unaware we had asked for one but Baz was very good; by now he just cracked on and let me know what was available. I was constantly computing in my head what I could do to bring the contact to a close. Options were limited, and the fire was not intense enough to warrant anything really. However, the Apache was returning to Camp Bastion after another operation and had a few minutes of fuel left. Baz brought the Apache into the overhead and the contact died completely. I asked the Apache to have a good look in the compound next over from us, and although he could see murder holes facing south onto one part of our patrol, he could not see any insurgents. He was running out of fuel and, content that we were not far from PB Khaamar, I cut him away and we all met back on the road and continued the move back to camp.

When I got back I wanted to be sure of what had just happened so I asked Baz what he had seen. He had not noticed the company commander backing into me, but he did notice that I had briefed up the entire group about getting inside that compound, and was pretty surprised to find it was just me and him who moved.

I went to see the company commander and we headed outside of the Ops room away from the men. I gently asked him if everything was OK. He immediately fronted up and didn't seem to know what I was talking about. It was disappointing. We were not from the same unit, I did not know him particularly well, but I was not in any way denigrating him, and seek not to now. I hoped for a candid conversation in return. It did not come.

Later that week I was unsurprised to be asked to call Adam Wilson, who by now had moved into the battalion second-in-command post after his predecessor went home with an illness.

'How's it going?' he asked, and I told him.

'The view from here is that we need to deploy further forces in your AO to try and get to grips with the insurgency there,' he said. 'The task force commander has requested the theatre reserve battalion and they are flying in next week.'

'Where will they go?' I asked.

'They will relieve your company, and your company will move back to FOB Shawqat for a rest before deploying further south for a deliberate operation in a fortnight or so.'

'I think that's fair. They're a good group but it's been tough,' I said.

'Do you think they've lost the will to fight?' he asked.

'I wouldn't like to say,' I replied, cautiously, with a very heavy heart.

'Are your team OK to stay on, show the new company the ground and act as the continuity?' he asked.

'Of course,' I lied.

24

It was early August now, and Britain was enjoying a blissfully hot summer, complemented by one of our national sides making the usual early exit from a World Cup – football on this occasion. The temperature in southern Afghanistan was intolerable – the heat of the day was like a furnace as the sun baked the desert floor. Baz and I settled into a new patrols routine with the new troops, fresh in from Cyprus. Handover patrols were generally not conducted in contentious areas, and we had three or four days out of contact with the enemy.

Despite the heat, I worked hard in the PB to stay fit. I had heard many times how some injured soldiers had stayed alive far longer than they medically should have done because of their fitness. My smoking and appalling diet probably meant I would not ever fall into this bracket, but I thought I should do everything I could to stack the cards in my favour.

On the welfare front, we now had an 'e-bluey' machine that could print out letters back in the UK and post them, cutting the postal delay down massively. I made sure I wrote to Felicity every day. Similarly, she could go to a website and write to me, and once a day the machine could receive a packet of data and download and print letters sent to theatre. We made plans for my return, when I'd be heading back to

29 Commando in Plymouth. I was going to be there for at least two years, and so for stability we would rent a small property about eight miles out of Plymouth, on the coast in a little village called Noss Mayo, Devon.

Noss was an idyllic place on the Yealm estuary, with a lovely pub overlooking the water. I had no doubt that when I got home, family life would be as perfect as anything I'd ever dreamed of as a boy. This made accepting the risks of operations ever harder. I wasn't sure if the letters helped or hindered my operational capacity.

One morning that August I was sleeping in my bed. It was a Sunday. We were right at the end of our handover period between the troops and we took a day off. It was just coming up for eight o'clock, when all seems bright and clean yet not too hot, before the sun can fully erode the coolness that hangs in the air from the night. I was dozing – I had woken, but for the first time in a long time I had not actually got straight up. I was relaxed and content.

Suddenly, I was stirred by enemy fire very close to the edge of the camp. Some of it was going over, and some was slapping into the eastern walls that faced out towards the Jungle – where all our trouble came from.

I was surprised – something wasn't right. It would require some real nerve from the enemy to attack the base in daylight, and from that side in particular, given the sparsity of cover available to them.

I sat up, fought my way out of my mosquito net and grabbed my weapon and webbing from the bottom of my bed. I always slept with a round in the chamber – as previously mentioned, a personal nightmare was waking up to a Talib at the end of my bed. This wasn't a false fear; it had happened in another patrol base already that summer, with a rogue ANA soldier targeting the FST tent and killing three. In pants and flip-flops plus body armour, balancing my helmet on my head, I raced over to the back gate.

I jumped up on a step in the HESCO bastion and peered over the top of the wall. I could see the Taliban firing onto a group of our people who were attempting to mend a small footbridge immediately outside the patrol base's back gate.

The company sergeant major appeared below me and asked if I could see any enemy. There were rounds coming into the PB, and I was loath to put my head above the wall to look again properly.

I had to force myself to do so. I had visions of that scene from countless war films where someone just looks over the trenches and immediately gets one straight in the grid. This was getting ridiculous. I had to get past this fear that was beginning to cripple me since Bing was killed, and stop thinking about getting shot like him. In that moment, on that compound wall, it was only my personal dignity and pride that made me look. Also, the knowledge that the company sergeant major would have most probably told everyone if I'd bottled it and the banter would have been intolerable.

I peered over the top, making myself as small as possible, and saw the enemy firing from a compound about 70m away from me. Rounds from his weapon were striking the patrol base – he was aiming at the blokes immediately below me. They in turn were frantically collecting their tools and trying to find some cover.

As I engaged him with quick single shots, straight into the window where I could see a muzzle flash, my legs were shaking so much I had to put nearly all of my weight onto the wall to still my weapon. I wondered what the fuck had become of the almost-fearless soldier I had once purported to be, when I now couldn't even control my own limbs in contact.

'Fucking get him, sir,' the company sergeant major encouraged me. I didn't say anything in return. I daren't look at him and reveal my fear. He had been joined by another senior NCO from the new company, and as I ducked to change magazines, I heard them crack a joke about my 'disco legs'.

After about forty seconds the team on the bridge made a run for it and re-entered the camp. The sangars had finally woken up by this point too, and were engaging into the compound with automatic 7.62 from their GPMGs. The excitement was over within perhaps a minute and a half, with, remarkably, no casualties.

I climbed down from the wall. Others had joined me further down the wall – perhaps about six of us were engaging in the end. Baz wasn't one of them. I could see him emerge from our tent in his army-issue Lycra pants and flip-flops, stretching like an old man on holiday. It would take more than that to get him out of bed on a day off.

'You all right, sir?' the company sergeant major said to me in his strong Scouse accent. 'Enjoyed that for a Sunday morning?'

'Yeah, I'm fine,' I lied, picking up my empty magazine from the HESCO and heading back to my tent. Inside my soul I felt like I was twelve years old again, lonely, nervous and child-like. My arm was shaking so much I struggled to unload my weapon.

I needed to sort myself out. This and the incident where I shit myself – what was going on? Something had changed in me since Bing's death.

Baz went for a shower. I went to my bed space and sat down. Fear was beginning to take hold. Real fear – the sort that you feel is going to suffocate you, take your breath away. The sort you feel when you wake up in the night having a violent nightmare. It wasn't passing as I'd hoped it would.

I put my running gear on and ran slowly around the compound for just under two hours in the now baking heat, until I almost passed out. I kept going, slowly plodding on while I thought about what had just happened. I wondered how this crippling fear had crept up on me, and started to feel angry. I couldn't talk to anyone about it – I felt too ashamed. I needed to sort it for myself – within myself.

I finished my run in a better place than when I started it. Not literally – I was on the loo for quite some time with mild heat exhaustion – but once I had got past that I went to find the OC and told him we needed to do a clearance of the compound from which the enemy had engaged us that morning.

This 2 LANCS company had a brilliant commander, who understood what I understood. If we did not get out of the PB and on top of the situation, deal with an enemy that thought it was entirely reasonable to try and attack the base during daylight hours, and reassert our authority, which had started to wane under the previous company, we were going to struggle significantly.

As well as getting the theatre reserve battalion, we had kept the 22 SAS team, who were now billeted in PB Khaamar with us.

Our first target was to stop the individual who had attacked us that morning from either shooting PB Khaamar himself, or facilitating the Taliban using his compound.

The new company commander, the company sergeant major,

the SAS team and myself chewed over a few options over a cup of tea. I wanted to sneak out at night and lace the place with Claymore mines, and as soon as we were engaged from that compound again, clack them off. This seemed like a good idea, but had too many downsides attached. We could not be sure there would be no civilians milling around the area at the time we wanted to detonate the Claymores. Also, planting the devices would be difficult given that the compound was used regularly, and any approach routes out of sight of the building were probably well guarded by IEDs.

In the end, we decided to put a patrol out to the compound that evening. We would approach using the main road that ran right past it, which was under the cover of the sangars from PB Khaamar. We would then have a chat with the owner, search his compound and see if we could persuade him to desist.

We headed out at about 4 p.m. that Sunday, placed a cordon around the area, and myself and a section commander – a good young lad – went with a new interpreter called Kush to have a look around the compound. The company commander was watching through a camera we had mounted in the PB as part of our defences.

We knocked on the door, which was answered by a man in his forties. He seemed to live there alone, in what was a fairly simple compound with two rooms. The room facing the patrol base had two curtains, which I pulled back to reveal two neatly made murder holes cut into the structure of the compound wall. Through the murder holes you could directly engage our PB. There were AK47 shell cases on the floor. He clearly didn't live there, and was as guilty as a puppy sat next to a pile of poo; or a Talib sat next to a pile of empty cases and a murder hole, if you like.

The section commander started to search the property, while I spoke to the company commander on the net to report our findings.

We then had a good look outside the property for concealed weapon caches, but had no joy. The man thought this was all a bit of a joke, and was laughing as he denied ever having even heard of the Taliban. I was getting a bit bored, and so when Kush and the man went back inside the compound, I followed him in.

Inside the compound it was considerably darker than it was outside. I couldn't really see anything so I started heading back for the door. The man continued to snigger and smile at me.

'Kush, ask him what's so fucking funny,' I said.

'No funny, no funny,' he started saying.

'You think this is all a laugh, don't you?' I said to him; Kush translated.

'He's Taliban,' Kush told me.

I told the man of my recent visit to Bing's parents and how devastated they were. He continued to smile at me. He either didn't understand, or he did, and was winding me up.

'In another time, in another place, I'd just kill you,' I said, matter-of-factly. 'Kush wouldn't help you. I'd say you grabbed my weapon – self-defence. Easy.'

His laughter dried up and his mood changed.

'But I thought this was all a game to you, right?' I said.

He started talking again, and as Kush paused to translate, I spoke again.

'Any more from this house and I will come back and see you on my own. You understand that?' I said.

'Yeah, we be friends, Johnny. We be friends!'

He knew some English, and he knew my name. This was

no ten-dollar Taliban; he had noticed what the lads were calling me and copied them.

'No, we won't be fucking friends, I assure you,' I told him.

The interpreter winked at me and we turned and left without saying any more. Outside, the section commander asked if everything was all right; I gave no hint of our conversation.

We patrolled back to the PB without incident.

After a contact about a month later, about 2km to the south of this compound, Baz and I were cleaning our weapons and having a smoke at the back of our tent when there was a commotion at the back gate. An injured fighter had been shot in the arse and wanted treatment. We took him in, as we always did, and I wandered over to the medical centre – a shipping container – to see what was going on. The Afghan male was lying on his front, with the doc treating a wound in his arse cheek. I was surprised when the enemy fighter looked up at me and said, 'Johnny! Johnny! My friend Johnny!' It was the very same bloke.

'Make sure you check him for gun residue,' I said to the doc, who by now was looking very surprised.

I turned around and left them to it. What a fucked up war this was.

25

The company commander who deployed initially with the theatre reserve battalion was replaced after just three weeks – I believe he had another posting to fulfil elsewhere. Either way he was a real loss, and I was pretty devastated to see him go. We worked like clockwork together and had started to achieve some tangible results. We spent his three weeks patrolling hard, day after day, in an effort to reassert ISAF dominance in the area. When he left he was replaced with someone not quite up to his capabilities, who became my fourth company commander in five months.

At that stage it became clear that myself and the senior NCOs in the company, under the guidance of the company sergeant major, were going to have to dictate battle tempo for the new chap, who wanted time to 'bed-in' that simply was not available.

Almost every single patrol came under contact that would require some sort of intervention from Baz or me. It was a busy time, and the days generally blurred into one. The moments that particularly stick in my mind are inevitably those in which I played a slightly more prominent role, but it would be wrong to say I was central to our efforts.

One patrol stands out as being particularly bizarre. Baz and I were part of an assault group that was attacking an enemy position from a flank. As we were moving into position we passed a chicken coop. With a loud crack, a round bisected me and Baz, hitting a chicken at our feet, which squawked in a flurry of feathers and keeled over. Baz found it hilarious. Anyway, later in this patrol we came under contact again.

Contacts can be all bullets, sweat and adrenalin. They can also be long, drawn-out affairs with sporadic fire over several hours, at which point they become more akin to a game of chess as both the hunters and the hunted try and locate each other. There can be time for a cigarette; there can be time to get out a small computer and download a feed from a jet in the sky that enables me to have a bird's-eye view of the battlefield.

This particular patrol was certainly one of the latter type. Baz and I were minding our own business in a bit of cover by a compound, waiting for a jet to come on station to engage the enemy position. All of a sudden, an insurgent popped up about 70m in front of me, firing an AK47 over the side of a compound towards another part of my split patrol, at a right angle to my position.

It was a gift. I slipped my safety off, raised my weapon and fired single shots at the back of his head. To my dismay he did not drop. Instead he looked confused for a second, then started turning around to engage me. I then fired three more shots at his body and somehow missed again! I was furious. Baz and I quickly shuffled backwards around the other side of the compound, out of his sight.

Baz was laughing so hard he could barely speak; I was embarrassed and humiliated.

Eventually the jet came on station, and my memory of the incident stops there, I think because I was too busy having a proper childish strop with myself.

When I got back to the patrol base I immediately went out to the HLS, pinned a handmade target to the HESCO bastion, paced out 25m and started practising my shot. It would never have passed UK standards (I was range staff qualified) but it enabled me to spend an hour sorting out my weapon sight. I had badly knocked it, so that rounds were completely missing the target. This gave me a bit of a shot across the bows in terms of equipment husbandry, and I spent the rest of that day stripping, cleaning and reassembling everything, from my radios to my magazines. It was embarrassing, but I had learnt another lesson and got away with it.

Amongst the enemy I had some sympathy for the moderates, who would pick up an AK47 and engage a patrol base for $20. They believed the screeching sermons and the promise of a better life that was to be had in the dusty desert of southern Afghanistan; more importantly, they needed the cash. The mullahs were a different matter, preaching their rubbish not because they believed in it, but because they wanted to keep their people oppressed and in their control. And then there were the enforcers; the local warlords. They spent the majority of their time going around the population cutting off hands and abusing the children of families they deemed to be assisting ISAF. They claimed a deep affiliation to their jihadist cause, but usually only when someone was watching. Almost all the warlords I had encountered during my 2008–09 tour had some sort of pornography and Western music on their phones, plus videos of themselves getting pissed up together somewhere in the Middle East. They, as ever, actually believed in nothing at all beyond themselves.

In early August 2010, I was holed up in a compound for

four days as we provided flank protection for some engineers who were building a new patrol base along the banks of the NEB Canal, about twelve kilometres from PB Khaamar. We were under sustained attack for a good proportion of the time we were there; the rest of the time we were all on guard anyway. It wasn't much fun, although the compound did have a well that we could wash in.

I remember after one particularly heavy engagement onto the compound, we received intelligence that the fighters in the area were having a prayer at last light before planning to overrun us that evening and 'slaughter all the infidels'. This was standard banter.

While on watch as the sun went down, a sniper on the roof called for me to come and take a look at what he could see. I crawled up and along the roof and lay next to him, looking down his sights. To my astonishment, we could see two men standing in front of about twenty others, clearly leading a service of prayer.

Without wanting to leap to the obvious conclusion, I rushed back down and collected a piece of equipment that essentially enabled me to see this target more clearly. It used thermal imaging, and allowed me to identify the distance and actually record on video what I could see.

With this better sight, I could clearly see that the two taking the service were armed with AK47s. Some of the others seemed to have them on their backs, but I could not identify them so easily. Some did, and some didn't.

This particular target was no doubt going to be hard to engage. I needed a very low collateral weapon that could have pinpoint accuracy, which was also silent so as not to spook the gathering – an airframe of some description might do that.

Fortunately, at the time the British Army had in its arsenal a now de-classified weapons system called Exactor. It was used rarely, had been designed in Israel, and was extraordinarily effective at what it did. Its missiles were ground-launched, manoeuvrable while airborne, and had an extremely small explosive charge. I was trained and qualified in its control, and I selected it as the weapon for this engagement. It also had a camera in its nose, so you could see the guy just before he got hit.

I had to move fast – this gathering was not going to last forever. But striking this group of Taliban in what was – given their brazen nature – quite clearly their 'safe place', with this degree of accuracy, was going to have a serious effect on their morale, and consequently their desire to attack our compound that night.

It was an extremely technical engagement which I will not go into, but I cleared the airspace and authorized the release of the weapon as I observed the target. On my imaging device, I recorded the missile going directly into the chest of one of the mullahs, and the rest of the group running away, indicating low collateral damage. The sniper with me (they are odd at the best of times) seemed disproportionately impressed!

26

By now we had initiated a much more targeted patrols plan that involved multiple patrols moving in different areas, in an attempt to channel and flush out enemy fighters into a dry wadi just north of the Jungle. It was hideously exposed for over 700m at its widest point – there was nothing there, just baked earth. I would have a joint fires plan ready to go, and as soon as the fighters were squeezed into the wadi, I could engage them at will. Here they had no cover and no civilians to hide behind. This more aggressive approach started to have significant success.

In mid-August, I was patrolling with a section just south of one of our satellite patrol bases, probing the Jungle in an attempt to squeeze some fighters into the wadi. Suddenly, RPGs whistled overhead and we came under small-arms fire. We began a controlled fighting withdrawal back to a main track that we had just left. From there we could patrol in an orderly fashion back to base, under the watchful eyes of the PB.

We were peeling one at a time back up the track, still under fire. I was running past the other members, looking for a place to break left or right, when I heard that fateful call come up the line behind me.

'Boss, boss, man down, man down.'

I spun around, and heard the section commander call for

us to go firm. I made my way back along the now stationary patrol. The call had come immediately after an RPG had detonated behind me. There was silence – no screaming. My blood felt chilly despite the forty-degree heat; I could feel the colour draining from my face as I prepared myself for the human mess I was about to encounter.

I was pleasantly surprised to see just one man on the floor, being spoken to calmly by the patrol commander. It was the company sergeant major, who had come along on the patrol for a 'treat'. His fingers were clasped onto the right-hand side of his neck, a fair amount of blood welling from underneath them.

The sometimes tricky relationship between senior rankers and junior officers has always been one of great amusement to both groups. I had a strong relationship with this company sergeant major. I thought he was a good fighting man who enjoyed experiencing all that the frontline operations had to offer. He clearly loathed me for my commission, my education and because I was from the south of England, but underneath he seemed to have a grudging respect. We had some fairly strong banter in camp, particularly after the 'disco legs' incident on the walls of PB Khaamar that Sunday morning.

The company sergeant major was taking his injury in good spirits. The medic pushed past me and started ripping open her pack and digging out the trusty British Army first field dressing. As soon as an injury was reported I would warn on my fires net that we may require the MERT. This was one of the important jobs on patrol, so obviously when I could, I left it to Baz! When someone has suffered a catastrophic injury and time is of the essence, we needed to clear the airspace and identify, mark and secure a landing site (possibly using attack helicopters to suppress enemy positions).

The medic called me over.

'Boss, we've got a tricky one here,' she said, and showed me the wound. Essentially a fragment from an RPG had taken off a fleshy part of the company sergeant major's neck. The wound was bleeding, but it wasn't the catastrophic bleed that one would reasonably expect. I soaked up the blood in the dressing, and each time, before the blood obscured my vision, I could clearly see his carotid artery still intact, pulsing away, with a small scratch on it.

The medic told me that in her mind this was a Category A wound, requiring the MERT. If the sergeant major so much as coughed too vigorously, that carotid artery might split, and he would bleed out within a couple of minutes. The trouble with this scenario was that we were still dealing with sporadic fire and had only just about escaped the clutches of a clearly pre-prepared ambush, and this meant it was too dangerous to conduct a helicopter extraction unless the casualty was actually dying.

I assessed the options with the patrol commander and my battery commander on my radio, and we got the MERT airborne from Camp Bastion with one of the emergency Apaches.

But Baz was clear, and eventually so was I, that we could not land the MERT into a hot HLS if the casualty was not in immediate danger of death, which strictly speaking he was not. The area was riddled with the enemy, but I contended that as our PB was due west of where we currently were, we might be able to extract north, quietly, handrailing the wadi. We would then have to cross the wadi ourselves before linking up with some armoured vehicles on a main road to transport the company sergeant major back to PB Khaamar. The rest of us would walk back.

Firstly, I had to stop the contact. I couldn't see the enemy, but I needed them to back off and give us some space and time to get this right. I ordered two rounds of 105mm high explosive into a field I could see, just next to the enemy position. We remained firm and listened for enemy movement. They had either left, or were now sufficiently put off from following us.

I told the sergeant major the plan. He was slightly unaware of the precariousness of his position, as he could not directly see his own wound. The medic told me that if we came under contact on the way back, she was seriously worried about him reacting in a way that would burst his artery.

The company sergeant major started arguing the toss with the section commander and the medic, saying he was fine and didn't need special treatment. The section commander was one of his blokes and revered him – he wasn't going to disagree. I intervened and told the sergeant major that we were sticking to the plan I'd outlined and that was that. I was going to make his weapon safe (unload followed by a load, to remove a round from the chamber) so that he could not use it, and he was going to walk next to me the entire way back to the road, as a walking casualty. There, he was going to be met by a vehicle and taken back to PB Khaamar.

'You can hold my hand if you feel you need to,' I finished.

With that, we started moving out. We patrolled north at a painstakingly slow pace. It's tougher than it sounds to walk slowly when you feel you are being hunted, but the HE seemed to have got the message across for now.

As we came to the top of the large north–south running wadi, it was clear that we would have to cross some open ground before turning due south and linking up with the patrol that had pushed out in armoured vehicles from the main PB. It was the same wadi we had been pushing the Taliban into to try and trap them, and the irony was not lost on me.

The first three British soldiers and the medic ran across the open ground at the top end of the wadi to secure the far side. Baz shuffled over on his own and came under contact. The ANA, in their usual fashion, legged it across the gap through the fire. How none of them got hit I had no idea.

That left myself and the sergeant major on the eastern side of the wadi by ourselves. We had a bit of a laugh as to what we were going to do now. The fire was not intense but sporadic, and the whip-crack was pretty loud, so they were reasonably accurate today.

Our options were limited. We could wait for some sort of joint fires platform that I knew Baz would now be requesting on his net; or I could launch some more HE into the bottom of the wadi. But I could not see the target area clearly, and at the southern end there were definitely family dwellings.

The sergeant major wanted to go for it; he was becoming impatient with a desperately slow patrol which, even before contact, he'd been finding tedious in the extreme. I remember at that moment thinking that impatience out here leads to mistakes, and someone getting shot. But he wanted to get moving, and gave me a wry smile with a little wink, implying that I would be a bit of a wimp if we didn't go now.

'Fine,' I said, 'but you cannot run. If that thing splits, you really have got something to worry about.'

We slowly walked out into the open ground, and I grabbed

his webbing with my left hand to stop him running. This was so that I could engage with my right-handed weapon, but as I remarked to the sergeant major at the time, it also meant that any rounds coming in our direction would strike him before they struck me.

We came under almost immediate contact. I returned fire in the direction of the firing point, although I could not identify it straight away. The remainder of the patrol engaged from their covered position and we slowly walked the seventy or so metres across the open ground, waiting to be shot.

I was extremely frightened, while the sergeant major clearly thought it was a laugh. To this day, I remember vividly the look on his face as he turned towards me with that crooked smile that had been punched a few times in his youth and said, 'You can run if you want, sir.'

'Fuck off, Sergeant Major,' I replied.

My entirely false bravado made me feel better, and eventually we reached the other side. It was a very odd experience, not running when one is under contact. I don't think I had done it before and certainly haven't since. I could feel the fear driving through my veins, urging my muscles to run. Walking required discipline and a courage I thought I had lost after Bing's death.

Since time immemorial, I suspect junior officers like me have always performed above their very average natural ability or fortitude because a sergeant major's wrath or disdain was more frightening than anything the enemy could do to you.

But this day something else clicked in my head. After Bing's death, I had struggled. I now knew the risks, and couldn't close my eyes to them in the way I perhaps had before. But slowly and surely I had forced myself to be brave again over the last month or so. Today, on my painfully slow walk over the wadi, I had retained the discipline to face incoming fire and operate at the standards I had always tried to achieve throughout my short and unremarkable career to date. I felt I had crossed a threshold. It had taken me a month or so, but I was now back and feeling up for the fight again, just as I had when Bing was with me. It's hard to put into words but I felt better, and confident, for the first time, that I might actually see out this tour.

27

Baz was not so lucky as he wrestled with the same feelings. Around the time of the sergeant major's injury, I bumped into him outside our tent after a morning patrol. I was heading off for a shit, and he had just got off the phone – it was breakfast time in the UK. Again, the moment is imprinted on my mind. He was in his combat trousers and flip-flops, no top. Every time I saw him like this it struck me how skinny he was. With his mop of spiky hair, he resembled a bog brush.

He said to me his wife was expecting. He had previously spoken to me about how he found it tougher and tougher to go out of the gate, and now he was concerned that the news might affect him further.

I took him inside, fired up the stove for a coffee and cracked open another packet of Maiwand cigarettes. I told him I completely understood and that I pretty much felt the same every single day. I thought about doing the whole officer piece, saying it was a noble fight and all the rest of it. But Baz deserved better than that.

'If I could go home right now I would,' I said. 'I fucking hate it. I actually shit myself on patrol when you weren't here.'

After a period of thoughtful silence watching the stove bubble away, Baz remarked how awful it would be if, having endured all that we had, we ended up getting killed right at the end of our tour.

'Yeah, thanks, mate,' I said dryly.

I said that I didn't feel we had an officer–soldier relationship any more and that our mutual experiences were so defining, so deep, that I was not going to tell him what to do, and neither was I going to tell anyone else about it. I said to him that while I felt exactly the same as him, I was in a different position, given my rank, experience and conduct expectations.

The truth was that in the Army I did have my suspicions that the officer corps could sometimes be too much about mess dress and sucking up to the CO, and too little about sacrificing your time and energy almost exclusively for those under your command. This is a terrible generalization, but I was coming across my fair share of examples. I saw my role very differently, but my way was not always the best way – I freely admit that. I was too involved, too close to the men, too keen to get stuck in.

The answer was probably somewhere in the middle. Most of the officers were much better than me, but I always felt the privilege of commanding men weighing heavily upon me. I felt unworthy in a way, and may have over-compensated.

I think a lot of it was to do with the fact that I saw myself as a soldier really, not an officer. I was not comfortable with people assuming I was above them. Perhaps this was because of my internal struggles, which were a great source of humility. It is tough to tell someone off when, as a grown man, you can't leave the shower block without washing your hands ten times.

I found that my natural home in the Army was with the corporals and bombardiers more than anyone else – including the senior NCOs and officers. These junior NCOs were my age; I went drinking with them; they knew about my oddities and didn't care; they were my mates. I loved being on patrol with them. They would call me Johnny and not 'sir'. I knew this was wrong, but throughout my time in the Army I cannot recall a single moment where I detected a lack of respect from anyone, even if from one or two it was begrudging. I had a sort of brutal honesty, which I think they liked.

I suppose, ultimately, I considered myself as one of them who had just got a bit fortunate because I had managed to bluff my way into Sandhurst and beyond. Above all I suppose I respected the junior ranks, and treated them accordingly. I would never let a soldier leave my office after a difficult performance review or conversation until they completely understood and agreed with me. This was, admittedly, odd; some in the Army seem to get off on giving a good bollocking. But I just did not feel it was my place to do so – I would far rather persuade someone of their errors, with them totally understanding what they had done wrong, thus giving them a chance to avoid doing it in future and improve on their performance.

I looked on other officers, who enjoyed losing their temper and ordering people around, with a mix of bemusement and sympathy.

'Baz, I can't change now, mate,' I said to him. 'You know what I'm like. I'm gonna go out. I can take both radio sets and do it myself, using you in the Ops room.'

We finished our conversation and I went for a run around the PB without my music, so I could think.

Baz was one of the bravest men I knew. I reflected on our time together. He was a deeply professional man. I had liked and respected him from the start, and indeed came to love him in the years ahead. He has more loyalty, devotion and courage than I will ever have and we shared some life-changing moments. He is just so selfless – always the one who would move position, potentially exposing himself to enemy fire, to get a better signal for our radios, as he barked orders that would rain death on our adversaries. He never wanted me to look bad (quite some task). He was a genuine privilege to command. I will never forget his actions that summer.

My first patrol without Baz felt extremely lonely. Up to that point I had been childishly reassured by the knowledge that Baz was there to sort it all out if I cocked up. Patrols were doing things that *relied* on me executing a joint fires plan to get us out of trouble, rather than being overrun and massacred. The sustained pressures of working with patrols who would deliberately do dangerous things because they knew that you – as an individual – would get them home safe, was extraordinary. Previously I had shared that with Baz. Now it was mine alone. I felt an overwhelming pressure on me to perform that I hadn't truly felt earlier in the tour, even though it was most certainly there.

As an officer, I could sometimes be lazy with my kit and equipment, but now it was all down to me I became obsessive about checking batteries, sights, firing pins and the like. The experience made me a better soldier.

28

My birthday had come and gone. I was twenty-nine years old. The Afghan summer was, perhaps, finally beginning to turn. The heat had come down to the upper thirties and, crucially, nights were cooler; allowing deeper, more restful sleep between patrols.

The patrol tempo itself increased, as we felt we were beginning to get on top of the enemy in the Jungle. As we headed out on one morning patrol I realized it was the August bank holiday weekend in the UK. The Barbican in Plymouth would be a scene of carnage by the end of the day.

We were conducting a standard doubled-up patrol (about twenty blokes), led by the company commander with the newly healed company sergeant major in tow. We patrolled into an area that had previously been heavily occupied by the Taliban, but was now much quieter after recent weeks of fighting. Arriving before first light, we watched the locals conducting their morning routine before revealing ourselves and chatting to a few of the landowners. They were happier, but stressed that the Taliban had not gone away for good.

We had just begun our extraction back west towards our PB when an RPG flew straight into a group of Afghan soldiers at the rear of our patrol, and was followed up with bursts of automatic weapon fire into all of us. Not surprisingly, the patrol immediately sustained multiple casualties.

At the precise moment of impact from that RPG, I was mid-way across a 500m wide field, ploughed and ready for planting. I followed the correct drills as I swivelled to my left in the direction of the lone firing point to the south, and dropped to one knee to start engaging the enemy with my weapon. After a moment, I realized I couldn't hear anyone else returning fire, and I looked around me.

For reasons I could not fathom then or since no one else returned fire. The troops in front of me had forgotten all their training and legged it to a ditch about 300m in front. Simultaneously, the troops behind me had run 300m in the other direction to a ditch we had passed before entering the field.

I was alone in the middle of a field, now the sole target of enemy automatic-weapon fire.

As I threw myself to the ground, I could hear that the group behind me were dealing with a Category A injury to an Afghan soldier; the others seemed to be walking wounded. The rate of fire from the enemy increased substantially – either because they knew we had taken a casualty, or they could see me alone in the field, I could not tell which.

I was lying face down in the dirt. I tried to get up a couple of times, but found myself instinctively ducking down again as rounds ripped past my head.

It took almost all my courage to change magazines and get up on one knee and put some rounds into the enemy position, but this seemed to anger the enemy and their fire increased, now from a second position.

The rounds were 'bracketing' me – meaning some were landing to the left of me and some to the right. The Taliban usually had very poor or no sights on their weapons, but if they bracketed the target, they could correct their fire until they hit it. It was clear that sooner or later one of these rounds was going to find me.

I was totally fixed in position, on my own, being used as target practice by the enemy.

I thought the only thing that would definitely stop a round with my name on it would be my helmet. I changed my body position to ensure that my helmet was facing the enemy, and got as low as I could between two ploughed furrows. I don't know what the fuck I was doing. I suppose I thought that if I hid, the enemy might stop shooting me. They were stupid, but perhaps not that stupid.

To my left, I could see a medical evacuation party who were now going to box round me behind some compounds, with their casualty. They clearly had no idea I was there, or had forgotten me in the mayhem.

I was convinced I was going to die. I could not move. I'd be dead if I had just got up and bolted. The rounds were now single shot from these two same enemy positions, trying to pick me off. They were kicking up the dirt around me. I hoped death would be painless but I suspected it wouldn't be. I've never been so scared, before or since. People talk about what comes into your mind when you are about to die. Some mention poignant things like their mother, or their children, some think of regrets. Well, I may be a bit too simple, but I just wondered how much it was going to hurt.

But then that old fighting spirit came to me again. For some reason, I thought of my forefathers, who had died so bravely at Normandy. I don't know why I always thought of them. I remember as a boy learning about the war, struggling to understand the commitment required to lay down your life on the altar of your country's freedom. I thought most of them probably died like this. Not in some glorious charge; not with others watching them sacrifice all they have for their freedom. Just shit scared. On their own.

Again, for some strange reason I thought to myself, Make sure you die like a man. Don't embarrass yourself.

I kept trying to crawl around into a fire position so I could see the enemy properly, but every time I did that the rounds seemed to get closer. While attempting this, I did finally spot some action in the fire team to my front. A young lad on the end of the patrol had seen me, and he was frantically calling his section 2IC to come and take a look.

The section 2IC just stared at me, mouth agape. It then clicked that the only person who was going to get me out of this was myself; no one was going to do it for me. The guys' immediate reaction to leaving someone behind was to panic; the patrol commander was busy sorting out the Cat A casualty. I had the radio on my back and the skills to bring down some heavy fire onto the enemy position. I resolved to blast my way out of this, or at least try.

I stopped using my personal weapon, and instead I pulled my map out of my trouser pocket. I had a good look at where I was and where the gun battery was located. I was so nervous my fingers were damp with sweat and my markings on the map smudged as I tried to read them.

The guns had performed so well for me on this tour. I could bring them to bear relatively quickly and land a couple of rounds of HE in the field to my front; that should give the enemy a shock and enable me to run.

As luck would have it, I was directly on 'line gun-target' – an imaginary line that you could draw on a map through the gun line and the target. This meant that any over-shoot would land directly on me, and given that I was in the 'beaten zone' (the oval shaped area that you draw in your mind over every target to allow for minor errors), the risk was extremely high.

I could drop the rounds short of the target, but then they would land in some dwellings, and I would not be able to see fall of shot. I grudgingly accepted in my mind that to use artillery in this engagement would be foolish.

My heart sank a little, as I couldn't think of another quick option that would give me an opportunity to escape. But now, quietly determined to try and fight my way out of this situation, I decided to go with the last resort. My radio was capable of being retuned and talking to aircraft. Retuning it would mean exposing myself to the enemy and increasing my chances of getting picked off, but if I did I could talk to the controlling air station and request some sort of emergency platform to assist me.

I was aware that this was a risk. I did not want to overplay my situation – was I really cut off? I would hate to cause a fuss for nothing. But I did not want to die.

I opened my bag and fiddled with the bloody annoying LCD display to flick onto the air net. Out were the days of dials and knobs; in were buttons and LCD displays, which were not particularly good when one is overcome by sweat and fear.

I calmed myself down, changed the net and put a call out to the controlling joint fires station.

'Hello, any call sign, any call sign, this is Witchcraft four-three. Requesting immediate emergency CAS. Man isolated on his own in contact.'

The fire from the enemy positions seemed to pick up a little, as if they were listening. I was focused now on getting out. I ignored it.

Nothing came out of my radio.

I took out my compass and made sure my SATCOM was facing south-west. It wasn't. I turned my body, exposing my front above the furrow, and tried again.

'Hello, any call sign, any call sign, this is Witchcraft four-three. I require immediate emergency CAS. Man isolated on his own in contact.'

'Hello, Witchcraft four-three, this is Widow four-zero. I have you lima charlie [loud and clear]. I will rebroadcast your call. Standby.'

Before they could talk to me again, a thick American drawl came over the net.

'Hello, Witchcraft four-three, this is Dealer one-four. I am a Cobra gunship and Huey pairing. I am currently supporting an operation to the south of thirty-one west, I am transiting now to you, confirm location of man left behind.'

I gave the pilot a brief, including my own grid position, trying desperately not to sound like I was as scared as I was. I knew this was again being listened to in headquarters, and I didn't want to embarrass myself.

'Witchcraft four-three. Roger. If you look into the area of that grid there is a lone figure in the field, he is in the prone position facing south, isolated on his own.'

'Dealer one-four. Roger. Looking.' He came back on the radio to say, 'I've got two firing points in two separate compounds. I have a good contact with firing points; I also have what looks like good contact with friendlies in the treeline, engaging those firing points.' The pilot failed to identify me. 'Witchcraft four-three, this is Dealer one-four. As I approach can you confirm I am clear to engage targets with twenty mike mike.'

'You are not clear to engage!' I shouted quickly into the handset. 'You are not clear to engage.'

I was not content that he knew exactly where I was. There was a critical difference between a US Cobra and a UK Apache that I was aware of. The main 20mm armament cannot swivel on the Cobra, and as such it can only fire in the direction that the helicopter is heading. The helicopters were approaching from the south; any splash from the target, or slight misunderstanding of my positon, and he would hit me.

I calmly (or so I thought) did a proper, line-by-line talk-on to my position. He finally identified me using his thermal imagery. I had no idea that UK camouflage was so good.

'Er. OK, I now have contact with a lone individual closer to the firing points to the south in the prone position. I believe he too is facing south, in the middle of that field.'

'Roger. That individual is me,' I said.

'Ah, OK, roger, roger.'

The pilot seemed not to have realized this before but now his tone became more urgent. I was feeling deeply uncomfortable with this particular control. You can often sense how an engagement is going to go by the nature of your conversation with a pilot or gunner. If you both quickly recognize the same points on the ground, and the talk-on to targets flows easily, you start to build confidence in each other. This had not happened in this case.

I gave the helicopter his five-line fire control orders as he completed a seemingly endless loop behind the target, out to the east, and lined himself up for a north–south line of attack.

All the while the enemy continued to engage. It was odd, because usually when a helicopter turned up the firing stopped, but with a casualty and a man isolated on his own, they thought we were trapped. It was bloody noisy, and I was struggling to hear everything on the radio.

Finally, in the distance I could see the Cobra slowly turn to run in. I still wasn't one hundred per cent happy. Fuck it, I thought, better safe than sorry. I threw a smoke grenade just in front of my position, even though I knew this would draw further fire.

'That red smoke, red smoke is me. The red smoke is friendly forces. How copy?'

'Roger. Red smoke friendlies. Am I clear to engage?'

I still felt uncomfortable but I was going to unleash him anyway. The stakes were too high.

'A-Firm. You are clear to engage twenty mike mike. Call engaging.'

'Am I clear to engage?' he shouted back, double checking. He was clearly uncomfortable as well.

'Witchcraft four-three, A-firm. Dealer one-four, you are clear to engage with twenty mike mike. Call engaging.'

'Roger. Engaging now.'

The sound was deafening. All hell broke loose as the gunship's Gatling vomited ammo right over my head. The rounds were not going into the target (later I found out there were families in the compounds the Taliban were using as firing points), but were tearing up the ground no more than 80m to my south.

For a second I was confused about who the fuck was firing where. I thought the enemy had wheeled out one of the 12.7mm Dushka machine guns they saved for special occasions. But then I looked up and could clearly see the Cobra spitting lead into the ground. It was now or never.

I got up and ran for the ditch to my front, where a collection of soldiers were now simultaneously engaging the enemy positions with machine guns. It was the noisiest battlefield I had ever heard.

I've never been very quick on my feet, and this was no exception. It was only 300m or so, but it felt like a bloody long way. I didn't feel out of breath but my legs were very heavy indeed and the ground was thick. As I ran I braced for the pain of a bullet ripping through me. I tried not to think about it, but it was tough.

With the terrain and the weight of the kit, it took me about a minute to cover the distance. It was a very noisy minute.

I dived into the ditch on my arse, behind the machine gunner.

'Fucking hell, boss, that was like something out of a film,' said a soldier I didn't recognize.

'Let's get the fuck out of here, lads,' I said. Oh, how I missed Baz.

The Afghan soldier who was hit in the initial contact was deteriorating fast. I made my way up the drainage ditch to find the company commander. He wanted to get an HLS into the field behind us, but although the firing had abated as soon as I hit the ditch I advised him that the MERT may well come under contact again. I did not think the enemy position had actually been hit.

'The ANA guy's not going to live, Johnny. I want you to use a precision weapon on that compound,' he told me. 'I need you to get the MERT in.'

The MERT was already wheels up from Bastion. The Apache that always accompanied it was now trying to get hold of me on the same frequency that I was talking to the Cobra on. I told him to stand by. I needed to give the guns new firing points too, but I'd been too busy to update them since I had been left behind. If it all went terribly wrong, I could potentially require them.

The Cobra was relieved by the Apache and requested leave from my call sign. I thanked the pilot for his efforts and then heard Baz take control of him as he exited my airspace and headed back to Marjeh, where he was supporting an operation. It was comforting to hear Baz's voice down the line. It was clear this Afghan's life rested on our ability to neutralize a couple of targets and bring in the MERT.

I walked away from the company commander and asked the gun line to wait for an update. They acknowledged and understood immediately.

'Hello, Ugly five-one,' I said to the Apache pilot, 'this is Witchcraft four-three, how copy?'

A posh British voice came back immediately. I was always surprised by the comforting calmness the Apache pilots projected to those of us stuck in the chaos of the explosions and the shootings.

'Hello, Witchcraft four-three, this is Ugly five-one. I have you lima charlie.'

'Witchcraft four-three, roger. Confirm you are happy with the AO and the situation update with this call sign.'

'Roger. I have had an update from Witchcraft four-three alpha [Baz] and am happy with friendlies, happy with possible firing points to the south.'

'OK. I am not the JTAC; I am close-combat attack-qualified, so I will give you a five-liner to confirm.'

'Roger.' Baz was the Joint Terminal Air Controller; I was not.

'I have a Cat A casualty requires immediate CASEVAC from an HLS I will mark to the west. Firing points in and around the south of that position. They are sporadic at present, but will no doubt increase once the MERT is here.'

'Roger.'

'Standby for five-liner – you are to call for clearance.'

With that I gave him the five-line engagement order. I repeated at the end of the call the request for clearance.

The MERT was seven minutes out. I ran (shuffled) back over to the company commander and told him. I indicated the HLS and asked for a man with smoke to mark it. I told him not to release the smoke until I said so – we didn't want to alert the enemy before the MERT was ready.

The MERT called to confirm the HLS and I shouted over at one of the lads to release the red smoke.

The MERT landed-on OK, but almost as soon as its wheels were down, a massive volley of shots rang out from the treeline to the south.

As a patrol, we were lined up along a berm with the Chinook behind us. We were slightly covered from view and fire, but not to any great extent. The blokes engaged these enemy positions, and a fierce firefight erupted. I looked at the company commander and requested clearance to engage with the Apache.

'Ugly five-one, you are clear to engage with thirty mike mike. Call engaging,' I shouted over the noise. Before I finished the call, the Apache's 30mm guns were rattling furiously.

'Engaging under card alpha [rules of engagement],' I could just about make out the pilot saying. 'The MERT is receiving incoming fire.'

Someone fired off an RPG from right next to me. I could not hear a thing.

I took a moment in the chaos and looked back over my shoulder at the Chinook. The boys were running a man on a stretcher out to it. Ahead of me I could see the splash of the 30mm eating into the wall of the compound. I scanned for any enemy 'squirting' from the target, ready to engage them with my rifle. We could not lose the Chinook.

The MERT pilot was ready to lift. He called for clearance on the radio. I was pressing it so hard to my ear that it must have looked like I was trying to insert it.

'Stand by to lift. Await my call,' I shouted. I yelled over at the company commander for an increased rate of fire. The patrol responded, as did the ANA. I could hear the Apache engaging as well. These enemy were giving it a good go. They wanted to down the Chinook.

'Ugly five-one, confirm you are engaging, I need to lift the MERT.'

'Roger. I have engaged three positions to the south. Do you require Hellfire?' he asked, talking about his guided missile system, which I could use as well.

I paused. The noise was insane – I could tell by the vibrations around my head more than anything, since the RPG had knocked out my hearing. The Apache was continuously firing above me. The MERT was turning and burning on the deck some 50m behind me. The entire patrol were engaging into the enemy positions from the berm-line I was crouched behind.

'Ugly five-one, no. Continue with thirty mike mike for now. MERT, you are cleared to lift. Cleared to lift!' I shouted.

In that one moment, I realized why I loved the Army so much. The teamwork was extraordinary. I distinctly remember thinking how brave those pilots were, sitting there with just a Perspex screen for protection, waiting for the command to lift. The lads all had their heads above the berm as they engaged the enemy position, determined to protect the helicopter. The pilot of the Apache gunship, coolly placing himself in harm's way to protect the MERT. Discipline; control; courage; professionalism; teamwork; sacrifice. The British Armed Forces codified in one moment of battle.

'Roger. Lifting now,' said someone very calmly into the radio.

The weight of fire increased – it was a bizarre incident. Usually the enemy would have desisted long ago. Usually if things kicked off to this extent it was because a commander was in the area and the local Taliban wanted to show off.

The Chinook raised and flared backwards. The noise remained intense. He continued to lift and eventually he was nose down, chugging away from the scene and back to Bastion. As the noise from the helicopter faded, so the enemy fire seemed to dwindle and stop.

By now we were only about two kilometres from PB Khaamar, and we started moving back in that direction, at a quicker pace now that the casualty was gone.

As we neared the base we came under contact yet again, but this was harassing fire and didn't feel particularly close. I stopped and urged the patrol to run past me back into the camp.

I could hear the Apache engaging.

'Ugly five-one, Witchcraft four-three. Can you confirm that is you into the original enemy position?' I asked.

'You've got enemy fire from one original position. I've engaged him under card alpha; I am going to put warning shots into the field behind you.'

'OK. Thank you. Cleared to engage under card alpha.'

The company commander ran past me. I told him what was going on and he was happy.

I was last man in. I hadn't had time to digest this manic

patrol when Baz came over to me, flip-flops and shorts on, with his radio in his hand.

'You are a fucking idiot,' he said to me. 'You are not going out again. No way. I'm not having it. These guys are a bunch of fucking idiots.'

'Calm down, mate. Not here,' I said, not wanting to cause a scene. He turned and stalked towards our tent.

I was slightly bemused that I was the 'fucking idiot', but was touched by Baz's concern for me. His behaviour was in stark contrast to the rest of the patrol as we stood and unloaded our weapons in the loading bay. After surviving a heavy contact, they had an overwhelming feeling of having got away with something, and the boys were understandably quite boisterous.

I headed back to the tent, unable to speak. I felt the blood run to my head.

I chucked my webbing and helmet onto my cot then flicked out the legs from the grip handle on my rifle and stood it up next to my bed. I looked at Mark's empty bed space. How I could have done with him today.

Then I wandered out to the back of the tent and sat on a brown 7.62mm ammo box. I pulled out my cigarettes – soaked with sweat and squashed. I tried to light one, but the sweat from my thumb had dampened the flint on the lighter. I couldn't get a flame out.

I put my head in my hands and shut my eyes, struggling to get a grip. I couldn't stop shaking. The stress of the joint fires as a solo effort; the experience of being left behind on my own; the repeated stamping on the monkey of fear in my head and keeping it under control – I think I was beginning to max out with what I could cope with. I could literally feel my head reaching saturation point.

Baz came in. He was never going to put his arm around me, but he silently offered me a lighter and I lit my cigarette. My hand was shaking more than usual; I couldn't get the butt into my mouth. Every time I closed my eyes I was back in the bloody field on my own. Baz sat opposite me, across the table we had made out of HESCO and plywood. He didn't know what to say.

I chain smoked three or four cigarettes and gently forced my mind to settle down.

I had, by this point, come close to being killed a few times, and my coping mechanism was very simple. The more I thought about it, the worse it got. So I forced myself to think about other things. If I was struggling to get out of the cycle of thoughts about dying, I would get up and do something else – physically move my body, go for a run. Eventually I settled down.

The company didn't do any more patrols that day, so Baz put a film on for us both to watch on his laptop. After the film had finished, the company sergeant major appeared at our tent door.

He asked Baz if he could come in – something quite rare from a fairly rambunctious Warrant Officer Class 2. He found me out the back in my usual place, cleaning my kit and clearing some markings off my map.

'All right, sir – mind if I sit down? You probably don't want to see another soldier from this unit right now.'

'Of course not, Sergeant Major – please do.'

'One of my blokes has just told me that we left you behind today. Were you ever going to say anything to me?'

'I didn't want to say anything – it was a genuine fuck-up in the fog of combat, and I didn't want to make a fuss.'

'OK. I'm sorry. I just felt I should come over and apologize.'

'Don't worry about it. I'm just going to try and forget about it and we'll go again in the morning,' I said.

'Do you want to come and talk to the company commander? He wants to see you. You did seriously fucking well today.'

'No – I'm going to spend some time with Baz, and then we'll go again tomorrow,' I replied. My relationship with the company commander was not strong, which is why he'd sent the sergeant major to see me rather than come himself.

'OK. Well, like I said, I'm sorry. Should never have happened.'

'No dramas. Move on.'

With that he left. He was clearly very uncomfortable.

In truth, I didn't need anyone to talk to me about it. I felt like I was now the senior, most experienced and – given my control of joint fires – the most capable soldier on the ground in this area of operations. If it was going to happen to anyone, it may as well be me.

And so much of this fucking war was luck.

29

Battle trauma, for me personally, was something I was simply not prepared to think about. I felt that if I opened that particular Pandora's box, I would not be able to shut it again. I had made a good friend early on in the tour. He was a good bloke – intelligent, thoughtful and a good soldier. He was brave, didn't flinch under fire. Baz, Bing and I would invite him into our tent to have a coffee and shoot the shit; we were all 'attached ranks' to this company group, rather than being a permanent part of the regiment, and shared a sort of camaraderie in that respect.

One day in July, one of the combat logistic patrols had issued us some new body armour plates. These were to complement our existing Osprey body armour system by slotting into our side pouches, to protect us from small-arms fire just under each arm.

I carried an awful lot of kit – plenty of ammunition as well as all of the comms kit and optics that I needed for my role – so I made the decision to not wear these plates. I assessed that I was slow enough as it was, and I did not want to be encumbered any more while in contact with the enemy. It was a calculated risk I was prepared to take.

My friend, however, decided the other way, carefully fitting his new plates into his Osprey to give him maximum protection. On our very next patrol he was shot in the side but the round pinged off his new plate.

Something in his head snapped. He had to be extracted as a casualty despite having no physical injury; he just could not compute what had happened to him. I went to see him as soon as we got back from the patrol. I can picture him now, sitting on the floor, leaning against the HESCO, with the medic, about to be evacuated by helicopter. It was perhaps the worst case of battle shock I had seen in a British soldier up to that point. I put my arm around him and consoled him, but spoke no words. It was devastating to see a man so strong, yet so completely broken by battle. It had a profound effect on me, and I suspect anyone who saw it. It demonstrated to me the vicious and unpredictable effects of trauma on the mind.

The Army had by now recognized that they must do something – anything – to try and mitigate the impact of mental trauma on our servicemen and women fighting wars overseas, very disconnected from the society from whose ranks they are drawn. But because the war was on the other side of the world and seemed so distant – despite attempts by our military and political leaders to relate it to domestic security – and perhaps because many just simply did not want to acknowledge what we were doing to keep them safe and to resource care correctly, mental health provision for armed forces personnel and their families at the time was woeful.

By 2010, the Army had introduced something called TRIM (Trauma Risk Management) practitioners – soldiers who would undertake a very brief training session before being expected to identify and report those at greatest risk of trauma in their unit for further attention from the medical officer or mental health teams in Bastion.

The first time I came across a TRIM practitioner was on a particularly bad day, back when the Royal Welch were still in PB Khaamar – right at the beginning of my tour. An engineering patrol was passing to the north of our patrol base along the road that runs alongside the NEB Canal when the road collapsed at a junction, and the armoured vehicle carrying six soldiers entered the water.

All of the soldiers managed to escape, except one who was trapped by his arm under the vehicle and could not get to the surface. Everything possible was tried to release him. It was a visceral struggle for life.

We landed-on an American MEDEVAC team at my HLS, and even considered using the helicopter to try and lift the vehicle just an inch, to allow us to get the soldier out. The Americans finally brought in some specialist equipment and we were able to free the man but by that stage there was no chance of resuscitating him. It was a devastating experience for all.

The man was brought back to the patrol base in a poncho – sometimes used as a body bag. The company commander and I picked him up and took him to the HLS, where we had called for a MERT to take the body back to Bastion. We had him on a stretcher, but the man and his clothing were almost entirely filled with water, and I could tell the stretcher was not going to take his weight for the short transfer to the helicopter.

As the helicopter landed, we picked him up again, but after a few steps the stretcher snapped. I caught the man's soaking and heavy body and, together with the company commander, carried him like a baby onto the CH-47 and gently placed him on a stretcher they had waiting in the back.

The helicopter took off and we ran back into the PB. The company commander asked if I was all right, and when I said I was he headed back to the Ops room. I went back to my tent and sat round with some of the boys, talking about what a shit day it was. I re-told the tale of the stretcher collapsing.

'You need to be trimmed, boss!' one of the sergeants piped up.

'Really?'

'Yeah. How did it make you feel?'

'Pretty shit.'

'There you go. You've been trimmed,' he replied, to inevitable laughter.

Funny, but not funny really. Tokenism dominated almost every approach to veterans' care and mental health, and the longer the tour went on the heavier the inadequacies of the care weighed on me.

30

As August turned to September, the fighting in northern Nad-e Ali did not simmer down as quickly as I had hoped. Instead, the Taliban adapted their tactics to keep us on our toes and we were faced with ever more complex ambushes involving IEDs and heavy machine guns. In the very north of the AO the sharpshooter, or 'sniper' as some persisted in calling him, was still operating and having some success in hitting his targets. This, along with other intelligence gathered by strategic assets, suggested that there was a specific cell of Taliban here, and that was why they were so robust and difficult to kill off. This was part of the reason we'd been given a small SAS team to help us in our mission. They had access to better intelligence, and would increase our capabilities when it came to targeting some of the key individuals in the area.

As mentioned previously, in my view the 'sniper' operating to the north of our AO was just a Talib who'd worked out how to use his sight and was a lucky shot. His comrades were fighters who specialized in the 'Beirut unload' method of engaging ISAF troops (firing an entire magazine around the corner of, or over the top of, a wall without looking through the sights), so I suspect he was slightly overrated. Nonetheless, we would be required to conduct dawn and night-time operations against a series of compounds in the area to try and find him, if not his cache of weapons. Sounds exciting. It wasn't.

In my previous tour, I had been attached to the Special Boat Service so I had some experience to draw on. The truth is, these types of units do extraordinary things on our behalf every single day to keep us safe. Nothing could ever diminish my high opinion and respect for them. They are simply the very best of us, and whatever time I spent with them was usually a privilege.

However . . .

On the second or third night after they arrived, a group of us were treated to a full and formal set of briefs for a very basic patrol to the north of the AO, from the sergeant major in charge of the SAS team. As we were listening to his orders, the PB came under a fairly sustained attack from small-arms fire. We weren't overly concerned, but I was granted an Apache that was on a neighbouring operation, to use if I required it.

The Apache turned up and the attack died down. The SAS sergeant major's orders resumed, but I was still exiting the attack helicopter out of our airspace after checking that there were no more targets available for them to engage. Subsequently, I came back halfway through the briefing.

The SAS 2IC stormed over to me.

'Where the hell have you been?' he said. I didn't think much of myself, but at the same time I wasn't used to an aggressive manner straight out of the blocks from someone I didn't know.

'Sorry, who the fuck are you?' I replied. Then I recognized him. 'Ah – you're the guy who's come up with the sergeant major. I've just been doing some controls – all that helicopter shit doesn't just happen by itself.' I was trying to be nice and diffuse his anger.

'Well, you need to be here from the beginning. It's orders. You're a fucking Rupert, right? You could learn a thing or two.'

There are not many occasions when I could legitimately say I was in the presence of greatness, but this was one. I was genuinely taken aback by how much of a cock the guy was.

I let it go. I wish I hadn't – I wish I could say I put him straight, but I was in shock. What actually happened on our patrol the following day was, therefore, beyond irony.

The plan was to push north into the area where the supposed enemy sniper was hiding out. Under cover of darkness, two sections of British and one section of ANA would patrol on foot into the village that the sniper was operating from. In my vehicle, along with Company HQ in their two armoured vehicles, I would patrol along the main road in the hope of coming under small-arms fire from said 'sniper'. The patrols on foot would then be able to identify the firing point and deal with the sniper in the village. Not a terrible plan.

The ground patrol duly went out and got into position. Upon first light the 'suicide squad', as I decided to rename us, started driving very slowly along the main road past the village.

No one shot at us, and under the pretext of visiting another patrol base, we continued on east until I was sure we were out of range of any small-arms fire from the village. We then 'leaguered-up' (found a good spot to park-up) and awaited our orders to drive back past the village again in the hope of drawing some fire, before returning to the patrol base.

I was watching my arcs, listening to the radio, when I heard of a contact come out of the village. I perked up and listened hard to the handset to work out what was going on. There's nothing worse than some guy coming on the radio and asking for a SITREP from you when you are in contact.

The three teams in the village had come under fire from a couple of firing points, and were looking to extract. I immediately moved our vehicles back onto the ridgeline and within range of our weapon platforms so we could provide fire into the village in support if required. While waiting, I also queued up some 105mm smoke to cover our imminent extraction.

Suddenly, a call came over the net asking the company HQ call sign to move into position directly in front of the village, on the road, to give the teams in the village some cover for extraction. Those on foot would then move in bounds to the vehicles and seek cover in the dead ground behind us, while those of us in the vehicles provided covering fire.

As we drove slowly into position, right in front of the village, on the road, the contact dropped temporarily. I saw the first man start heading for my vehicle. Both Brit teams were coming one after the other; apparently the ANA team had 'extracted another way' and were on their way back to the PB under their own steam. (They had legged it, again.)

Just as the last man exited the village to cover the 150 or so metres to the vehicles, the vehicles themselves came under more accurate heavy-weapons fire; the rounds were pinging off the outside of my Mastiff. I engaged with 105mm smoke to cover the withdrawal.

For some reason, the lads who had reached us had not immediately gone down into cover behind our vehicles. Instead a few were on the road itself, covering the remainder of their patrols.

'Open your fucking door, and tell them to get off the fucking road!' I told my driver, shouting to be heard over the noise of the bullets.

As the door opened I heard three 'Man down' calls, one after the other, from different soldiers. We had multiple casualties. That familiar feeling in my arms and legs started almost every time I heard that phrase, let alone three times.

The company sergeant major, who was providing top-cover from the vehicle with a .50 calibre, was yelling at his blokes to 'get the fuck off the ridge', and I remember hearing one of the soldiers encouraging his mate, who had clearly been hit, although I could not see any of this from my position in the passenger side of the second vehicle.

A guy just in front of my vehicle was attempting to set up a GPMG position to engage the enemy when he too was hit, and he dropped the weapon. He was picked up and dragged back over the ridgeline.

The SAS 2IC ran forward and grabbed the machine gun. He started firing it from the hip into the village. But what I couldn't understand was why he was still on the wrong side of the ridge – exposing himself to the enemy while firing the weapon in a way that meant he was never ever going to hit anything he was aiming at.

'Fucking hell, tell that twat to get off that ridgeline!' I shouted at the sergeant major.

The rate of fire was not dropping as the smoke started to take effect. I was not sure how but the Taliban always seemed to recognize when you had taken casualties. The SAS guy was still horribly exposed, trying to load another belt into the machine gun. I adjusted the point of aim for the three guns I had laid onto the smoke target and engaged with rounds of HE. We had now put in a call for emergency close-air support as well, and Baz was sorting that out. In the fog of war, it can be hard to recollect the exact sequence of events, but I remember what happened next as if it was yesterday.

I gave the order to fire, and while I did so the SAS guy in front of me ran back out in front of my vehicle to engage the enemy again, firing once more from the hip. He was either fucking stupid, or trying to win a medal. I said to the driver, 'Watch this, he is about to get hit.'

He was immediately hit and rolled forward; it looked like his right arm had been shattered.

'For fuck's sake!' I shouted, not only pissed off with him for getting shot but also because I was – irony of ironies – now going to have to go and get my friend from the night before. I opened my door, and as I did so a burst of automatic fire shot up the wing mirror inches from my face. I shut the door again.

'Don't go that way, sir!' shouted the sergeant major on top-cover.

'Thanks, sergeant major,' I replied. I think he was joking, or else he hadn't noticed the wing mirror incident. As I went to exit the Mastiff on the other side, another soldier bravely ran out and dragged this SAS guy back to my vehicle.

He was not unconscious, but was clearly in a lot of pain. He was pushed up to me and I grabbed him by the scruff of the neck and dragged him inside. He was covered in blood and pretty unresponsive. Making a quick assessment of the casualty, I told the driver and sergeant major that we would have to make a single vehicle dash back to camp to get this guy on a MERT.

The 105mm HE landed. I was going to be fully employed

with emergency first aid, so I yelled into the handset to Baz back in PB Khaamar.

'Those rounds are good but you are now the controlling station – I have taken a casualty in my vehicle.'

Baz had never fired the guns in his life. Should be interesting, I thought, as I started getting to work on the injured soldier. Finding that I could not move properly around the cabin, I quickly took off my body armour and helmet, completely trusting in the vehicle to provide my protection. The guy continued to be unresponsive, and there was a great deal of blood coming out of his arm.

I was worried he had been hit somewhere on his torso that I couldn't see, as had happened with Bing. Every time I touched him he recoiled in pain, and it was a struggle to check him over. I started looking down his back and ran my hands over his chest, feeling for blood; after a while in theatre one can easily tell the difference between the sticky, viscous nature of blood, and the slippery, cleaner nature of sweat. He groaned. I told him he should talk to me and I wouldn't have to move him so much. I asked him if he had been shot anywhere else other than his arm, and he said no.

His arm was limp. I tried to get a tourniquet on it to stop the bleeding but there didn't seem to be much bone matter there and I could not get it on properly. I sat behind him, pulled him into me and rammed my hand up into his armpit as tight as I could to try and stem the blood, even a little bit. It worked. I told the driver to get us back to camp as soon as possible, and the sergeant major to make sure the MERT was mobilized to pick the guy up. Over the speaker in the cab, I could hear the guns report to my call sign that they were ready to fire again, and I wondered what I should do – I could no longer see the target.

Unbeknownst to me, Baz had got eyes onto the target through a fast jet pod, and was happy to engage to break the contact permanently.

'You okay for Baz to engage?' the sergeant major asked. 'You'll have to decide between you.'

The sergeant major said the engagement was needed, and Baz got the rounds away. He told me later he had never been so nervous. I was nervous too, as I hugged this wounded soldier into me as tightly as I could, listening to Baz giving the order and waiting for the rounds to land and hear the result. Remarkably, they landed well, with one round directly onto a firing point. I knew Baz would never shut up about that, so if he hadn't seen it through the jet pod, we all agreed not to tell him.

We got back to the PB, where I passed the injured soldier out of the vehicle and made his weapon safe. He was taken in by the medic, given some morphine and stabilized. I thought he might lose his arm, but he would live. Baz controlled the MERT into the HLS and the three other casualties were all extracted. They had been very lucky – one suffered a shrapnel wound to his knee from an RPG, one was shot in the body armour, and one was shot in the helmet.

That evening the company HQ had a wash-up from the patrol. The SAS sergeant major was over in the corner of the room on the phone to his boss, explaining what had happened. I cringed as he used the line 'took it like a Special Forces soldier'.

After a week of normal patrolling, the company was asked to conduct another patrol under the auspices of the now lone SAS sergeant major. He was adamant that he had intelligence (that he couldn't possibly share) that there was a particularly unpleasant individual in a compound directly south of the NEB Canal.

To cut a long and tedious story short, we patrolled there before dawn and tried to wake the guy up with a few flash-bangs, before entering the compound and discovering it was, in fact, empty. This was becoming a bit of a theme. While I was waiting on the cordon, holding off an Apache to the south, far enough away that its noise wouldn't disturb the operation, I decided to scan the surrounding area with a device that can pick up heat signatures and has extremely good night-vision capability.

Looking along our planned route out, I found twelve areas of disturbed earth in the space of 200m – the most obvious IEDs one could hope to find. The reason this place was deserted was because it was an old IED factory, mined every-where. There was no one here. And there hadn't been for some time.

I told the sergeant major what I had seen on the radio, and asked him to come out of the compound to my position on the perimeter and have a look.

In agreement, we stopped the operation immediately, and he asked me if I would lead the teams out of the area by a safe route, given that I could use my device. It couldn't be used on the move, though, so while the rest of the patrol gathered themselves up, I mapped out where the IEDs were on a bit of card and plotted a route around them. It was night-time, and we were quite some way from the PB. If I brought the Apache into the overhead it would expose us, and while we were unlikely to come under contact, diving for cover – or any other slight deviation from the route – would set an IED off.

We moved out, everyone following me in single file as I

tried to remember where each of the signs of disturbed earth were. I ended up walking as close to the canal's edge as I possibly could without falling in, and remarkably we all got out of there safely.

Suffice to say, my confidence in the operational surge with this particular team was waning. It was a wildly different experience to my SBS tour.

Two days later the sergeant major conducted a small patrol to another ANA patrol base and, unfortunately, he didn't think to tell the ANA that they were coming.

The patrol was leaving early in the morning, and perhaps sensing my reticence, the sergeant major had not asked me to provide anyone to accompany them. The first I heard of it was when I was woken by a frantic signaller telling me that a patrol was under contact, with a British soldier seriously wounded, and could I sort out a MERT. I ran to the Ops room to discover that almost no one knew anything about this patrol, that it had been engaged by the ANA from the base they were heading to, and that one of the British soldiers had been hit by a 7.62 round in the shoulder in a so-called 'green on blue' incident.

After the patrol returned, and as the MERT lifted off with the wounded soldier, I had had enough and I got the senior NCOs around me for a chat.

'What the fuck is going on, lads?' I said.

Some of them were clearly a bit star-struck by the SAS team and were simply going along with it.

'I don't care who they are; we've been here for months now. You know how it works; you know we don't hit compounds like we did two nights ago – it was obviously a bad place. You know what the ANA are like. Now one of your blokes has been shot by them?'

The SAS sergeant major wandered over.

'Look, buddy,' I said, 'this is all turning into a bag of shit. I respect you and what you guys were trying to achieve, but this is nonsense.'

Nobody backed me up, seemingly too much in awe of the SAS team.

'What do you mean?' he replied, taken aback.

'I just completed a tour with a Special Forces Task Force. This is not that; this is not a company of SF soldiers. The Afghans are not Afghan SF soldiers – they are fucking stupid and they nearly killed a Brit this morning. We do not have the resources or the assets to properly conduct the sort of patrols you are trying, with a realistic chance of success, in a reasonably safe manner. We've been to half of these compounds before; we know where the IED belts are. Let's pause today and work out a better way forward tomorrow.'

'But the blokes want to come out,' the SAS man said to me.

'Of course the blokes want to come out with you. You're a warrant officer in the SAS. Don't be fucking stupid.'

He disagreed with me, and told me he planned to hit another compound that night in the north of the AO. I had been to precisely that compound before; it was deserted and had been for some time. Whatever intelligence he had on it was wildly out of date.

'I personally wouldn't, but I'm just the fires guy,' I said. 'Speak to the OC.'

That evening Baz came to find me in the Ops room.

'Boss, can I have a word?'

I assumed he had run out of porn or something, but instead he told me that the SAS sergeant major was waiting in our tent, demanding that Baz give him some joint fires kit so that he could 'drop' (some bombs) on his mission.

I went over to the tent.

'Everything OK, sergeant major?' I asked.

'I want to control the joint fires on this one, so I just want your lad to give me his 352 [radio].'

'No, buddy, we do the fires for this company in this AO. If the remainder of your squadron come up, then that is a different matter; you guys crack on. But while you are working with the company, I'm afraid that is my team's job.'

He exploded.

'You are starting to really piss me off, Johnny. I'm a fucking sergeant major in the British Army.' He stepped towards me.

I stood firm. 'Calm down,' I said, raising my hands, thinking the guy was going to lay me out. It was strange that he had got so cross, so quickly. 'Whatever happens now you are not going to get any kit off me or control any fires in this AO. Let's chat later,' I said, conscious I did not want to have a scrap with the guy in front of Baz. Baz stood up from his bed.

'Come on, let's chat later,' I said again. The sergeant major left.

To be totally fair to the guy, later that day he came over to me in the Ops room and we went outside for an 'Officer–senior NCO' chat. He apologized, stated he was under pressure, and that he'd felt I was deliberately trying to wind him up.

I promised him I wasn't. I told him of my first encounter with his 2IC, that had got us off to such a bad start, and I apologized because I had regrettably let this cloud my judgement. I also said I had been in the AO for nearly six months now – I knew it very well, and I was not prepared to take the risks he was prepared to for so little reward, because I knew them better than him. He accepted that.

We ended the conversation on good terms. A bizarre interlude in a bizarre war.

31

By September, we were beginning to get a bit more 'freedom of movement' across the AO. We could run logistics patrols to neighbouring patrol bases and even the ANA were beginning to get the hang of it, setting up a couple of shuras (meetings) in a nearby village for us to attend.

One day, right at the end of September, a logistics patrol was transiting along the main road running next to the NEB Canal, on their way back to their home base to the north of our particular AO. I was in the Ops room watching them through the base cameras. They were passing a dangerous spot, where I had been struck by an IED earlier in the tour. I wanted to react fast if we needed to assist them. I had also conducted multiple strikes into the uninhabited compounds just to the south of that 'vulnerable area', or VA, so had the targets on record.

Being hit by an IED is a strange experience. I was very lucky on all three occasions. I was caught in one that went off at the rear of the vehicle in front of me back in July. On another occasion the detonator went off under my vehicle but the main charge did not explode. On another occasion, it happened just behind me and I was not caught up in the blast.

The blast is a deafening bang, followed by darkness as the mud and smoke falls around you. The next seconds are horrible, as you call out to those around you to see who has been hit, and what carnage you might have to get involved with. But, like I said, I was lucky, and mine were all when I was in one of the new armoured vehicle fleet. If I'd been in a Snatch Land Rover, particularly for the first one, I and the soldiers I was with would probably not have survived.

I was watching this patrol both through a jet that Baz had on station, and through a balloon with a powerful camera on it that was now stationed on my PB. As the patrol went past the VA, they were caught in a complex ambush initiated by quite a small IED but followed up by accurate and sustained small-arms fire, suggesting pre-prepared enemy positions.

I continued to monitor by listening to the radios and watching the feeds on two TV screens in front of me. The patrol commander requested some sort of smoke screen to the south of his position, to enable him to extract.

One of the smoke rounds came in and malfunctioned, its white phosphorous capsules failing to eject. The round landed with some of the capsules still attached, seemingly onto the back of an enemy fighter in the prone position, engaging the patrol with a machine gun. It was complete luck; good in my case, bad in his.

Somehow he survived the initial impact of the carrier shell, perhaps it had actually landed right next to him, but now he was burning alive. All I could see on my screen was this guy rolling around on the ground, burning to death.

The Ops room was paralysed. The company commander looked at me.

'Johnny . . . ?'

I knew there was nothing I could do except hope the guy died quickly.

'Fuck it, he'll have to burn,' I heard myself say to Baz, and we watched him die on the screen.

The contact ended soon afterwards and we went back to the tent to have a brew and a smoke.

I think Baz was a bit taken aback.

'Do you ever wonder what we've become?' he asked.

'Not really,' I lied, and scratched another mark on the board where we recorded our 'kills', trying not to think about it. 'Don't feel bad, mate; they choose the fight, not us.'

I had come a long way; from the choirboy of my Strict Baptist youth to racking up my kills on a wooden board.

I got my trainers on and went for a run.

By late September, as the summer drew to a tired end, the fighting surge finally started to wane and we were coming under contact about once every other day. Initially I missed the daily contacts; time seemed to pass more slowly and I was getting bored.

I found myself starting to do that most awful of things; counting the days until I could go home. I had well and truly had enough, and I could feel the sands shifting inside of me. Now I was going out of the gates hoping not to come under fire; not a good place to be mentally.

I remember the first day that I did three patrols in a row without any contact with the enemy – they seemed to have had enough as well, and some would be heading back to the poppy fields. Winter was on its way, and so was the end of my tour.

I wondered what it might be like to return to England, to my home, to Felicity. I wondered how I would adjust.

32

The day we left PB Khaamar was a hard one. It was tough to leave because it was where we had been with Bing. His bed space had remained empty, with no one taking his place.

Baz and I had built a memorial to him. I'd had a brass plaque sent out and we mounted it on a concrete plinth surrounded by four 105mm carrier shells that had been brought in by the locals, trying to claim damages. We spent hours polishing up those shells with our small weapon-cleaning kits.

It felt surreal to be back in Camp Bastion. It was a totally different environment and I hated it. I was very grateful to all those there who had supported us so well on the front line, but I couldn't stand the place and all its formalities. Fortunately, I was not there for long, and before I knew it I was flying home.

We flew into Teeside Airport in early October. After the heat and dryness of Afghanistan, the immediate cool of England in the autumn was invigorating. Felicity met me at the airport. She was wearing her beautiful blue dress again. I can remember my first glimpse of her as if it were yesterday.

We got in the car and tried to talk about how she was. I did not want to talk about me, or explain anything that had gone on. I wanted to forget about it. I felt like I had landed on Mars.

We stopped at the first services we came to where, once again, I ordered about £15 worth of McDonald's. Again I had a couple of bites and couldn't eat any more. We had a long drive ahead and I just wanted to get home and get out of my uniform. I knew it was going to be a difficult transition back to a normal life. I wanted to get on with it.

Regimental post-tour shenanigans are always a drag. I found dealing with the return home from war a very personal struggle, and these collective social events did very little for me.

Baz and I went our separate ways as soon as we touched down in the UK, as he was returning to the Queen's Royal Lancers. I missed him painfully. During the waiting in Bastion and the journey home, we had spent hours in each other's company without saying a word, just grunting to each other, trying to make each other laugh. Once we were 'off the line' we felt Bing's absence acutely.

It didn't help that many people in my regiment did not know how to treat me, and seemed very wary of me. I couldn't work out why at first. I thought I had had a very ordinary tour, but it seemed that mine had been rather extraordinary; not through any skill or doing of my own, but simply because of the sheer amount of time spent in contact with the enemy. I later learnt that I had fired more HE rounds than the rest of the FST commanders in Helmand put together. At a lunch for me to say goodbye to 3 RHA, the CO said in his speech about me that he had done some research around the Army, and that in his mind I was 'probably the most combat-experienced terminal controller in the Army today.'

It wasn't much to be proud of. The reality was that I was the one coming home without my Ack, and the duties associated with that would remain with me for life.

I had already seen Bing's parents, Mike and Ann, during my mid-tour break, but that did not make it any easier when I saw them again at the regimental homecoming. We marched through Sunderland – the adopted home city of 4th Regiment Royal Artillery – and were then treated to a horrific night out, as an entire nightclub was hired for the blokes. I drank myself into oblivion, and Felicity carried me back to our hotel.

I was shortly leaving the regiment to return to 29 Commando in Plymouth, where I was being posted to a desk job as the Regimental Signals Officer. It was a joke to all – me and a desk didn't produce much work – but it meant I would have three years' stability with Felicity after three Afghanistan tours in four years.

We were eventually relieved of duties and put on post-tour leave. I had six weeks off to gather myself before embarking on the Regimental Signals Officer Course.

Once you leave the men you have been fighting with, there is an all-pervading sense of loneliness that engulfs you like a dark cloud. Baz and I had said goodbye to each other, not knowing when we would see each other again. We were not similar people; we would perhaps have drifted apart had we not gone to war. But we had endured the same formative experiences, side-by-side, day-in, day-out, and without having each other there to say the right thing to help cope with an intrusive and frightening thought, it suddenly felt very lonely indeed.

During those first few days in Noss Mayo, I felt my soul struggling to come home from theatre. I kept telling myself that home was the real world, that theatre was exceptional. There were a lot of tears, in random places and at random times. I found this embarrassing.

For those first few nights I hardly slept. I would go and have a cigarette on the balcony overlooking the little inlet that runs into Noss Mayo from the Atlantic Ocean. Sometimes, as I stared into the darkness, a little tear would run down my face, although I wasn't feeling sad. I was so happy to be home; away from the heat, the shit, the blood and the smells of southern Afghanistan.

But from here, Afghanistan all seemed so fucking pointless. We had sacrificed so much of our bodies and minds, but it felt like no one in my village even knew where Afghanistan was. And of course Bing would never be coming home. He had been required to make the ultimate sacrifice. For what?

I decided to buy a boat, so I could get out on that ocean by myself and spend some time coming to terms with what was going on. With my post-tour cash, I went to a nearby dealer and bought a rigid inflatable boat with a powerful 125hp outboard engine.

The dealer asked me if I knew what I was doing. I said yes. I had actually driven a RIB before, but only in the military, and knew nothing of the upkeep, maintenance or skills required to keep her on the water.

I managed to get her home, and after finding a local farmer's field where I could leave her full-time, I took her down to the water. I chucked her in, fired her up, and in a couple of minutes I was a mile out to sea. I turned the engine off, and for the first time since I had returned I genuinely felt a little calmer.

Off the water, though, things were not easy. Remembrance Sunday quickly followed, and I found that I simply could not bring myself to dwell on losing blokes in war. I had a terrible attitude, feeling that while the nation respectfully remembered, most could never begin to understand the sacrifices made on their behalf. And particularly not the politicians at the Cenotaph on the TV. I switched it off and went for a run along the cliffs.

Maybe we should have booked a holiday, but I don't know if it would have made things any easier. I thought of Bing four or five times a day; of Afghanistan itself hourly. As soon as that happened, I would immediately stop myself and do something else. So even if I was in bed, I would get up and read a magazine or go and watch some sport on the TV. I would steadfastly refuse to let my mind go down that path.

Intimacy with Felicity was off the table – I could not even consider it. If she so much as touched me, or sat on my lap, I felt uneasy. It was different with our little girl, Amalie. She was a truly beautiful little human being. I could watch her just potter around for hours. I took pleasure from the simple times I shared with her; watching the dying sun reflect off her shiny, perfect nose as we sat down the local pub on our own, her drinking her usual Fruit Shoot and me nursing a pint of West Country ale. We must have looked like an odd couple indeed.

The boat was a big distraction for us, and I would often take Amalie out for a spin up the river Yealm – sometimes it was bitterly cold but she never seemed to make a fuss, or bore of our time together.

On these trips I often thought of the compound Baz and I had entered thinking it was a firing point, and the little Afghan girl we encountered there. I remember looking at her over the barrel of my gun; the expression in her eyes was not one of terror, but almost acceptance that men with guns storming into your house was part of growing up in Afghanistan. I wondered what the future looked like for those children and their families. Now it would be winter, and hopefully a bit quieter for them, but the Taliban would return and the brutalization of their generation would start again next year.

But there was also a whole generation of young men and women in my country who had been brutalized by this conflict. Baz had called me a couple of times; he was finding things really tough. I thought I was struggling, but Baz told me he had seen the doc and he was now being treated at his local Department of Community Mental Health. I asked him what he was struggling with specifically, but he wouldn't really open up on the phone, understandably. He preferred recounting stories from our tour, and laughing with me about some of them. His favourite was the story of the patrol when a fighter presented himself right in front of me and I tried to shoot him three or four times and missed. Baz thought that was hilarious; he thought I got just a little bit too excited. The funniest part for him, what really cracked him up, was that chicken's squawk as it died at our feet. Baz was recounting this story to me over and over again, almost every time I spoke to him.

It was 18 December 2010, the night of the BBC Sports Personality of the Year Award, when I came off the phone with Baz and finally realized what was going on. He was struggling to let go of this particular event, which could have killed either one of us, and seemed to have something resembling post-traumatic stress resulting from it and some other incidents he mentioned. The laughs were hiding the private tears, and I know he was grieving hard for Bing, having not allowed himself to do it in theatre. I went back to the sitting room, where Felicity was waiting for me.

'Baz OK?' she asked.

'Not really,' I replied.

She didn't know what to say. Neither did I. We turned back to the TV and watched as they gave a Lifetime Achievement Award to David Beckham. I had first seen David Beckham when I was fifteen – on my birthday in fact. My dad, who is one of those classic Manchester United fans who have no connection to Manchester, took me to watch them play Wimbledon at Selhurst Park. Man Utd were 2–0 up in the last minute and we were getting up to leave the ground when Beckham got the ball just shy of the halfway line, looked up and lobbed it in the net. The crowd went mad, and my dad could not believe it. It was a quite brilliant goal.

Before I knew it, I was formed in my father's own image as a Manchester United fan with no links to Manchester, and a fan of Beckham through his career. So I was more than a little disappointed that when he came out to visit the troops in Afghanistan in the summer of 2010, he was not prepared to hop on a helicopter and come and see me personally on the front line (!). Instead, he went to Camp Bastion and mingled with soldiers there. He went down a riot – he was down to earth, 'one of us' apparently, who had done well, got lucky and seen the tough times through.

When he was awarded the Sports Personality Lifetime Achievement Award I was pleased for him – a good guy, getting acknowledged. He went on stage, thanked his wife and children, but then paused. What he said next seemed completely unprepared.

'This year I went to Afghanistan, and I saw the bravery of our troops . . . they risk their lives to save so many people . . . I dedicate my award to the men and women serving our country in Afghanistan: be safe, have a great Christmas and thank you.'

With that I burst into tears and went to my bedroom. What the fuck was going on? David Beckham had made me cry? I was properly in tears this time. Sobbing my heart out, sat on the bed. I wasn't crying for Mark; I wasn't crying because of guilt; I wasn't crying for myself. I think I was weeping for our generation. Nothing really prepares you for the reality of repeated visits to war.

And I felt decimated. I felt totally destroyed inside. I felt that I had nothing else to give. I felt that I used to be a good man. Someone who cared so much for other people that I didn't have time to care about myself and really address the scars from my childhood. Yes, growing up had been tough, but I had finally got there, and found a family and a home in the Army that I was content with. But now the ride was going too fast, and I wanted to get off. This Afghan stuff was getting out of control.

And I only had myself to blame. It was all entirely self-inflicted. I did not have to join the Army. I did not have to be a Joint Fires Controller. I didn't have to go on patrol twice a day, every day, for seven months. I did not have to laugh at the Taliban's stupidity as I ended people who stood up in front of me in a contact.

I had become totally brutalized; I was ashamed of what I had done, ashamed of what I had become and wondered how life would ever be the same again. My relationship with Felicity was suffering too. I kept taking Amalie off for walks on our own, or staring into space in the pub, alone, and she became convinced I was having an affair. I tried to explain that I was finding things tough, but she genuinely did not know how to treat me.

If I was having a good day and feeling robust, I did not want her to sit me down and ask me softly how it was all going. If I was having a bad day, I just wanted the world to leave me alone – particularly her – lest she prise the lid off the jar and make it worse.

Felicity slowly began to realize the negative impact she was having on my re-adjustment to normal life, and through sheer hard work and love, she sought to understand the experiences I had been through but was so reticent to talk about.

And yet during these difficult winter months, as 2010 became 2011, I still considered myself deeply fortunate. My fiancée was committed and resilient – she was not going to cast me adrift to the darkness no matter what. My daughter was sublime – a gift – and one with whom I could always find a deep solace. I had some money – albeit not much – and I lived in a beautiful little cottage by the sea in Devon. I was acutely aware that some of my soldiers were not so fortunate.

33

Bing's parents, Mike and Ann, were calling on an almost twice-weekly basis. Someone at the regiment had furnished them with an account of the day Bing died, and made out that I did something heroic and retrieved his body under fire from an advancing enemy. Extremely overblown. In their kindness, they kept telling me how proud they were of me, and how they did not blame me. They wanted to visit me and Felicity in Noss Mayo, and we had them down to stay.

Mike drank for the first time since that knock on the door from the Army on 8 June. He drank the whisky like water, and before I knew it was demanding that we head down the road to the local pub. I ceded to his request and we made our way down the road. As we passed some steep steps that led down to the harbour side, he collapsed from the alcohol and fell down them, hitting his head badly on the stone and knocking himself unconscious.

I flagged down a passing van and lifted him into the back of it, to transport him back up the hill to my house. When we got there he had come round, and wanted to go back to the pub. When I told him we hadn't quite made it to the pub, he thought I was lying. Ann then got cross with him, and they went to bed.

(The severity of this injury was not fully realized for some months. He actually suffered a very slow, very small bleed on his brain that resulted in him collapsing some months later, and nearly passing away in Gloucester hospital. He had an operation and was saved, but it still remains the most serious drunken injury I've seen!)

Mike and Ann were suffering a deep loss. Back then, I did not see an immediate way out of it for them. They would sit endlessly in their sitting room, staring at the little cross made up of brass 30mm shell cases from an Apache helicopter's gun in theatre, given to them by the Army. I accompanied them to anything they asked me to, including the dedication of the Armed Forces Memorial at the National Memorial Arboretum by the Queen. As a family, we were sat at the front, almost right next to the Queen. She kept looking over at us throughout the service. I wanted to talk to her. She looked as if she understood, as if she had seen it all before. I wanted her to come and speak to Bing's parents and thank them personally for their sacrifice.

Present that day were the mothers, fathers, wives and daughters of all those lost during the summer of 2010. We met some stoical fathers, some devastated mothers and some inconsolable wives and children. The scale of their loss was epic; it was raw, and it was painful to watch. We spoke to many that day, but one that stood out for me was a lady in a soldier's ceremonial jacket.

She was in her mid-forties, and was by herself. She had got her son's No.1 Dress tailored into a jacket for herself, and she looked very smart. Felicity struck up a conversation with her and we discovered that her son had been caught in an explosion, and despite everybody's best efforts he died on the stretcher as he was being evacuated. He knew he was going to die, and the last thing he said to those treating him was: 'Tell my mum I love her so much.'

There was an element to all the grief that day, an over-whelming feeling of 'why?', that I simply could not address.

Mike Chandler repeatedly asked me if I had killed the man who killed Bing. I told him the truth – I had no idea. I fired the guns, I fired all six of my magazines containing twenty-eight rounds each, but I don't know if I killed the individual who shot Bing. But Mike wanted that closure, he wanted vengeance, because he did not believe in the broader mission. He thought it was a waste of time; Afghanistan was a long way from Gloucester, and he could not make the link between our national domestic security, which Bing had joined the Army to protect, and the death he had suffered on a dusty track thousands of miles away in a conflict that understandably did not register with a lot of people going about their daily lives in the UK.

It struck me that during those years that I was either training for or going to war, the military was almost a subculture in our country. The military community was acutely aware of the price of conducting a high-intensity war. People were dying every day, in truly horrific circum-stances, to protect the freedoms that were enjoyed in mainstream society. Yet outside that community, life continued untouched. The music festivals, the sports tour-naments; life ticked on regardless.

Even within the military community, there were sub-groupings. A lot of us would be pleased to never hear the word Afghanistan again, whereas some wanted to volunteer to go there – to 'do' it and get the medal. The big regret I felt was that the Army did not discourage this, but almost commercialized the war. Those who ticked the 'commanded on operations' box were promoted, regardless of their per-formance, and so their peers wanted to keep up. What they had done in their command, and indeed how their soldiers coped with or perceived their time at the helm, was almost disregarded.

Whenever I thought of this, I would remember a pre-deployment training serial at a base in Yorkshire, where an ambitious company commander regaled us with his exploits the previous summer in a way that actually made me feel quite ill. He was seemingly, albeit probably not intentionally, taking a sort of strange pride in the fact that nine of his soldiers had been killed the previous summer.

The state honours system's list after the summer of 2010 did not help this. Of course, honours do a vital job of recognizing our service men and women's actions on operations. However, the difference in what was required to win an honour of any kind varied wildly from the early days of Iraq – when the Army had not seen any significant combat for a quarter of a century – to the height of the fighting in Afghanistan in 2010 and again to the end of the conflict in Afghanistan for our Regular Forces, in December 2014. I saw men win awards in battle which, when I read about them afterwards, brought me great amusement. The official records didn't quite tally with my recollections, but good for them.

I also saw many more men and women conduct themselves with the highest degrees of bravery and self-sacrifice every single day, and simply return to base, clean their kit and get ready for the next day, never to be recognized.

I remember passing through FOB Shawqat back in Afghanistan in September 2010 to be met by my then battery commander, who was talking about operational awards. He told me I was to be put forward for one. I was surprised and felt awkward. I simply could not in all conscience go home – without Bing – and be publicly commended for my work. What would I say to his parents? Besides which, my strong view was that during that tour I never did anything above and beyond what is required of a commando captain in combat, for which I was paid a fair wage. I asked that he take me off the list.

34

I started back in the Army on the Regimental Signals Officer's Course at Bovington in Dorset in January 2011. It was another classic Army course – four weeks crammed into fourteen. The lack of interest in 'normal' Army life, which inevitably follows a tough tour, was a struggle to shake off. I took the time to get fit and indulge in the paltry nightlife of southern Dorset in the spring.

I was struggling to settle and sleep in Noss Mayo, so we decided to move north of Plymouth into a small 300-year-old miner's cottage on the edge of Bodmin Moor in Cornwall, where we could entirely get away from it all.

It was perfect for what I needed at the time – the sort of place where no one would think you strange for getting up at 0430hrs and going for an eight-mile run across the moor. The sort of place that takes you a while to break into. The locals are suspicious of outsiders, but once your presence is proved not to be the standard 'give Cornwall a go' before returning to London, and you have shown you are committed to the moor life, it is very peaceful and soul-settling indeed.

I took real satisfaction from simple physical tasks, such as deforesting my garden, cutting my acre of grass by hand (it took six hours a go) and the outdoors upkeep of the property in general.

I could cross a stream and be up on top of the moor in

five minutes, run for an hour and then swim in the river at the bottom of the Tor that loomed over our small valley. I could loosen off by walking up to the pub and drinking with some new local friends – the pub really was the centre of the community in the nearby village. From this account, it would seem that I was largely spending time by myself, and that is true, but eventually I began to feel my soul healing.

I still thought of Bing two or three times a day. They were intrusive thoughts – the sort one cannot control. I could never shake the feeling of my cheek on his in the back of the Husky that drove us back to PB Khaamar for his extraction.

I struggled with sleep – I would often wake in a sweat. When I dreamt of Bing I didn't mind too much; I enjoyed the thought of being with him, albeit briefly. The tougher dreams were when I was left in the middle of that bloody field on my own. Then I really did wake in a panic. The dreams could be vivid, but I had a fervent desire to stave off the darkness, and countered them by immediately getting up and going downstairs, making a coffee and having a smoke by the back door as the wind and weather screamed in across the moor and battered my little house.

The effects deepened when I was around my other Army comrades. Many spoke of a desire to return to Afghanistan, or go there for the first time to experience it. I found this very difficult. Equally, I did not really want to engage with some old Army friends who had been deployed on different tours and had some horrendous experiences themselves. I felt talking about it was feeding the beast, and it was best to do something else.

This was a grave and selfish mistake.

I had a very close friend who had returned from his tour

when I was still on my second one in Kandahar. He came back a changed man. Selfishly focusing on my own return to the UK and my preparations for my third tour, I had not tried to find out what was really going on with him. When I got back from theatre in 2010, he sought me out for a pint.

We went for a drink or three, and he told me about a horrific incident in Afghanistan in 2009, where women and children had been killed as a result of his actions. I had become so brutalized by my conflict that I did not understand why he was letting this affect him in this way. The deaths were clearly unintentional; how on earth could he have known they were there? But he did not see it that way. He kept telling me the story over and over again, in excruciating detail, and I failed to spot the symptoms of what this clearly was – PTSD.

In the years that followed he became very distant indeed. We fought when we were drunk and I heard of his unhappiness in our relationship through others. At the time, I couldn't work out why. Some years later, I was told that he had hoped that I might be able to help him with his problems, and was bitterly disappointed when I seemed to trivialize them.

I was extremely ashamed – and remain so to this day – of my behaviour towards a man who was a brother to me in my formative years. My lack of awareness and understanding of how combat stress affected other people was abetted by an entirely selfish navel-gazing exercise; making sure I was winning my personal fight before taking care of others. I am not proud of it.

I continued in my role with 29 Commando in Plymouth for a while, happily doing the minimum amount of work my career required. By autumn 2012, I realized I had sunk into some level of contentment for the first time since I returned from my last tour. We decided to have another baby, and Joey was born at home on the moor in June 2013. By now I realized I was unlikely to ever recover the military bug that had so dominated the last ten years of my life.

My life's priorities were changing, and I had to have a frank conversation with myself about the future. By now Felicity and I were unbreakably strong again, having forged our bonds through some dark times. I was at a crossroads. I could continue in the Army; my reports and promotion prospects were above average. I received an A– (top 10%) on my Officer's Joint Appraisal Report – meaningless generally, but the only indication of what kind of esteem the chain of command held you in at the time.

But inside I knew my time was up.

I was never in the Army for anything other than the operations. I enjoyed leading blokes in combat – I found it the ultimate 'man test' and that was a major part of why I did it. Every human wants to test their limits; leading in combat was me testing mine. To do that you must be cognisant of the risks and yet prepared to take them. You must work out what is risky and what is not – what wins in a 'risk vs reward' scenario – and then lead men through dangerous times to ensure a successful outcome. Failure in combat operations involves dying a pretty nasty death. To accept this fact requires belief – in the mission, in oneself, in the men and women around you, and crucially that it is worth it.

Now, with a little family of my own and roots on the moor, the scales had, after twelve years, finally tipped. No longer could I justify entering compounds not knowing what was there, with a partner and two children at home. No longer could I justify missing so much of my children's lives. And no longer could I justify putting Felicity through another combat tour like that in 2010.

A realization like this takes a couple of months to solidify in your mind (Am I being weak? Am I a coward?). It was during this time that I bumped into Cooper, the soldier I'd trained back in 2007. He had completely transformed himself from a problem character into a better soldier than me. More importantly, he had just returned from his first tour in Afghanistan, where his stock was held in extremely high regard.

He made a point of telling me how important those early days in training had been; how somehow I had taught him humility, courage, discipline and resilience; how he often thought of me, and knew of plenty of others who felt the same way. He is now a successful special forces operator; happy and settled. This meant more to me than almost anything else I might have achieved in my time in service. Of course, I didn't tell him that.

The Army has its shortcomings, like any other institution, but in terms of getting a rough bit of rock and turning it into a stable, strong, disciplined and committed diamond of an individual, in my view, it remains second to none.

Seeing Cooper reminded me how rewarding it had been to help him, and many others like him, make something of themselves. I started to think about where I might be able to make a difference now, and considered my very personal insights into the rather desperate narrative of how we were looking after our men and women when they returned from a tour like I had done in 2010. In 2012, more British service personnel took their own lives than were killed in combat. Some of the tales were horrific; descents into substance abuse, homelessness and violence. For some, it was a short trip from the parade ground to the morgue.

Lance Sergeant Dan Collins was one individual whose tale had a profound effect on me, because he reminded me of so many of my own men. Hailing from the proud Welsh Guards, he had found life so difficult upon his return from a terrible tour – during which two friends were killed – that he took his life on a wet, clouded hillside in Sennybridge. Before he did so he made a video on his mobile phone for his mum. In the grainy footage, he says: 'I'm so sorry, Mum. I've tried everything, but nothing seems to work.'

I did not know the guy, but he could have been any one of the thousands who use that training area every year before heading out to Afghanistan for yet another tour. He could have been any one of my soldiers, any one of my friends. It was the look in his eyes on the video – that look of total resignation and desperation – that I could not accept.

Servicemen and women were fighting mental trauma everywhere. I thought of Baz, trying to deal with everything that had happened during our tour, and of a SBS operative I knew, distraught because he had killed a woman on target (she was wearing webbing and carrying an assault rifle). I remembered a female officer, who had identified a decapitated corpse with me when we were training young soldiers, scrubbing herself raw in her bedroom with a nail brush because she could 'feel the death'. I remembered a senior NCO struggling with an alcohol problem.

I felt an unbreakable bond with these soldiers – I had been through these things too, I knew what they were like. I hadn't suffered in the same ways; I was lucky. I went running and spent days at a time outside on the moor to cope. But these people should be provided for. They were wounded too – you couldn't see it, they weren't missing limbs, but they should be looked after as much as anyone who had a physical injury. But the Army and state provision simply was not there, nor was there much interest in improving the situation.

In the late 2000s, seeing the endless conveyor belt of physical and mental trauma arriving back on our shores, the charitable sector filled the gap. The charities brought the public with them, and so followed an explosion not just in levels of donations, but in the number of service charities set up. This was helping a great deal of service men and women, and their families, cope with some dark times both personally and professionally; our nation will owe them a debt of gratitude for some time to come.

But this sector was proving wildly inconsistent. Some of the charities did not get along. Some relied on evidence-based, proven treatments; others on the whims of their directors, usually a retired senior military officer. There was no regulation beyond the Charity Commission's extremely light touch, and some sad cases materialized.

In 2010, we all wore the wristbands to support the 'Afghan Heroes' charity, set up by Denise Harris after her son Lee was killed in Nad-e Ali a year before I was there, in that terrible summer of 2009. The Charity Commission had opened an inquiry in 2013 after it was discovered that Afghan Heroes had raised over half a million pounds, but spent just 3 per cent of it on veterans. Some charity founders, in another case, went to jail.

The landscape was a mess and it needed sorting out. And the Lance Sergeant Collinses of this world, along with thousands who had stopped short of his tragic point of no return, were paying the price. They were my mates – my soldiers – and they were the best of us. I had seen these young men and women conduct themselves with such unfathomably deep wells of courage that one feels truly humbled to be in the presence of them, both then and now. They are not the loudest and they are not the intellectual giants or fame-seeking characters that usually dominate our newspapers. Sometimes they fuck around; sometimes they get carried away in the pub. But they truly are our finest product; special people in a dangerous world fixated upon self-promotion and selfish desires. And they deserved so much better.

Their Britishness runs deep; their compassion, their teamwork, their ability to operate under the most extreme pressure because it is 'their duty'. It's something I have been privileged to witness and will carry with me throughout my life. Not once in my operational service – whether it was the lad being sick in the ditch before we advanced to combat or the sergeant major who had been shot in the neck – did I see someone begrudge their service. (I saw plenty of people moan about being in the Army while stood on a wet, piss-soaked range in Sennybridge or elsewhere, but that is another issue!)

But herein is the crux; they sign up knowing that some things are – or should be – a given. That they will be well led; that they will be equipped correctly; that they will not be asked to conduct immoral wars founded on things that aren't actually real; and that they will be looked after both during and after their service by the nation, if required.

This contract was simply not being honoured by the nation. People were trying – the charitable sector were over-performing. But when it came to post-combat care specifically, I felt strongly that the government had singularly failed our service men and women. It was not something I could let lie.

This thought process coalesced with another in my mind. I remembered being part of the briefing team for British ministers while on tour in Afghanistan in 2008. I had been extremely impressed by the discipline and focus of the unit I was working for, tactically and strategically. But I was also struck by the supremacy of the political command system that ultimately made things happen, or not happen, as in the case of veterans' care.

And when it came to foreign policy, you had to look pretty hard at what was going on to find a strategy. British foreign policy was based on one thing only – the British election timetable. How on earth could senior officers really achieve results on the ground if political leaders were so naive as to specify when wars would end, to appease a domestic audience?

And the equipment with which we were asking people to do this?

All this left me with a desire, one day, to be at the level where I could make decisions and have a deliberate and direct effect on these things. Ultimately, I was and remain a patriot. I had personally fought to protect our country's freedoms. Back at home we just had a nasty habit of forgetting how hard-won these freedoms were; the commitment, sacrifices and courage required.

In 2012, when the idea first dawned on me, it seemed ridiculous. I knew nothing about politics, and I didn't want to know anything either. I had never voted before, and still couldn't quite work out what a 'hung parliament' was. I regarded some politicians as a rather inept breed – more in love with the trappings of office than dedicated to delivering for their men and women. Like some Army officers could be, admittedly.

But it was not always thus. This 'career politician' thing

was become a relatively new phenomenon. In the 1950s, most MPs had seen military service of some sort. Parliament's timings were specifically set so that one could keep up another job while doing the job of governance in the evenings or at weekends. Some genuinely saw it as I saw it – simply as a vehicle for getting things done that needed to be done, rather than a career. It gave you a position, a reach, a platform. It looked like an enormous privilege.

If I really wanted to change things, could I try and be an MP? I did genuinely feel that I could change things for people who needed it. I believed in the system of parliament, and I believed in some core causes. Veterans' care and Defence were undoubtedly my key drivers but, drawing on my experience of training soldiers, I also felt this bond with kids from tougher backgrounds who didn't have the friends I'd had, or the breaks I'd had, to help them grow up. For some, life's path, through no fault of their own, was an interminable struggle, and I wanted to help them. And I wanted to help end the unacceptable stigma and lack of genuine commitment to mental health.

My mind was made up. I was going to leave the Army and become an MP. Plymouth was the place to do it. I had grown up here; made my mistakes; spent many nights in the bars and clubs of the town; loved, lost and grown up. Now I wanted to help define the future of the city I called home, where I had settled with my family, and where I had so many wonderful friends.

I broke the news to Felicity. I was going to leave the Army. She was unashamedly happy, right up until I told her I was leaving to go into politics.

35

I resigned and would be leaving the Army at Christmas 2013.

I had no idea where to start in terms of becoming an MP, but had heard of Bob Stewart, who had made the transition from the Army into politics. I wrote to him, and he invited me to come to London and see him.

He showed me around the House of Commons as we chatted about why I was doing this. He advised me to work out which party I wanted to be in, as independents do not get elected. He thought I would stand a better chance standing for Labour – they were not stuffed with ex-military types, and could do with the expertise. After lunch, Bob gathered a small group of Labour and Conservative MPs on the terrace, as we sat outside and had some afternoon tea. We talked about the Labour Party; I respected them and we had similar broad ideas, but there were slight differences in our views on the military and foreign policy, and very different views on tackling poverty. I'd done some research and been surprised to learn that I could leave the Army and, with my particular domestic set-up, walk into a life on state welfare receiving 50 per cent more income than I would if I had got up and gone to work every day for the average wage in Plymouth. I didn't think that endlessly pouring more money into the welfare state was particularly fair, either on the recipients or wider society. The Labour MPs just kept talking about these welfare cuts, while I sat there thinking that it was about time we cut some of these welfare payments down, and focused them more on people who really needed them, or on services that were woeful, such as mental health provision.

On the train back to Plymouth, my gut was telling me to join the Conservative Party. Accepting I knew very little about it, and was basing my decision on a brief meeting with some MPs, I thought hard about my beliefs. I didn't dislike other parties' values, I just felt more broadly at home with the Conservatives. It was not a Damascene conversion, or anything like a cut-and-dried decision; I was never going to be a rabid loyalist. But if I wanted to change things I would have to be elected; independents never get elected. I had to go to my nearest home, and that would be the Conservative Party.

I joined Plymouth Moor View Conservatives, expanding their association numbers from fourteen to fifteen in the process. The chairman, John, seemed a very nice chap, as was Jack, the treasurer, but after our first Conservative Association meeting, Felicity and I had sat in the car in silence. For the first time, I wondered whether or not I was making the correct decision. The members of the association were terrific; older, resilient and determined Conservatives. But they were definitely at a different stage of life to me; there was no one there under the age of seventy.

Leaving the Army is undoubtedly a tricky transition. Leaving the Army and going straight into politics was going to be a challenge. The local association – the vehicle from which one launches oneself at parliament – had been decimated by years of infighting. Jack had just about brought it out of special measures, but it was not the well-oiled machine that would make my campaign easier. Still, I got the feeling everyone in the association wanted me to succeed, even if they had no idea how I was going to do it, and mostly thought I was mad.

I saw out my last few months in the military under a sympathetic CO in Plymouth, who entirely got what I was doing. Some others didn't, which was good practice for me. It tested my belief in myself and what I wanted to do, and showed me I had the ability to withstand detractors.

The transition was one that I had to manage closely. And by manage, I mean lie about.

I was not, under service law, allowed to be involved in politics until I had finished my period of resettlement and left the armed forces. But sticking to the rules meant I would miss the dates for the 2015 General Election candidate selection for Plymouth. I also wanted to sit my Parliamentary Assessment Board before I left so that, should it all go pear-shaped, I could bail out of politics and stay in the Army.

My CO was extremely good, but I had learnt a few things in the Army – chiefly about asking forgiveness rather than seeking permission. So, in the end, I faked a family commitment on a Friday and Saturday in September 2013 to attend a Parliamentary Assessment Board in Cambridgeshire.

The assessment was a two-day event held in a hotel, designed to discover whether or not one had the elusive and as yet unquantifiable qualities required to be a Member of Parliament for the Conservative Party. I was grouped with a broad mix of candidates. Most were quite clearly more qualified than me. It was a strange atmosphere, as though we were all competing against each other.

I was having to change as a person to excel at things like this. Naturally quiet, and happy to keep myself to myself, in politics this behaviour would be interpreted as unfriendly or bad-mannered. After attending a few events with the association, by now I was getting better at judging the mood of these sorts of occasions. At the assessment, I forced myself to be more outgoing during the general meet and greet stage, but kept myself to myself as I went around the various stands, where the candidates were interviewed, did presentations and group exercises, and even sorted a mock MP's post bag.

It wasn't testing in the slightest – it seemed as though a lot of the candidates had had a rather long run-up to this event, and had over-complicated it in their minds a great deal. I just took it as I found it, and didn't know whether to expect success or failure. I got the train home without much feel for it, having no metric to judge it against.

My journey home that day was more eventful than the Assessment Board itself.

Knowing that from January we'd be surviving on my paltry savings, Felicity and I were committed to living a financially austere 'good life' on the moor. I had sold our cars, which were becoming old and expensive, and bought a battered motorcycle for £550 and a Peugeot 205 for £700 cash, in the hope that it would prove to be one of those magic cars that just kept going. It was not to be, and on the way home from dropping me off at the station that morning, it had broken down on Felicity. Fortunately, she had been able to thumb a lift back to the cottage, and had called to assure me that the car was left in a very safe and inconspicuous place for me to sort out when I got back.

I was therefore a little surprised in the taxi home from the station to be violently thrown from side to side as the driver cursed a Peugeot 205 that had been left abandoned in the middle of the road – the straightest, darkest part of the road across the moor.

The police had taped it off, and it was clear that it was going to cause an accident. I got home at about 10.30 p.m., and without any other transport available, jumped on my motorbike in my suit to go and move it. I got to the car and rolled it into the obvious layby, some fifteen feet back from its original position, and removed the police tape so that they didn't tow it away in the night. I was resigned to picking it up the next day with one of my friends from the village.

As I remounted my motorbike for my second trip home, I was cursing Felicity, feeling unreasonably and disproportionately cross about the fact that I had to ride across the moors on a wet and cold night to move a car that my soon-to-be wife had abandoned in the middle of the road.

So cross, in fact, that I missed a turning and got catapulted off my motorbike and through a hedge, landing in a field, face first. I had not at that stage bought myself a proper helmet, and had one that protected my head but not my face. (I had for some months been driving around in a parachutist issue helmet and goggles from the Army.)

I laughed at myself, face-down in the undergrowth. Then I limped back to the road, on which no cars had been seen for a few minutes. My motorbike was largely OK, except for a smashed front light and some bent handlebars. I straightened the handlebars, but then was left with the option of returning home across the moor with no lights.

I managed to get the thing restarted, and arrived back at my village at kicking-out time. The crowd leaving the pub went rather quiet as I passed them, grass and hedge still clinging to me and my bike, before howling with laughter as I disappeared further down the lane to mine. When I got home I had the imprint from the handlebars on one leg, in the shape of heavy bruising. I could even read the name of the manufacturer for a few months afterwards.

After a long day trying to act like an MP, I cracked open an ale with Felicity and we toasted our combined stupidity at leaving the security of the Army to take on this mad new life in politics.

Later that weekend, I received an email saying that I had passed the Assessment Board and that I was welcome to apply for seats all over the country.

36

Being on the candidates list, while talked up by many, essentially meant very little. I did ask how many were on the list, but was told this was 'top secret' information. To me top secret information meant details of live national security operations or similar; not who was on a list of possible but unlikely MPs.

In the end, it transpired that the selection dates for the Plymouth seat that I wanted had not been confirmed yet, and as such I had to wait. The Plymouth Moor View Association was still recovering from 'special measures' and enduring a particularly difficult time.

I was a little deflated; I had given my notice in the military and, while I accepted that my strategy of becoming a member of parliament carried a heavy degree of risk, I did not feel like stretching the plan out indefinitely.

I was advised by the local party agent to put in for selection to another local seat, North Cornwall, for the 'experience'. They already had someone they wanted who had been lined up two years previously – a strong local lad – but for some reason I needed the experience of losing.

I didn't agree.

As the selection for North Cornwall was only two weeks away, I eventually caved in and agreed to do it while keeping my eye firmly on the Plymouth selection, which now seemed likely to be in the New Year.

I received the papers for the North Cornwall selection meeting but didn't really understand what was required; I was asked to go and speak for five minutes and take questions for fifteen. The subject was deliberately not mentioned, so I telephoned the local Conservative Party staff member to find out more.

'What's the talk supposed to be on?' I asked.

'You'll have to work that out, Johnny,' he replied.

'No, seriously, can you just give me a guide as to how these things have run in the past?'

'I can't really do that, I'm afraid; it's for you to work out and we'll see what you come up with.'

How very cryptic.

I drove over to Wadebridge on a wet and windy Cornish winter's evening and went to my first ever full Conservative Association event. It was an experience.

I was kept downstairs by myself when I went in, so I bought a stale half pint of ale to keep me company. Largely left alone with my thoughts, I wondered what the hell I was doing. I knew nothing about politics, the Conservative Party or why there seemed to be so many people here introducing themselves by their title and not their name (deputy political secretary; deputy chairman political; secretary general; membership chairman). I wondered if I should refer to them by their title instead of their name.

They asked me about Europe, and I said I thought it was a nice place that I was hoping to visit the following summer on a family holiday.

Eventually they returned to their seats – I had turned up at a half-time interval – and I was summoned upstairs. I walked into a room with some 120 people in it, and was clapped in and shown to the lectern.

Having spent years briefing soldiers and statesmen, I was a confident public speaker. But on this occasion I was extremely nervous, because I had no idea what I was doing. My chosen subject in the end was the benefits system; how the bill had gone from £120bn in 1997 to £210bn in 2009, and that it was now at a point of not delivering for the most vulnerable who needed it because too many people were claiming it.

Simple stuff, or so I thought.

It did not go down very well, and there was an awkward moment when I sensed people looking at each other just out of my field of vision as I carried on speaking. No doubt they were asking each other if I had walked into the right bar that evening.

One lady, who must have been at least in her nineties and seemingly without much time for other people's feelings, said rather loudly to her neighbour, 'What is he talking about?'

I took this as my cue to change tack. I told my story, briefly and poorly, and spoke about what I thought politics meant to me – improving life for people, our most vulnerable, our veterans; our young people and our mental health communities, both carers and sufferers.

In Cornwall, where the most important issues were farming, Europe and the single market, I had misjudged the mood.

I was pleasantly surprised by the questions at the end. The younger contingent clearly liked me, and I felt much better after fielding some of their questions than after my five-minute rant. Fortunately, the questions had very little to do with my speech.

I was thanked for my time and then I got back in the car and headed home. I knew what was coming when the phone rang that night. I remember the call now – I hadn't got it.

The thing is, no matter that you never really wanted that seat because you knew nothing about it, no matter how much your partner tells you that it's 'not part of the plan', no matter how badly you know you did, to some degree, the rejection still stings.

That evening I suddenly felt very vulnerable. I had left a stable, good career against almost everyone's advice; I had two children – one of whom was six months old; Felicity and I were planning on getting married the next summer; I had no family wealth to fall back on. It suddenly seemed like a very bold (stupid) decision to 'leave the Army to be an MP'.

It's times like that which define you, I think. I was lucky; I had an immensely supportive partner and to be frank, anything was better than getting ready for another tour of Afghanistan with the Army – I was sick of that.

That evening, Felicity and I stayed up late talking. We resolved to stick to the plan, to hold on for the Plymouth selection and go for that. In the meantime, I would get a job in the local area, and we would seriously cut back the scale of our impending wedding.

In the end, the Plymouth selection came around relatively quickly and I was given a date in the autumn of 2013. Then on the day itself I received a phone-call to say that all of the other candidates had pulled out, and the selection event would not be going ahead. For a moment I wondered, yet again, what the hell I was doing. However, the delay did give me a fantastic opportunity to get to know the association, and I spent some time in the intervening couple of weeks – while a new selection was convened – speaking with the personalities involved. It was a small and modest association, who were very friendly indeed.

The selection evening eventually took place two weeks later. Eleven people were eligible to vote for me on the evening (having been members for more than three months). Based on how seriously the process was taken by the central party, and how little national interest the seat seemed to attract, it was clear that the chances of winning this seat in a general election were not good.

I was, however, up against some very interesting characters. One conversation stood out.

'I've just got back from conference,' she said.

'Oh yeah, what's that?' I asked.

'You know, conference. I'm still high from it.'

I thought this was a stitch-up, or a joke. It wasn't.

'What do you mean?' I asked.

'Lynton's given me the secrets of passing these things,' she said.

'Who's that, and what are they?' I asked, excitedly.

'I can't tell you that. I'll tell you when we've finished,' she replied.

'Oh, OK.' I shut up.

This was going to be a very interesting journey. Remarkably I was chosen, and late that October evening in the Futures Inn in Plymouth, I assumed the position of the official candidate for the Conservative Party for Plymouth Moor View at the 2015 General Election.

Even though this was what I wanted, leaving uniform for the last time that December was an odd experience. I had trained hard in that uniform, I knew what I was doing in that uniform and I could put it on and assume the role that I was asked to play. Taking it off for the last time is disarming, making one feel uncertain and nervous about the future, both immediate and longer term. This feeling was particularly strong for me. The Army had become my family – my home and my security after I had left my parents' house. I could handle the internal thoughts and challenges that were hangovers from my upbringing by simply donning my uniform and being 'someone else'. But life was very different for me now. I had won my mental battles for now – no doubt they could return. I had a family and home of my own for the first time. I was settled and stable. I was that person I wanted to be, and I told myself I could do it.

37

New Year's Day 2014 brought the new challenge into focus, and I was looking forward to it already. The year ahead was going to define the next ten years of my life. I needed to find a way of combining a job that I was yet to find, that could support a wife and two young children, with campaigning for a seat as an MP that no one thought was winnable.

From my savings, I paid the bills for the wedding in advance. I came up with a finance plan that would give us £105 per week in cash to get by. Bills and rent would be paid; we would just have to feed and clothe the kids and put a bit of fuel in the Rover 400 we had bought for £400 to replace the knackered Peugeot, which never recovered from its night on the moor.

But the fuel soon became too much of a drain. Felicity and I decided that we would sell the remaining car and instead get a baby trailer that attached to her bike. She would then cycle six miles, twice a day, to get Amalie to and from school. This would save us money and give us some wriggle room if we needed it.

I would remain on my motorbike. The fuel on that worked out a lot cheaper, but riding it everywhere was so bloody cold. My fingers, in particular, felt the cold quickly after getting frost-nip in Norway all those years ago. As well as being painful, the bike looked ridiculous. I had repaired it myself after my encounter with the hedge in the autumn and it reminded me of one of the motorbikes the Taliban used to ride around on in Helmand. This was confirmed on a trip into Plymouth in early January: I was riding past the dockyard in Devonport when I was hailed by two kids at the side of the road.

'Oi! Oi! Mate!'

I slowed down to speak to them.

'You've got a really shit bike, mate,' the older one said.

'I know,' I said. 'Sorry.'

I carried on. Running for parliament as a Conservative in Plymouth was going to be an abusive year. I'd best get used to it.

As winter turned into spring, a friend from the village offered me some work. Phil didn't think it was good for me to have the male banter from the military disappear all at once, and asked if I would work on his building site with him.

He picked me up outside my house at 7 a.m. each day in his van. We would wind our way across the moor in the morning haze that dominates the Tamar Valley in the early part of the year. We mostly worked on one new-build property. However, on the way home we would often pop into someone else's house to help them out with a piece of DIY, such as sealing a chimney or building a wood store.

It was bloody hard graft. Phil taught me how to lay a wall with breeze blocks. I dug out a garden. He would set me to work and come back three hours later. The manual labour was perfect. We sometimes worked with other unskilled labourers, and the banter was intense. From an army officer to the building site in three months – for some reason they found that hilarious.

But not as hilarious as when I told them I had left the Army to be an MP, and I was standing in May 2015. They truly thought I was joking. They wondered why on earth I would do that. Once they got over their initial shock I was belt-fed politics from their view on a daily basis, and it was intriguing. My knowledge of small business, business rates in general, accounting, employment law, imports and exports, material prices, immigration, the NHS and state welfare was, until this time, very limited. This was the perfect education. It quickly became apparent that all I knew about was defence and foreign affairs. But as one of them said to me – better to know what you don't know.

Spring turned into summer and Felicity and I got married. It was a very small but very idyllic wedding. Amalie and Joey were our beautiful but disruptive bridesmaids; Felicity designed everything from the table covers to the candle-lit first dance under the stars. There were only eight of us. Karl, the Padre from 29 Commando, married us. My best men were Adam, my boss from the 2010 tour of Afghanistan, and Charlie Fisher, the mad one who had married the maid of honour from his cancelled wedding. That story would never get old.

We got married in Altarnun Church in Cornwall, colloquially known as the Cathedral on the Moor, and had our reception at the Endsleigh Hotel, just the other side of the River Tamar in Devon. It was an extraordinary day. My thoughts were all over the place. When first my children, and then my stunningly beautiful wife-to-be, walked down the aisle to me, I realized I had achieved all I ever wanted in life. I only ever wanted a family of my own – the other stuff was just filling time. Now I had them. And they were perfect.

I also thought a lot of Mark Chandler. I don't know why, but whenever I had one of those moments when I realized how lucky I was, I thought of Bing. He would have been married by now and had children, I suspect. He would have built a life and a family, just like me, had I not commanded him in Afghanistan of course, so the monkey on my shoulder wanted me to believe.

I went to the hotel toilet and remember glancing at myself in the mirror – dressed up in a suit, still a bit scruffy despite my best efforts. I looked at my face, at the lines around my eyes, the scars, and watched as a tear rolled down my cheek.

I heard Baz saying, 'Do you ever wonder what's become of us?'

I wiped the tear away, left and walked back out into a beautiful sunlit garden that sits atop the hill that runs down from the house to the Tamar. I would have to carry these thoughts for many years, but I was happy to.

The honeymoon would have to wait. Throughout this period, I was working out my relationship with the Conservative Party Central Office. During the selection process, I'd made a real effort to engage with the professionals from the party. In their view, the seat of Plymouth Moor View, having been 'eminently winnable' before my selection, became a 'lost cause' as soon as I was named as the candidate. I tried not to take this personally.

'Well done, Johnny. We're really pleased for you,' the local agent said on my selection evening.

'Thanks. Shall we get together next week and talk about what we are going to do? I've got some ideas,' I enquired.

I had analysed the past results from the previous two elections. There was clearly a core group who voted for one of the main two parties; the majority did not or were not interested. If I could get just two or three per cent of them interested in me and my campaign, I might get over the line.

The agent and I met the following week for a coffee in the association office.

'Johnny, we don't want you to campaign for your seat. You've got to understand that our priorities are elsewhere, and you must campaign for one of the other candidates, in a seat with a better chance than you – a 40/40 seat this time round for the General Election. We'll see how you do, write a report and after that we'll take it from there.'

The 40/40 Campaign was a strategy used by the Conservative Party to target forty seats to hold and forty seats to win, in order to gain a marginal majority in the House of Commons. The targets for 2015 were mainly based on a Liberal Democrat collapse, and because I'd be standing against a Labour incumbent I was not on this list. I understood the 40/40 strategy of course, but did not understand that it would stretch to other parliamentary candidates abandoning their own associations and constituencies.

'I'm terribly sorry,' I told the agent. 'I left a good career in the Army, which I loved, to be an MP and sort out veterans' care. I can't simply abandon that.'

I also felt bad for my association. They had worked bloody hard at the previous election and almost won. They had been through some very hard times, but a few stoic souls had kept it going, and they were desperate to run their campaign around me.

'You will campaign in a 40/40 seat, Johnny, or we will have a few problems,' I was told.

I was deflated. The night before the meeting I had been up late with Felicity working through ideas. We would focus on membership first. We wanted to change it so that joining the Conservative Party in Plymouth meant more than paying a subscription and being given hundreds of leaflets and a map of where they needed to be delivered. We wanted it to be a team, a social group, something people wanted to be part of again.

Immediately after this meeting I went into Plymouth and got another coffee. I was left feeling rather isolated. I had a family to support, very little money, had left the Army to pursue these ambitions against all advice, and now the pillar upon which I was going to so heavily lean – the Conservative Party – was not the support I had hoped for.

I called the agent back.

'Look, I'm terribly sorry, but I'm not just going to give up on this,' I said to him.

A few weeks later I was asked to come to London and hoped it might be good news. I found Conservative Campaign Headquarters (CCHQ) in Millbank for the first time, and made my way upstairs. I was greeted in silence and shown through to a boardroom with two members of the candidates board. I greeted them with a smile. It was not returned.

'Johnny, I hear there is a bit of a problem,' said one.

'We need you to give up on your campaign and get on board with supporting Oliver across town,' said the other.

Oliver Colvile was the MP for Plymouth Sutton and Devonport. He had been elected in 2010 and was facing a tough fight to keep his seat in 2015, despite all the good work he had done for Plymouth in his tenure.

'I'm so sorry,' I said. 'Of course I'll help him. But I cannot abandon my campaign. The association would be devastated. But above all I left the Army to be an MP, and I can't give that up. You did give the impression, deliberately or otherwise, that this 40/40 strategy was malleable, and that I might be successful in attracting attention to my seat.'

I knew I would not be a priority. But to my mind there was some distance between that and abandoning my association and giving up on becoming an MP.

'Johnny, we will not be allocating any resources to your seat. Now or in the future. I'm sorry you have got that impression but it's simply not going to happen.'

I was obviously not amused, and the atmosphere got worse.

'Why do you think you should be supported?' one of them said. 'Who do you think you are? What have you done with your life?'

I never for one minute came into this career change expecting anything and I didn't mind that these guys clearly thought nothing of me; they didn't know me from Adam. But I did not expect the arrogance and the sudden, sharp hostility. This belittling fired something off in me. I thought of Felicity, the girls, everything we had sacrificed to achieve this. I had cycled to the station this morning with a suit bag banging against the spokes of my bike because we did not even have a car to our name. I had heard from other candidates that CCHQ was like this, but I had given them a clean slate with me, hoping it would be different.

'Let me stop you there,' I said.

She carried on. 'Why do you think you should be an MP? You say you want to do it better, for veterans. You need to be really careful. Really careful. You're implying that it's not being done well enough now. And who are you to question the standard of MPs?'

'There are clearly some terrific MPs,' I said. 'I'm not saying that at all. I just feel we owe these guys.'

'What do you think is going to happen to you after 2015?' the gentleman asked me, with a wry smile.

'I've no idea.'

'Well, we assess you.'

'What on?' I asked.

'We assess you,' he replied, again, nodding his head and smiling at his partner in crime.

'I'm going to leave now,' I said, rising to my feet. The lady walked out in front of me without saying goodbye and I was shown out of the building.

The Thames was at low tide as I walked back along the Embankment to Westminster tube station. I felt pretty cut up. Felicity had got up early with me that morning and made me a packed lunch as the food in London was so expensive; she had hoped some good news was coming. It took me a while to tell her how the meeting had gone; I was too embarrassed. Similarly, my chairman was hoping for some good news. I told him we were unlikely to be made a 40/40 seat, but lied and said we could be hopeful for some support. I couldn't disappoint him.

Fortunately, I had made a friend in this process. His name was Gary Streeter, and he had been an MP since 1992 for South West Devon – the neighbouring seat to Plymouth Moor View. While I was learning that politics is a game in which everyone gives you advice and you can't listen to or agree with all of them, you could never argue with someone who had been elected five times in a row.

On hearing of my selection, and always on the lookout to help an ex-serviceman, Gary had invited me for a pint over Christmas 2013. He was a very kind, religious man – driven by principle rather than an outright blind commitment. But he had a steel underneath; he wasn't 'wet' with it. He remains my primary mentor to this day. Somehow he had been assessing me.

'I think you might just do this,' he had told me. 'Stick to your guns. Don't change. I will see what I can do for you in London to get you some support.'

Those words ran through my mind as I rode the tube back to Paddington. I called Gary from the station and told him what had happened. He asked for the names of the people I had been in with.

'Johnny, you've got to understand there is a difference between the political party and the professional party. I don't even know who those two people are. Don't worry about it.'

I felt a little better, and the journey home helped. The train ride from London to Plymouth is special. It goes rather fast to Exeter but then slows down, seemingly in deference to the stunning route it takes, which hugs the coastline, most spectacularly at Dawlish. As you get past Exeter and chug past the Atlantic on your left, and the tors of Dartmoor on your right, London seems to leave you. There is no phone reception either, which I quite liked.

I was going to bloody do this, I decided. I had put up with worse. I had committed myself to this path; my young family were relying on me to make a go of it.

I thought again about the data from previous election results in Plymouth Moor View. The largest collection of voters in the constituency was those who didn't care who won; who weren't targeted and who were thoroughly disillusioned by politics. If I could go out there and knock on their door; if I could meet them, make the effort and show I cared about *them*; if I could give them something to vote for, then perhaps, just perhaps, they might come out for me.

Of course, I would have to show my face in the Conservative

parts and meet and woo the local party faithful. Given there were only fourteen members of my association, not all of whom could walk any more, I figured this part wouldn't take long. I would have to also try and 'convert' a few Labour stalwarts; many in Plymouth were fed up with the Labour Party.

Through all this scheming, one course of action leapt out as giving me the best chance of winning. *I had to knock on every door. Every single one.* If I did that, then at least no one could say, 'you never tried to speak to me.'

Next I needed a strategy. I had no money to spend on my campaign, but I would need some. So I needed to put myself in enough places to meet enough of the 'influencers'. I would have to be across every medium; social media, print media and those who didn't have anything to do with any media. When I left the Army I had no personal mobile phone, and although I had accounts I didn't use Facebook or Twitter. I avoided journalists and newspapers at all costs. I rarely even read them. That would all have to change.

Felicity and I sat down that night. I would have to set about finding donors – that's what they did in America. I would have to sell my vision of Plymouth – the potential of the place was huge if we could just get the politics right.

I had never bought the line that Plymothians were somehow less gifted than others, and hence we never really achieved much. We had the finest military history in the nation, contributing more in blood and treasure in the cause of our country than anywhere else. We had the most beautiful natural harbour this side of San Francisco. And if that wasn't enough, Dartmoor was a fifteen-minute run away, described by Steven Spielberg as the 'most stunning natural landscape' he has ever worked on after he filmed *War Horse* there.

The people were the city and the city was the people. The people of Plymouth had a special breed of resilience blended with an optimism and pride that you don't find in many places. We just needed better governance. Our settlements for health, transport, the Arts, education and the NHS from the national government were woeful. There was a real opportunity here, and Gary's optimism had confirmed this to me. So I went back to my military roots. Cheerfulness in adversity was commando quality number four. I would need it.

Felicity and I made a timeline for the next fourteen months. Until December 2014, I would focus hard on finding money – either earning it or persuading people to give it to me – and getting myself out and about and known in Plymouth. I would do the less time-intensive, more strategic meetings with the 'influencers' in 2014. From 2 January 2015, I would stop working and would campaign full-time, including the time-intensive tactical door-knocking. I bought six A–Zs of Plymouth and cut them all up to make one big street map of the constituency with, most importantly, all the houses on it marked.

I visited donors regularly. I would go to London and meet ex-military men I knew who were now executives. I tried to sell them my vision with the aim of walking away with a few hundred quid. Similarly, I would try and engage local businesses with this vision, and elicited services when cash was not appropriate. Politics wasn't dead at all.

I telephoned my local agent regularly as the campaign wore on, wanting to make sure I was abiding by the rules. He never returned my calls – I was *persona non grata* now – and so I phoned the Electoral Commission for guidance. The rules were not complicated, but one must stay within them. They generally concerned levels of spending many times larger than mine would ever be, but I thought I should play safe.

Felicity and I went out with the children on a couple of Saturdays to gauge how many doors we could knock on each day. We then pored over the maps and marked out every day between 2 January and 7 May 2015 in terms of zones. We would do one zone a day, five days a week, for five months.

We would need a van for the door-knocking stage, and we hired the cheapest one in Plymouth. It stank so much I was scared to open the back doors when we picked it up, and we spent a cold Saturday afternoon in December giving it a deep clean. The girls had great fun painting my name on it. We also spent a little bit of cash on some bike and advertising trailer combinations that we could trundle around in to keep fuel costs low. A plan was coming together.

38

On 2 January 2015 the campaign proper started for us. We went out in all weathers. We would draw up to an area in the morning, get Joey in the backpack and get door knocking. I said the same thing thousands of times: 'Hello. My name's Johnny and I've just left the Army to be your MP. Can I give you something to look at, please?'

With that I would hand over my self-designed leaflets, printed on a budget by a local firm. The weather in January was freezing, and if it was not freezing it was wet. Joey seemed happy with the situation and Felicity was resilient. We often had help from John, the chairman of the association, who had been exceptionally loyal and hardworking since I started this process.

We did every door meticulously, marking off streets as we went. We braved some extremely challenging areas and were told to 'fuck off' more than once a day. If someone was particularly rude to Felicity I would knock on their door and speak to them. I didn't really care if they were unpleasant to *my* face.

I was summoned to London again, because Gary had persuaded CCHQ to poll my constituency.

'I'm not paying my transport and hotel if it's just another bollocking,' I told the agent.

'I'll sort all that out, Johnny,' he replied.

I walked into CCHQ and had a meeting with Lynton Crosby, who I now knew was the election campaign director, and a few others.

The results were disappointing.

'You ain't gonna win, mate,' Crosby said.

But on the way home I compared my results with other similar seats whose polling data was in the public domain. I was doing much better than them. I kept checking the data meticulously – the make-up of the constituencies, the previous election results, answers to key questions. But overall, yes, I was doing significantly better than my comparable contemporaries. On that journey home, I thought for the first time I could win, while accepting that this view was not shared by anybody else! Now I was up for the fight, and the disappointing poll did not have a long-lasting effect on me.

Throughout that spring into May 2015, the tide seemed to tangibly turn in Plymouth. People started recognizing me before I knocked on their doors. Some started waiting in to see me. I would put on social media where I was going and what I was doing each day. For the first time, I could feel something in the air, and so could Felicity. The media started getting interested and our rate of progress around the 35,050 households in Plymouth Moor View slowed somewhat, as we made time for interviews.

Local businesses became involved. They helped me with a website and leaflets, and design. There was some serious goodwill towards me. I worked hard, but simply would have got nowhere without this help.

The week before 7 May, we started standing on main roads and roundabouts during the rush hour, holding signs. We had allocated Saturday afternoons for me and Al – a friend from the village – to drive around houses on main roads asking if we could put up posters in their gardens. And the reception was very good. Surprisingly good.

The local Labour Party had started getting upset. Some of the posters were defaced. One encouraged people to 'cull the Mercers' and 'cull the Tories'. Undeterred, I organized nine public meetings in each of the social clubs in Plymouth, and these were surprisingly well attended.

Felicity was my rock. The Army, and nature of some of the jobs I had done for it, made me hesitant to engage warmly with people I didn't know; I was even a little shy. But Felicity was brilliant at talking to anyone. Her commitment to this project was humbling. It was a slightly mad idea of mine but she just got on with it, in all weathers. The cycling to school in the rain; the peeing in a cup in the back of the van; constantly ensuring Joey was fed and watered on my back; her commitment was deeply affecting, and I shall never forget it.

On 7 May 2015, I didn't really know what to do with myself. The count didn't start until 10 p.m. that night, leaving a lot of hours to fill. I didn't want to go around hassling people to vote for me. I felt I had done all I could in that respect. In the end, I went into town and drove around the polling stations, thanking the council staff for their time and efforts.

By now we had a little network of helpers who fed and watered us and gave us a hand with childcare and leaflets. The day passed very slowly indeed for all of us. That evening we went for a curry and a couple of pints. I thanked them so much for all they had done. The news was on in the corner of the Treasury bar next to Plymouth Guildhall when, at 10 p.m., an exit poll conducted by the BBC suggested a result no one had predicted; a Conservative majority. I put my pint down and made my way back to Council House.

I got there in time to hear the local BBC announce that the swing would not be enough for me, and they were declaring a 'hold' for my opponent. I hugged Felicity. I told her the worst thing was not losing. The worst thing would have been not having done all we could to ensure success, and we had done that. We were exhausted, and I was so proud of her and our efforts.

But, suddenly, the atmosphere started changing around us. The local opposition – there seemed to be lots of them, all with suits and clipboards – started getting agitated. They were demanding recounts in certain wards. I didn't know why. The young council staff on the tables started smiling at me. They wanted us to win.

We were called into the centre of the room. Candidate and agent. Felicity was mine. We were read the result.

We had won.

Felicity started shaking. I tried to compose myself. We walked back through the crowds, unable to reveal the result, and waited at the side of the stage. I nipped behind the curtain for a minute. I thought of Bing. I thought of what we had achieved. I could feel some bastard tears welling up (what the hell was wrong with me?) and I composed myself as best I could. Felicity came to find me and gave me a hug.

'This is all because of you,' I said. 'I could not have done it without you.'

She kissed me.

We went out and were all lined up on stage and the result was read out. The opposition activists started crying. They took it very badly indeed. Not my problem. Next came my speech. I hadn't prepared anything, so I thanked my team, the people of Plymouth, and, of course, Felicity.

EPILOGUE

The next few days were surreal. There were many, many engagements, particularly with the media. The Conservative Party seemingly did not have any contact details for me, and so the Whips' office got in touch with me on Twitter. I went to London on the following Sunday night, and on Monday stepped into Portcullis House, the large glass building that sits opposite Big Ben, where MPs' staff and their offices are housed. I was very impressed that Westminster had its own tube station built into the complex. I was shown around by a 'buddy' who was allocated to me; she was very kind and very helpful.

The rules and regulations of parliament were almost mind-boggling. I felt a bit of a fraud; the unease with privilege I had felt at school, Sandhurst and as an officer in the Army was back again. But people were very friendly. MPs on all sides of the house would take time from their schedules to show you where to go if you looked lost and there was advice in spades about staff – that most crucial of decisions when one becomes an MP. I remember being made to feel very welcome.

But you weren't really settled in this place until you had made your maiden speech on the floor of the House of Commons. We were advised to talk about our predecessor and about our constituency, but keep it light and funny. I wanted to get mine done and out of the way, so I had asked to speak on the following Monday and my parents were going to come up for it, as was Felicity.

Back home that weekend, Felicity got up early on Sunday with the girls to give me a bit of a lie-in. Eventually I got up, feeling full of energy, opened my laptop and just typed away.

I thought of the advice I had been given, including the requirement to pay tribute to my predecessor; I thought of making myself look good with some strong political Conservative statements about a long-term economic plan. I cringed a bit.

That wasn't really me. I deleted and started again. I thought of Plymouth – how it was time to get the city and its people what they deserved.

But chiefly I thought of my lads. Those whose voices are never heard loudly enough in parliament, who are either too proud or too loyal to ask for a better deal. I wanted, if only for a few minutes, to bring into that chamber what we had asked a generation to sacrifice, in order to safeguard the privileges we enjoyed. I didn't want to complain about it, but to shine a light on it, in the hope that it might change something for our service men and women. I would find it hard, but I was going to talk about Bing. I was going to talk about his parents and our endless debt to them as a nation. I was going to talk about Dan Collins, who had killed himself on Sennybridge Training Area after suffering the demons of Helmand. I was going to talk of the duty and pride with which we served this nation of ours; I was also going to demand that that duty was matched by the House of Commons and the Government in their treatment of our veterans, service personnel and their families.

It was a risk, and I felt nervous as I went into the House. This place runs on traditions; it is not wise to break them on your first day.

I took my seat at 2.30 p.m. on 1 June 2015. As the afternoon wore on, I became more and more nervous. Most MPs were praising the Conservative Party and their election victory, as well as making people laugh. I was up next. I felt like changing my speech.

But in that moment, I thought of Bing again. It was one week shy of five years to the day since he lost his life. This speech was an extension of my duty to him and the hundreds of others like him. I looked up into the empty gallery and I imagined Bing sitting there watching me, along with the other service men and women who'd given their lives. I felt the pressure – I was sweating and my knees were weak – but this time there were no tears. I had made it. I had made it to a place where I could be their voice. I would carry the torch. I would not let it go out.

At 6.54 p.m., I rose to my feet.

APPENDIX

Johnny's maiden speech

I want to start by thanking my predecessor, Ms Alison Seabeck. She worked hard in the course of the past decade to help some of the most vulnerable people in Plymouth. She never wavered in her commitment to her party, albeit a different one from mine.

The great city of Plymouth, which I have been sent here to represent, has a history and stature to rival our nation's capital. Some of our country's defining moments have occurred in the 'jewel of the south west' that is Plymouth. It has a recent character, defined in some of the darkest days of the conflicts that dominated the previous century.

In the carnage of the Second World War, the sacrifices of those on the home front in cities outside London cannot always be first recalled. During the war, more than 1,100 souls perished on Plymouth's streets, with a nightly exodus to Dartmoor keeping as many children alive as possible. I mention this because that period of war defined our modern history in Plymouth. From the ruins of those dark days sprang the spirit of a modern Plymouth. A huge period of regeneration saw the building of 1,000 homes a year in the 1950s under the Homes for Heroes plan.

It was those days of regeneration and rebirth and the spirit of discovery that engendered what we affectionately call our Janner spirit. In the general election just passed, I tried to knock on every door in my constituency – and I almost succeeded. I am pleased to report that the Janner spirit is truly alive and well: from local community projects to saving our football club; from pioneering mental health and substance misuse treatments to a world-class hospital at Derriford; and from cutting edge businesses growing an increasingly resilient local economy to the plethora of ambitious and socially aware social enterprises in the city, we truly have a special place on the southern shores of this country that has recently seen a new dawn and is in serious danger of realizing its potential.

We in Plymouth have contributed to this nation's history as much as any other major city. This has continued through recent conflicts. It cannot be right that our transport, health and other spending settlements are less than half of what they are elsewhere. In a seat that once elected Michael Foot, I do not underestimate the burden of trust that the people of my city have placed at my door to ensure that we as a government deliver a more resilient, stable and fair economy that must include better funding settlements from central government for our core services in Plymouth.

I want to speak briefly about my two main missions in this Parliament. First, mental health provision in this country remains poor. There are some extremely dogged and determined characters who fight night and day to improve the services offered to those who struggle with mental health problems. Often, those who struggle with mental health problems cannot shout for themselves, and suffer in silence because of the ridiculous stigma placed on mental health. That stigma ends in this Parliament. It is not good enough to have sympathy, empathy even, or simply to understand these issues when they affect someone close to us. It is time to get this right and I look forward to starting this crusade in Plymouth.

Secondly, the past decade and a half has defined a whole generation of us in often unseen wars against enemies of the state that only seem to grow darker. We have no complaints about the duty that we have chosen. It formed many of us; indeed, it made many of us who we are today. We were proud to defend this great nation in the same traditions of the immense sacrifices of our forefathers. However, last week my right honourable friend the Prime Minister spoke of the gravity of the end of combat operations in Afghanistan. For many families, that marks the end of the sleepless nights by the phone and the ever-dreaded knock at the door.

I am sorry to report, however, that there remains a great stain on this nation of ours when it comes to conflict. In 2012, we reached a very unwelcome threshold when, tragically, more soldiers and veterans killed themselves than were killed on operational service in defence of the realm. It goes without saying that there are some genuine heroes in our communities and charities up and down this land who work tirelessly night and day to look after and assist those who have found returning to a peaceful life the biggest challenge of all. A great many of these veterans are not only from Afghanistan.

My key point is this: there has been a fundamental misunderstanding by governments of all colours over the years that veterans' care is a third sector responsibility and that the great British public, in all their wonderful generosity, support our troops well enough, and any new initiative is met with the response, 'Well, there must be a charity for that.' That is fundamentally and unequivocally wrong, and I make no apologies for pointing it out to anyone of any rank or position who may be offended by my candour.

I am not a charity and neither were my men. We gave the best years of our lives in defending the privileges, traditions and freedoms that this House and all members enjoy. It is therefore the duty of this House to look after them and, crucially, their families, when they return. I would be grateful if you granted me your patience, Mr Deputy Speaker, to bring just two of them to the attention of the House this evening.

Lance Sergeant Dan Collins of the Welsh Guards was typical of the soldiers I was privileged to command in my tours of Afghanistan. His story had a profound effect on me. I implore members to look him up tonight before they go to bed and to read his story. He endured events that were atypical of a fighting man's deployment in that theatre. He returned to Britain's arms a deeply scarred man and entered a dark, dark place that too many are familiar with. Dan worked hard to try to find treatment that worked for him, but repeated changes of staff and six-hour round trips for appointments did very little indeed. He fought his demons with the same spirit and courage that he had demonstrated on a daily basis against the enemies of the state in foreign fields. When he returned home, however, unlike when he was in his battalion, we did not have his back.

Dan liked to take on his demons alone in the mountains, where perhaps the outside arena made him feel more empowered. However, in 2012, during the period of new year's celebrations – that time of year when all the world is celebrating – Dan recorded a video message for his mum on his mobile phone. He said:

'Hey, Mum. Just a video, just to say I'm sorry. Ever since I

came back from Hell I've turned into a horrible person and I don't like who I am any more.'

He went on to say: 'I've tried everything, and there's nothing that seems to be working. I love you, and I'll see you, okay? I love you.'

With that, our nation failed one of her bravest sons once more, as yet another victim of the Afghanistan war lost his life, not bleeding out in some dusty foreign field in the intense pressures of combat but in his homeland, which he had fought so hard to defend.

Next Monday, it will be five years to the day since I conducted a particular dawn patrol in southern Afghanistan with my troops. We were enduring one of the most contested fighting seasons of that campaign in 2010, and fear was rife. I was particularly blessed to have with me in my small team a man of colossal courage called Lance Bombardier Mark Chandler, who in our role was duty-bound to protect me in close-quarter combat while I continued in our primary trade. While most people in this country were still in a morning slumber, we closed in on an enemy position, and in an intense close-quarter gunfight Mark was shot in the face right next to me and died in my arms.

In the five years since, I have become intimately familiar with another quiet yet very stoical group of casualties of this country's war.

Mike and Ann Chandler, Mark's parents, like parents, wives, sisters and brothers up and down this land, now endure a daily sacrifice. It is very difficult for those of us who have not experienced it to truly grasp the bottomless well of grief that comes from losing a child, husband, brother or sister in war as a result of a grave decision made in this House. Theirs is the greatest sacrifice on the altar of this nation's continuing freedom, and it is a price that is paid daily. For many families up and down this land, it is indeed at every going down of the sun and every morning that we remember them.

I come here, unapologetically, to improve the plight of veterans and their families. The last government under this Prime Minister did more than any before it in this cause, but there is still some way to go. It is a deep privilege to come to this House with the hopes of tens of thousands of Plymothians, and I do not underestimate the duty that is incumbent upon me in the years ahead. I cannot promise anything but noble endeavour, relentless positivity and an abounding sense of duty to look after those who, through no fault of their own, find themselves on the fringes of society, and who find life an interminable struggle. I look forward to the challenge.

GLOSSARY

2IC second-in-command
3RHA 3rd Regiment Royal Horse Artillery
Ack closest assistant, right-hand man
AK47 assault rifle
ANA Afghan National Army
ANGLICO Air Naval Gunfire Liaison Company (US Marine Corps)
AO area of operations
AQ Al Qaeda
BDA Battle Damage Assessment
Bergan rucksack
CamelBak hydration pack
CAS close air support
CASEVAC casualty evacuation
CH-47 Chinook helicopter
CO commanding officer
CPR cardiopulmonary resuscitation
de-confliction the separation or organization of airspace to allow airframes to operate safely
ECAS Emergency Close Air Support
FOB Forward Operating Base
frag grenade fragmentation grenade
FST Fire Support Team

GPMG general-purpose machine gun, the standard infantry machine gun of the British Armed Forces

Grot military slang for accommodation room and/or bed-space

HE high explosive

HESCO bastion system of wire-cage blocks used to create a protective barrier or perimeter wall

HLS helicopter landing site

Huey an attack helicopter

Husky landmine and IED detection vehicle

ICOM handheld radio system used by the Taliban

IED improvised explosive device

ISAF International Security Assistance Force

jet shorthand for any fixed-wing air platform delivering close air support to troops in contact

joint fires co-ordinated air, artillery and mortar fire

JTAC Joint Terminal Attack Controller

Kandak company of the Afghan National Army

Kevlar plate body armour

MEDEVAC medical evacuation

MERT Medical Evacuation and Response Team

monkey walk walking in a crouched position

NCO non-commissioned officer

NEB Nahr-e-Bughra (Canal)

OC officer commanding

OMLT Operational Mentoring and Liaison Team

on point in the forward position in a military formation

Ops room operations room

ORBAT Operational Order of Battle

Pan/flight Pan – the area in a camp separated for the operation of aircraft

PB patrol base

pulk sledge used to carry equipment in the Arctic
QRF quick reaction force
R&R rest and recuperation
RFA Royal Fleet Auxiliary
RPG rocket-propelled grenade
RSM regimental sergeant major
Rupert derogatory term for a military officer
RV rendezvous
sangar protected sentry post normally located around
  the perimeter of a base
SATCOM satellite communications
SF Special Forces
SITREP situational report
tab march (from TAB, tactical advance to battle)
TiC troops in contact
TRIM Trauma Risk Management
uptick small or incremental increase
VA vulnerable area
wadi dry river valley
wash-up informal debrief
WMIK Weapons Mount Installation Kit, a stripped-down
  Land Rover
yomp the Commandos' word for **tab**.

extracts reading groups

competitions books new

discounts extracts extracts

competitions

books new events

events books

extracts books reading groups

new titles reading groups

interviews

reading groups books events new

discounts

new books events events

events new interviews books extracts

discounts extracts discounts books

www.panmacmillan.com

extracts events reading groups

competitions books extracts new